My Home, My Land

My Home, My Land

A NARRATIVE OF THE PALESTINIAN STRUGGLE

Abu Iyad

WITH ERIC ROULEAU

TRANSLATION BY LINDA BUTLER KOSEOGLU

Times
BOOKS

Published by TIMES BOOKS, a division of
Quadrangle/The New York Times Book Co., Inc.
Three Park Avenue, New York, N.Y. 10016

Published simultaneously in Canada by
Fitzhenry & Whiteside, Ltd., Toronto
© International ABC 1978

Translation copyright © 1981 by Times Books

Library of Congress Cataloging in Publication Data

Abū 'Iyād.
  My home, my land.

  Includes index.
    1. Abū 'Iyād. 2. Palestinian Arabs—Bibliography.
3. Jewish-Arab relations—1949–   4. Lebanon—
History—Civil War, 1975–   I. Rouleau, Eric,
1926–   II. Title.
DS119.7.A6263   956.94'05   80-5144
ISBN 0-8129-0936-4

Manufactured in the United States of America

Contents

Preface

From the first, I was tempted by the prospect of interviewing one of the "historic leaders" of the Palestinian Resistance, the first who had ever agreed to cut through the secrecy which continued to cloud the movement, even twenty years after its creation.

Salah Khalaf—better known under his code name Abu Iyad—is without question one of the key figures of the movement. One of Fatah's principal founders and a former head of its security arm, he is a leading member of its highest body, the Central Committee. Since 1970 he has been chief of the PLO Special Services, which coordinates the information gathered by the various groups comprising the fedayeen umbrella organization. Denounced as the head of Black September by Mossad, the Israeli Intelligence Agency, and by the CIA, he is accused of having organized some of the bloodiest terrorist operations of recent years, including the one at the Munich Olympics which monopolized the headlines in September 1972. But precisely because of this prominence, I was reluctant to take on the task of writing this book with Abu Iyad. I was afraid he would sidestep questions. I wondered if it would even be possible for him to go beyond the natural restrictions imposed on him by his responsibilities. It seemed unlikely that he would be ready to speak with the necessary frankness: It would be all too easy to end up with a political pamphlet or, at best, a hagiography, instead of the desired historical work.

Abu Iyad's commitments and assurances concerning his intentions went a long way toward alleviating my doubts. He said he didn't want an autobiography or memoirs, but would speak of himself and his personal experiences only insofar as they shed light on the psychology, aspirations, and struggles of the Palestinian people or the ideology and structure of the Resistance. He would answer frankly all questions of a political nature, even though such frankness was likely to earn him "antipathy and hostility." He did reserve the right, however, not to answer questions which could compromise the security of the movement or its leaders. Considering that the book would not be his own, he asked that the proceeds and royalties go entirely to the Martyrs' Foundation, the organization that provides for the families of fedayeen killed in action.

Having known Abu Iyad for a decade and listened to him numerous times in public and private, I had reason to believe that the book wouldn't lack interest. He is known for his frankness, and there is no question that he has made as many enemies as friends through his habit of saying aloud what many of his compatriots or colleagues keep to themselves. In this regard, several of our past meetings come to mind. The first took place in June 1969 at the residence of Lakhdar Brahimi, the Algerian Ambassador to Cairo. Before a group of prominent foreigners including several representatives of Arab governments, Abu Iyad propounded a view that was shocking at the time: To wit, that the Resistance posed a much greater threat to the Arab regimes than to Israel. To illustrate this statement, he indulged his taste for allegory: "A man vigorously shook a tree in order to make a splendid orange he had seen fall to the ground; but, while the fruit he wanted remained solidly attached, all the others—thirteen in all—fell one after the other." The rotten oranges, the Fatah leader explained, represented the thirteen members of the Arab League, while the one that wasn't ripe enough symbolized the Zionist state. Several months later, everything seemed to indicate that Abu Iyad's prediction was about to take place in Jordan. The showdown which pitted King Hussein against the PLO seemed to be turning in the latter's favor. The fedayeen virtually controlled the streets of Amman as well as the main wheels of government. The provocative or triumphant declarations of the Palestinian leaders seemed to confirm that the Hashemite power was living its last days.

Abu Iyad alone failed to share the general euphoria. Receiving me in Fatah's information office on September 3, 1970—two weeks before the

Jordanians launched their offensive—he said that the fedayeen were heading straight for a catastrophe. He told me not to be deceived by appearances: The Palestinian movement, whose power had been "blown up like a balloon by the press," would not be capable of resisting Hussein for long. In any case, he went on, the King—who was prepared to "bury his own capital under mortar" to save his throne—would be supported by Israel and the United States. The Resistance, on the other hand, could rely only on its own forces: The Iraqi units stationed in Jordan at the time, he assured me, would not come to the aid of the Palestinians despite the formal commitments given him and Yasir Arafat by the Baghdad leadership. The tragic events which followed—described at length in this volume—showed how right he was.

Back in October 1968, Abu Iyad was the first Fatah leader to outline the Resistance's "strategic objective," the transformation of Palestine into a "democratic state" where Jews, Christians, and Muslims could live together as equal citizens—in other words, the dismantling of the Zionist entity. But he was also the first to publicly advocate—in February 1974—the creation of an Arab "mini-Palestine" next to the Jewish state. "We should be frank with our masses," he told me in November 1972. "Not to tell them the entire truth is a way of scorning them." He was more explicit during a conversation that took place in Cairo on October 31, 1973, a few days after the Yom Kippur war. Realism, he explained, consisted of taking the balance of power into account. "What's the good of being pure and uncompromising if you have to end your days in exile, like Haj Amin al-Hussayni?" he said. Although he thought it improbable that Israel would agree to negotiate a settlement with the PLO, he was counting on fedayeen participation in the Geneva Conference, provided Security Council Resolution 242 was amended to stipulate that the Palestinians were not merely "refugees" but also, and especially, a "people" with "national rights."

Abu Iyad is undoubtedly one of the best-known political thinkers of the Resistance. He is also one of its best orators. His mere presence on a speaker's platform is enough to unleash the enthusiasm of the crowd. Yet he in no way resembles a fighter or a revolutionary. Of medium height, stocky and even tending to fat, he prefers the prosaic business suit—generally badly cut—to the martial battle dress that distinguishes other fedayeen. His physique is more in keeping with the philosophy teacher he was before devoting himself full-time to the Resistance. His face is round and full, his eyes—topped with thick coal-black brows—sparkle with intelligence; his thinning hair, greying at the temples, scarcely conceals the baldness at the top of his head.

In fact, Abu Iyad is a many-faceted and complex personality. If fate had been otherwise, perhaps he would have been a writer—and indeed he wrote two successful plays as a young man. Endowed with a prodigious memory, he is an excellent storyteller. During the long evenings he spent in front of a tape recorder answering my questions, he gave some measure of his gifts of observation and sensitivity through the anecdotes, images, and humor of his accounts.

Always on the move, constantly threatened, Abu Iyad has lived apart from his family since 1967. His wife and six children—three boys and three girls ranging from seven to seventeen years old—live in a Cairo suburb. Since he practically never takes a vacation he sees them only rarely: Throughout the entire eighteen months of civil war in Lebanon he was too involved in his responsibilities to get to Cairo even once. Yet his eyes soften each time he mentions a telephone conversation with one of his children, particularly his fifteen-year-old daughter Jihane, a polio victim who plans to become a doctor. For all the tenderness he shows his loved ones, his warmth toward his friends and indulgence toward his adversaries, Abu Iyad condones the death penalty—in the exceptional cases of a traitor to the Palestinian cause or an Israeli agent.

In practice, his attitude toward violence is ambivalent. He is a strong advocate of armed struggle, yet never took part in any military action. In this respect, he probably doesn't differ much from most leaders of national liberation movements, who generally don't participate in the guerrilla activities they plan and direct. Menachem Begin, for instance, former head of Irgun Zvei Leumi and accused of spectacular and bloody terrorist attacks, is reputed to be a nonviolent person by nature. Like the Palestinian leader, he is said to hate the sight of blood.

Abu Iyad and I had long and sometimes heated discussions about terrorism while preparing this book. The reader will doubtless find his position on the subject somewhat curious. Basically, he makes a distinction between the operations he approves of—which he calls "revolutionary violence"—and those he condemns, which he relegates to the domain of "terrorism." Among the acts of terrorism, he includes in particular hijackings which endanger the lives of innocent civilians. On the other hand, he condones as legitimate the Munich operation, the seizure of American and Arab diplomats at Khartoum, and the March 1978 bus operation along the Haifa-Tel Aviv highway.

There are two categories of hostages, he says, one "innocent" and the other "guilty." He adds that in every instance it was the Israelis who assumed the heavy responsibility of having the captives killed rather then giving in to the commandos' political demands. But doesn't fedayeen blackmail inevitably lead to the killing of the hostages if their demands are not met? Abu Iyad insists that the fedayeen never intended to execute their hostages—a statement that has yet to be demonstrated.

Abu Iyad's arguments are not likely to convince most Western readers. It must be noted, however, that they are in line with the reasoning of other guerrilla movements throughout the world, from the Mau Maus of Kenya to the Tupamaros of Uruguay, from the *fellaghas* of Algeria to the Patriotic Front of Rhodesia. Isn't terrorism, as atrocious as it is, the last weapon of the weak? Abu Iyad's statement that the Black September organization was born of the despair engendered by the defeat and massacre of the fedayeen in Jordan seems to bear this out. It is significant that the organization disappeared after the Arab "victory" of October 1973 and the PLO's success on the international scene.

Abu Iyad vehemently denies that he was ever chief of Black September. This is possible, since the name in fact designates a loose agglomeration of commando groups rather than a structured, strictly hierarchical organization. These groups were headed by various Fatah officers who for security reasons acted autonomously. Perhaps the entire enterprise was presided over by Yusuf al-Najjar, alias Abu Yussuf, Fatah's security chief at the time who was killed in the Israeli raid on Beirut in April 1973.

Regardless of his roles in the organization, Abu Iyad describes in great detail the planning and execution of Black September's principal operations, especially the one at the Munich Olympics and two rather incredible plots to eliminate King Hussein and the Jordanian regime. Although he doesn't assume responsibility, he does claim the "honor" of approving them. He says he learned of these actions after the fact in his capacity as chief of the PLO Special Services, but the minute detail of his revelations could lead one to suspect that he was not entirely foreign to the operations.

Abu Iyad has escaped a number of assassination attempts, one of which is described in these pages. He knows that his life is in danger and that the threat doesn't come from Israel alone. Several foreign intelligence services, particularly those of Arab countries, would gain from his elimination. Subjected to draconian security measures, especially following the rupture between the PLO and Egypt in the wake of President Sadat's Jerusalem trip, he leads the life of a hounded man, even in Beirut, the last fortress of the Resistance. He no longer has a fixed residence. He maintains several offices, visiting them only unexpectedly. Four bodyguards armed with submachine guns take turns protecting him around the clock. He no longer appears in public. He never has a meal in a restaurant. He is unable to go to the theater or cinema he so enjoys.

Numerous precautions surrounded our meetings. They took place at night in the houses of various friends, generally non-Palestinians sympathetic to the Resistance. The car that brought Abu Iyad to the meetingplace—most often a Peugeot 504 with drawn curtains—left immediately after he crossed the building's threshold so as not to attract the attention of the neighbors. His bodyguards, too, would vanish. Practically no one knew where he was: The operator of Fatah's telephone network, which is separate from that of the Lebanese state, kept him posted on vital calls, and a most selected and trusted few men could contact him via the radio transmitter in cases of extreme emergency. These security measures seemed to annoy Abu Iyad, who considered them useless. They were imposed on him by the Fatah leadership after the April 1973 Israeli raid on Beirut claimed the lives of three PLO leaders. His skepticism was based on the conviction that "any man is capable of assassinating whomever he likes so long as he is prepared to die doing it."

As paradoxical as his natural antipathy for violence is his aversion for Intelligence. For this reason, he preferred the term "surveillance" or "security" to designate the PLO department he heads. A question of semantics, no doubt, but nonetheless significant of the mentality of a stateless person and militant who has experienced the repressive power of numerous regimes ever since childhood.

Abu Iyad is clearly far more at ease in his role as a political leader than as a soldier or terrorist. His accounts of his meetings and dealings with various heads of state attest to this fact. Known as a formidable negotiator, he was often assigned delicate missions. During the Lebanese civil war, he acted as spokesman for some twenty Lebanese and Palestinian parties, organizations and factions of various leanings, and was called upon to extract a common position before coming to the bargaining table with the Lebanese rightist parties. I watched him negotiate a draft agreement over the telephone with considerable skill, remaining even-tempered, patient, sometimes joking. The agreement was aimed at effecting the withdrawal of Maronite militias from South Lebanon, and Abu Iyad was skeptical. "We know in advance that these negotiations won't lead to anything," he confided. "But at least they enable us to sound out the intentions of our adversaries and especially their protectors, the Israelis . . ."

Abu Iyad has the reputation for being the leader of Fatah's hard-line faction, but his differences with his more "moderate" comrades are of a tactical nature. While it is true that he favors cooperation with the Rejection Front organizations at a time when the Resistance as a whole is threatened, he unequivocally condemns at the same time the diehards who reject the compromise of a ministate in the West Bank and Gaza. He was against the secret talks in Paris between PLO representative Issa Sartawi and various prominent Israelis, including General Peled, Ari Eliav, and Uri Avnery. On the other hand, he specifies in this book that he does not oppose the principle of negotiations with the Jewish state or even a "mutual recognition" between the two peoples. These seemingly contradictory attitudes can be reconciled. In his view, "a negotiated settlement is out of the question as long as the balance of power doesn't change significantly in our favor." Unlike certain other Palestinian leaders, Abu Iyad believes that only from a position of strength is it possible to make concessions without renouncing the essential. Otherwise, he maintains, compromise can only be capitulation.

It was undoubtedly this conviction which led him to vehemently denounce President Sadat's trip to Jerusalem. Above and beyond an emotional reaction, which he freely acknowledges, he criticized the Egyptian leader not so much for the act itself as for Sadat's belief that he could get his way while in such a weak position. After hearing Sadat's and Begin's speeches in the Knesset on November 20, 1977, Abu Iyad reread the Likud leader's autobiography, *The Revolt.* Shortly thereafter, he told me bitterly: "I respect Begin because at least he knows how to defend the country. But Sadat offered to sell the inalienable rights of the Palestinian people for practically nothing." Yet he was still unable to imagine that the Egyptian president would go so far as to conclude a separate peace. "No Arab state would dare conclude a settlement without us, much less against us," he said, barely a week before the Camp David summit.

During our interviews, Abu Iyad never tired of evoking the successive betrayals of the Arab regimes, which he summed up in the colorful saying, "All revolutions conceived in Palestine have aborted in the Arab capitals." In the epilogue of this book, he is frankly critical of the Resistance, laying bare its "mistakes, shortcomings, and errors" over the past two decades. No doubt this picture leaves something to be desired, but it is bold compared to the apologies most often heard from the Palestinian leadership. Abu Iyad does not exclude the hypothesis that the Palestinian movement as it stands will be paralyzed or even destroyed. But while expressing this "realist's pessimism," he also demonstrates a "revolutionary's optimism," stating his conviction that his people will eventually see the realization of their right to a country, a sovereign and independent state.

My Home, My Land, though rich in revelations, is not and could not be an objective work. But the text constitutes a precious document, the only one of its kind, which will unquestionably contribute to an understanding of the Palestinian problem.

Eric Rouleau

My Home, My Land

1

Seeds of Hatred

MAY 13, 1948, is a day that will remain forever engraved in my memory. That day, less than twenty-four hours before the proclamation of the Israeli state, my family fled Jaffa for refuge in Gaza. We had been under siege; the Zionist forces controlled all the roads leading south, and the only escape left open to us was the sea. It was under a hail of shells fired from Jewish artillery set up in neighboring settlements, especially Tel Aviv, that I clambered onto a makeshift boat with my parents, my four brothers and sisters, and other relatives.

Hundreds of thousands of Palestinians started for exile that day, often under tragic conditions. Not yet fifteen, I was overwhelmed by the sight of this huge mass of men, women, old people and children, struggling under the weight of suitcases or bundles, making their way painfully down to the wharfs of Jaffa in a sinister tumult. Cries mingled with moaning and sobs, all punctuated by deafening explosions.

The boat had scarcely lifted anchor when a woman started shrieking. One of her four children wasn't on board and she implored us to put back to port to look for him. Caught under the heavy fire of the Jewish guns, we couldn't turn back without risking the lives of the several hundred people, many of them children, crushed together in the small craft.

The piercing cries of the poor woman went unanswered. She broke down into sobs. Some of us tried to calm her by saying that her young son would surely be picked up and later brought to Gaza. But in vain. Her nerves finally cracked and she straddled the rail, throwing herself into the sea. In an apparent effort to save her, her husband jumped in after her. It soon became clear that neither knew how to swim. The angry waves finally swallowed them up under our very eyes. We all remained rooted to the boat, paralyzed with horror.

At the time I didn't even ask myself why we were so hastily leaving our homes and belongings for the adventure of exile. It wouldn't have occurred to me at my age to question my father's authority, and besides, like everyone else, I was convinced that to stay would have meant sure death. News of the Deir Yassin massacre, which had taken place on April 9, 1948, still rang in our ears. Militants of Menachem Begin's group, the Irgun Zvai Leumi, had stormed the peaceful village west of Jerusalem and wiped out most of its inhabitants: More than 250 defenseless men, women, and children had been shot down, buried alive, or had their throats slashed. Numerous bodies had been mutilated with knives; pregnant women had been disemboweled. We had no reason to doubt the news of this savage killing, confirmed by Jacques de Reynier, the representative of the International Red Cross, who personally conducted the investigation at the scene.

Like Deir Yassin, Jaffa was at the mercy of the Zionist forces which completely controlled the hinterland of the city. The Haganah, the "official" army of the Jewish Agency which closely coordinated its activities with those of the so-called dissident groups like Begin's Irgun, had unleashed a full-scale offensive at the beginning of April aimed at cleaning out the Arab "pockets" within the territory set aside for the Jewish state. Before each attack, the population was warned that it would suffer the same fate as Deir Yassin's if it didn't evacuate the area.

The news of the genocide had spread like wildfire throughout the entire country, helped along by the Zionist mass media which amplified it as part of its campaign to terrorize the Arabs. But there's no denying that the massacre was also used by Palestinian agitators trying to mobilize the population. For example, they stressed that Deir Yassin women had been raped by the Zionist forces and called upon their compatriots to defend their most precious possession, the honor of their wives and daughters. But in most cases the strategy backfired: In a profoundly traditional society such as ours, many men rushed to remove their women from the reach of the Zionist soldiers instead of staying to resist the aggression. I often remember hearing in this connection that "honor is more important than land."

The decision of most of Jaffa's approximately 100,000 residents to flee the city for temporary refuge seemed all the more logical in that the Jews had an overwhelming military superiority. Better armed and better organized than the Palestinians, there was no question that they had the upper hand. The population began to take fright when Great Britain announced at the end of 1947 that it was relinquishing its mandate over Palestine and withdrawing its troops before May 15, 1948. So we couldn't even count on the protection—such as it was—of the British troops. Fright changed to panic when, after the Deir Yassin massscre, the Zionist forces began to pound the city, especially the port and business district. Everyone thought that the economic suffocation would serve as a prelude to the conquest of the city and doubtless new and atrocious killings.

If someone had told me as a young boy that we would one day be driven out of our country by the Jews, I would have been shocked and even indignant at such a preposterous idea. My family had always enjoyed excellent relations with Jews and had many Jewish friends. My grandfather, Sheikh Abdallah, a man of religion at Gaza, had raised his children in a spirit of great tolerance. One of his sons had married a Jewish woman and as a child I often remember hearing of romances developing between various boys in our circle and Jewish girls.

My father had picked up Hebrew through daily usage and spoke it well. In 1920 he had left Gaza, where his family had lived for ten generations, and moved to Jaffa, settling in the al-Hammam al-Mahruk quarter overlooking the sea. As an employee of the surveyor's office, he traveled continually throughout the country and thus got to know the Jewish population. When he quit his job in 1940, he opened a small grocery store in Carmel, a mixed neighborhood near Tel Aviv. About half his customers and suppliers were Jews, with whom he was on excellent terms. In keeping with the traditions in our part of the world, my parents exchanged visits with their Jewish neighbors and friends on Jewish and Muslim holidays.

My brother Abdallah, who was three years older than myself, and I used to work at the store during our lunch periods and after school so my father could take a few hours off. It was while serving the Jewish clientele that I learned to get along in Hebrew. Although my school, Marwaniya, was for Arabs, I had many friends from Jewish schools. Most of them were either born in Palestine or from Arab countries, especially Yemen, so their Arabic was better than my Hebrew. We used the two languages almost interchangeably. We shared the interests of all children our age, and I remember distinctly our games on the beach of Tel Aviv, our long walks during which we spoke of everything except the problem which was soon to catapult us into enemy camps.

I first became aware of the Jewish-Arab conflict a little before the end of the Second World War. I was on my way to visit some close relatives in Sumeil, an Arab village in the Tel Aviv region. Rounding a bend in the road, I saw a group of young people on a hill in the distance being trained in the use of weapons. After the initial shock, I watched astonished as they went through various exercises, following orders in Hebrew with perfect discipline. I was eleven years old at the time and the scene made a powerful impression on me. Why were these Jewish boys and girls (who must have been about sixteen to twenty-five years old) preparing for war? Whom were they going to fight? What group did they belong to? When I told one of my teachers about it, he said they must belong to the Haganah. That was the first time I ever heard the name, and the first time I vaguely understood that we were heading toward a confrontation.

It was just about that time that a Palestinian paramilitary organization, the Najjadehs, was created under Muhammad al-Hawari. The principal of my school, Rashid al-Dabbagh, was one of its founding members. On his encouragement, I joined the youth section, the "lion cubs," where, along with a few comrades, I got my first taste of militant activity. Meanwhile, some of our professors tried to give us a political formation. They told us about the history of Palestine, the Balfour Declaration, Zionist colonization, the popular uprising of 1936–1939. Our duty, they told us, was to struggle for Palestine's right to be independent, like the other Arab states of the region.

I began to take an interest in the issues that were increasingly on every tongue: the Zionist's demand for unlimited Jewish immigration, their massive purchase of Arab lands, the huge stores of weapons they received from abroad with the active or passive complicity of the British authorities.

The defeat of the Axis powers, which immediately reactivated the Palestine question, marked the end of the careless friendship we enjoyed with our Jewish comrades. We continued to see them, sometimes in secret, despite the advice we each received from our respective elders. But our ardent discussions took on political overtones, and sometimes became violent.

I clearly remember a particularly unpleasant incident which took

place in October 1945. I was with a group of Arab and Jewish boys—
there were about twenty of us in all—when a heated argument degen-
erated into a veritable pitched battle during which we actually threw
stones at each other. I dismissed the episode and the next day set off to
visit relatives. My father had just given me a new bicycle and I was
proud to use it for the ten-kilometer trip.

While I was peddling through Tel Aviv on my way to Sumeil, four or
five boys a little older than myself suddenly started following me. They
were shouting at the top of their lungs: *"Aravit! Aravit!"* which means
"Arab" in Hebrew. They caught me, threw me on the ground, and
began punching me in the face, stomach, and back. Since I had never
seen these boys in my life before, I had no idea what I had done to
deserve the beating. Unable to defend myself, I was so frightened and
surprised I couldn't even cry for help. But when two of them grabbed
my new bicycle and started tearing it to pieces, I did manage to let out a
yell. Some passers-by rushed to snatch me from the clutches of my
aggressors, who got away. An older man helped me stand up and led me
to a nearby pharmacy where they bandaged my cuts.

My bicycle was ruined. Heartbroken, I left it at the side of the road
and took the bus to Jaffa, limping home from there. Aching all over and
worn out from the ordeal, I went straight to bed. Some hours later we
were awakened in the middle of the night by a loud knocking at the
door. When my father anxiously asked who was there, a stentorian voice
thundered: "Police!"

Our three-room apartment, hardly big enough for the seven members
of the family, was certainly unable to accommodate the ten or so Arab
policemen and the handful of officers—mainly British—who crowded
into the doorway. One of them handed my father a warrant for my arrest. I was ordered to follow him to the security police headquarters for
questioning.

My family had never had any trouble with the police before. The sud-
den invasion of our apartment by the police at this hour of the night was
in itself a shocking thing. What would the neighbors say? What crime
had I committed to deserve such a large police contingent?

I can still see my father, white as a sheet, asking what I had done. The
officer replied curtly that he didn't know anything. We all recognized
the officer as al-Habbab, for he was well known in Jaffa even though he
belonged to the secret services. A Palestinian and a servile defender of
the colonial power, he had been charged by his British superiors to fight
against "subversion." He carried out his task of spying on his compa-

triots and punishing any deviation which might upset the established order with such zeal, not to say cruelty and cynicism, that he was feared and detested by all.

My father pleaded my youth, saying that it was impossible to take a twelve-year-old to the police station in the middle of the night. Protesting my innocence, he promised to bring me to al-Habbab's office the first thing the next morning. He literally begged, but al-Habbab wouldn't budge. He finally conceded, however, that my father could come along.

The interrogation began as soon as we arrived at security headquarters. Seated importantly behind his desk, al-Habbab asked me where I had gotten the cuts and bruises on my face. When I finished telling him what had happened in Tel Aviv, he called me a liar. He then summoned a plainclothes policeman into the room, who proceeded to accuse me of having stabbed a Jewish boy in the foot during a riot which had taken place that day in Jaffa. I told him that I couldn't have committed this aggression since at that very moment I myself was being attacked in Tel Aviv. Al-Habbab then had two Jewish boys whom I had counted among my good friends brought into the office. Without blinking an eye, they confidently confirmed the policeman's version, adding that I was the leader of the gang that had attacked the group of Jewish schoolboys. I was flabbergasted, crushed, and revolted. Had they seen me take part in the battle with their own eyes? Yes, they replied in chorus. Since I couldn't provide any counterwitnesses, my protests were useless.

When the confrontation ended, my father, still trying to get permission to take me home, was bodily expelled. I clenched my teeth, tears welling up in impotent rage and humiliation at the sight of my father being brutally shoved aside while loudly proclaiming my innocence and appealing to al-Habbab's sense of fairness. Locked up in a cell for juvenile delinquents, I couldn't sleep a wink all night.

The next morning, al-Habbab tried to extract a confession by beating me on the fingers with a ruler. My silence, which he took for arrogance, made him beat me all the harder. "You don't want to confess? All right then! You'll go on trial!" he finally shouted.

I was then led under guard to a juvenile court set up on a lower floor. The Englishman who presided over it asked me a few questions in his limited Arabic. Once again I recited my woes, which obviously didn't make much of an impression on him. The hearing lasted only a few minutes. After I was taken back to the office where I had first been questioned, al-Habbab made me stand for about ten hours until late in the evening, at which point he delivered the verdict in the presence of my father. Naturally I was found guilty, and to atone for my misdeeds was sentenced to a year of house arrest. Among other things, this involved reporting to al-Habbab once a week with a detailed account of my activities.

For the first time in my life I felt frustration and hatred—hatred for the English who oppressed my people, hatred for those of my compatriots who served them, hatred for Zionism which had driven a wedge between Arabs and Jews. The sense of despair I felt at the injustice was nonetheless partially compensated by the prestige I enjoyed among my peers, who considered me more a hero than a victim. Hadn't I held up in the face of the oppressors and their repressive apparatus? Rashid al-Dabbagh, the school principal, immediately gave me a week off from school so I could recover from my wounds and traumatic experience. When I got back to class, my comrades welcomed me with open arms and I was more than ever the uncontested leader of the Najjadeh "lion cubs."

As for my parents, I had the impression that their protective tenderness toward me increased. My father didn't say much about the ordeal we had been through together, but given his deep patriotism I knew I could count on his complicity. Like my mother, he had approved my joining the Najjadeh, even though he himself was not a member of any military or political organization. Still, he acted rather strangely in the months following my arrest. My brother Abdallah and I noticed that he had begun to lock one of his closets to which no one had access but him. From time to time, he shut himself up in the room where the closet was located, and always emerged without saying a word. Intrigued, one day we decided to watch him through the keyhole. I can't even begin to express our astonishment as we saw him open the closet and take out a magnificent submachine gun! My father, the mildest and most peaceful of men, meticulously cleaning and oiling a lethal weapon, caressing it affectionately! Abdallah and I were thrilled. The gun was well beyond the means of a needy grocer like my father. Surely he must be a fighter in some underground unit!

The reality was quite different from our fantasies. When we finally got up the nerve to confess our indiscretion about a year later—it was toward the beginning of 1947—he told us he had paid for the gun out of his own pocket. It was not inconceivable, he said, that the British would withdraw their troops from Palestine, in which case the Arabs would have to defend themselves against the Jews who were arming themselves to the teeth. Most of the people in the Arab quarters of Jaffa bordering on Jewish settlements had done the same. With no one to count on for their defense, they were fearfully preparing for the day they'd be at the mercy of the Zionist fighters.

The Palestinian organizations were cruelly lacking in weapons. The guns the Najjadehs were training their members to handle were made of wood! During the whole time I was in the Najjadehs, I never had the chance to see, much less touch, a real weapon. The bulk of our training consisted of physical exercises and theoretical classes on the art of guerrilla warfare taught by former soldiers who had fought with the British during the Second World War.

The brutal suppression of the great rebellion of 1936–1939 had decimated the ranks of the Palestinian national movement, and dispersed the surviving leaders, most of whom were either jailed by the British or forced into exile. Obviously I had heard of Hajj Amin al-Husayni, the Mufti of Jerusalem and leader of the Palestinian movement, but at the time I knew little about him aside from his aversion to the Najjadehs and his insistence on safeguarding his full autonomy vis-à-vis the "historic leaders." But I do recall the return from exile of Jamal al-Hussayni, the Mufti's cousin. A huge popular meeting was organized in his honor in Jaffa's main square, and I was one of the thousands of demonstrators who chanted slogans proclaiming the will to fight for an Arab and independent Palestine.

Jamal al-Hussayni was a secret leader of one of the Palestinian organizations of the day, the Futuwa. Shortly after his visit to Jaffa, efforts aimed at merging the Futuwa and the Najjadeh began. To this end, the Arab League dispatched an Egyptian officer named Mahmud Labib, whose links with the Muslim Brotherhood were well known. His mission was a tricky one but met with apparent success since the two groups formally merged to constitute the "Youth Organization."

Far from breathing new life into the movement, the operation threw the members of the two artificially united organizations into utter confusion, paralyzing their activities. Muhammad al-Hawari, the Najjadeh leader, ceased all activity to protest the merger which he had bitterly opposed. A matchless orator and born leader, Hawari had been a passionate nationalist and contributed to demoralizing many of his admirers and followers by sliding from passivity into collaboration. Indeed, he actually went over to the Israelis when Jaffa fell to the Zionist forces. The Youth Organization petered out during the same period.

I am convinced that the British had a hand in this ill-conceived merger. Working through numerous channels, including their agents in the Arab League, they tirelessly intrigued to weaken the Palestinian movement either by stirring up divisions or by making it inoperative, as in the case of the Najjadeh and Futuwa.

The Palestinians were unanimous in demanding the end of the British mandate and the full sovereign independence of their country. So the colonial authorities stepped up the measures and initiatives aimed at justifying and prolonging their power. To that end, they had to foster dissensions in Palestine, exacerbate passions among the Jews and Arabs, and when necessary stir up armed clashes. In the spring of 1946, the London government virtually suspended the provisions of the 1939 White Paper by authorizing the admission of 100,000 Jewish immigrants into Palestine and the purchase of Arab lands by the Zionists. At the same time they proclaimed that Great Britain would continue to exercise its mandate over Palestine so long as conditions didn't permit the country to become independent.

At the beginning of 1947, I saw with my own eyes how the English sought to make their presence indispensable, how they tried to demonstrate that their withdrawal would lead to a bloodbath in Palestine. On a number of occasions, my friends and I watched a light tank stationed in Jaffa fire on the Jewish quarters of Tel Aviv. Thinking that the Arabs had opened fire, the Jews fired back. The British went through exactly the same procedure in reverse, firing on Jaffa from Tel Aviv. Skirmishes escalated between the two components of the population until November of the same year, when the United Nations General Assembly, noting that coexistence had become impossible, decreed the partition of Palestine into two states.

Britain's policy of clear-cut partiality toward the Jews was designed to counterbalance the potential means at the disposal of the Arabs, who constituted the overwhelming majority of the population. While the authorities pursued a pitiless repression against the Arabs, they treated Jewish terrorists guilty of atrocious crimes—even against the English themselves—with an indulgence which taxed the imagination. The forces of order turned a blind eye to the massive influx of arms the Haganah and other Zionist organizations received from abroad, but didn't hesitate to jail an Arab found in possession of a simple firearm. Indeed, we were forbidden to carry so much as a knife, an offense punishable by six years in prison.

The balance of power, which had seemed in our favor during the first two years following the war, was soon reversed in the Zionists' favor. It is true that the Zionists also enjoyed support and complicity from abroad that we lacked. The Arab states had a largely platonic sympathy for us, promising a great deal but in fact giving a merely symbolic assistance. The Palestinians had no organization comparable to the Jewish Agency, which centralized the funds and provided the coordination needed for the purchase and transport of arms. They were likewise devoid of a political and military leadership which, had it existed, could have organized their resistance.

Left to their fate, fearing massacres like that of Deir Yassin, hundreds of thousands of Palestinians decided to leave their country for temporary refuge. The decision was made all the easier by certain "national committees," notably at Jaffa, which assured those who wanted to leave that their exile would be of short duration, a few weeks or months, the time necessary for the coalition of Arab armies to overcome the Zionist forces. The Arab countries' loudly-trumpeted decision to resist the creation of Israel with the force of arms had given rise to an immense wave of hope among the Palestinians.

In retrospect, I think my compatriots were wrong to have believed the Arab regimes and in any case to have left the field open to the Jewish colonizers. They should have stood their ground, whatever the cost. The Zionists could never have exterminated them to the last man. Besides, for many, exile has been worse than death.

My parents decided to leave. After all, they were going to Gaza, my father's hometown. Confident of a speedy return, they left all their furniture and possessions behind, taking with them only the bare necessities. I can still see my father, clutching our apartment keys in his hand, telling us reassuringly that it wouldn't be long before we could move back. Thirty years have passed, and I have never again seen the house where I was born. I still don't know whether or not it was destroyed.

2

Years of Gestation

THE YEARS WE SPENT IN GAZA were among the saddest of my life—years of uncertainty, despair, years of misery. Yet for all that, our situation wasn't bad compared to that of others. While most of the refugees were huddled in makeshift camps, living in tents or tin shacks, we were lucky enough to have relatives living in the city, and one of my uncles took us in.

My uncle was of humble circumstances, having to support a large family on the meager wages he earned building wood frames for the construction industry. We stayed in a minuscule room crammed with seven mattresses for my parents and us five children. We barely had space to lie down. Clinging to the irrepressible hope of returning soon to Jaffa, my father extended our stay at my uncle's from month to month. In any case, he didn't have the money to move us anywhere else, so we lived in this suffocating closeness for two whole years, until my uncle told my father that he was unfortunately unable to keep us any longer.

The number of schools in Gaza was limited, and what with the enormous influx of refugees there wasn't room for us in any of them. It was only after months of repeated applications, pleading, and countless visits to various authorities that my father was able to get us all in school. His efforts might not have succeeded if the Egyptian authorities hadn't introduced emergency measures to facilitate the absorption of school-age

13

children: The schools were divided into morning and afternoon shifts so that the teachers could handle larger numbers of students.

My brother Abdallah and I were enrolled in the morning session, which began at seven o'clock. Since we didn't have enough money for public transportation, we went on foot with other children our age who lived in the nearby refugee camp and had to leave the house at about five-thirty to arrive on time.

One night during the winter of 1948–1949 Abdallah and I were awakened by the sound of low voices. My father was complaining to my mother that all his attempts to find a job—any job—had failed and the unemployment rate in Gaza was so high that he'd lost all hope of earning his living. The savings brought from Jaffa were almost gone. How could he feed his five children? My mother tried to reassure him, but without much conviction. His future seemed a dead end.

On our way to school the next day, Abdallah and I decided to look for work to help with the household expenses. Since our classes let out about midday, we figured we could do something in the afternoon. Knowing how proud my father was and how horrified he would be at the very thought of us working for money at our age, we decided not to breathe a word to our parents. We discreetly approached two of our cousins. One of them, a carpenter, hired my brother as a clerk. The other, who made wicker furniture, took me on as an apprentice. My monthly salary was two Egyptian pounds, which seemed enormous since a normal rent at the time was about four or five pounds. Inevitably, my mother soon guessed what we were up to. We handed our earnings over to her, which she used, unknown to my father, toward household needs.

My brother failed his exams that year and quit school to become a mechanic, which he had always wanted to do anyway. My father wasn't told, since he would have taken it very hard. He had come from an educated family. His father, Sheikh Abdallah, was a much revered religious leader in Gaza who had completed his studies at Al Azhar university in Cairo. My father, growing up before the First World War, hadn't been able to follow in his footsteps because the Ottoman authorities at the time made it difficult for Arabs, and particularly Palestinians, to seek an education. As a result, my father barely knew how to read or write. He never quite got over his lack of education and was more anxious than most for his children to complete their studies. In fact, Palestinians in general—especially in the diaspora—attach tremendous importance to the education of their children and make great sacrifices to see that they get one. It's a way of assuring their survival in a hostile environment. It isn't a coincidence that Palestinians today have the highest literacy rate in the Arab world.

My father didn't have cause for complaint on my account. He saw me studying late every night, and at the end of that first year in Gaza my report card showed that I had passed all my exams. Naturally he didn't suspect how much effort it cost. My job as an apprentice to my cousin took up all my afternoons, and was both demanding and tiring. Also, my wages seemed to shrink as the family savings dwindled.

One day I went to see a cousin I particularly liked who owned a large coffeehouse, the Al Kamal. After listening to my account of our money problems, he offered me a job in his coffeehouse for ten pounds a month, five times what I was making at the time. The offer was very tempting, but I hesitated since my family was extremely strict and considered working in a coffeehouse shocking. I knew my father had never set foot in one in his life, but I was afraid he'd get wind of the outrage since the Al Kamal is at the center of town and very crowded. Still, I decided to risk it.

The first weeks on my new job were painful. Each afternoon I spent six or seven hours on the lookout for familiar faces and trying to go unnoticed whenever I saw one. It didn't take my mother, who was highly observant, long to notice that something strange was going on. One day when she questioned me closely, I ended up by blurting out the truth. She was horrified, and begged me to quit immediately. She could get along without my salary by selling her jewels, she said, since the money I brought home could never make up for the trauma my father would suffer if ever he discovered the dishonor. I held my ground. I explained that I only had a few months before taking my baccalaureat exams and that after that I'd look for another job. She finally gave in, reluctantly, and promised to say nothing to my father. And when he began to wonder at our relative comfort, she pretended we were living off money she got from one of her jewels. A little while after that we left my uncle's house and rented an apartment.

Six months passed since I'd started working at the Al Kamal. Then in February 1950 the unthinkable occurred: My father entered the cafe. He walked along the counter behind which I was sitting, and without seeing me took a table. He stayed an hour, which seemed an eternity. I was paralyzed with fear, not daring to move for fear of attracting his attention even though he was at the opposite end of the room which was huge and crowded. He finally got up to leave, and while going down the steps leading to the exit, he heard one of the waiters call my name. He stopped dead, turned around, and saw me. Our eyes met for a few seconds and my father, seemingly unruffled, went out.

When I got home, my mother—trembling like a leaf—was waiting at the door to warn me that my father was beside himself with rage. My younger brothers and sisters were keeping as far out of the way as possible in a corner of the living room. He, meanwhile, was saying his prayers and completely ignored me. When he finished he asked icily if I were even capable of understanding the baseness of my behavior. When I tried to explain that I had taken the job solely to help the family and mentioned the conversation about the financial difficulties we had overheard two years earlier, he cut me short: "I would rather die of hunger than see you working in a coffeehouse!" I don't remember exactly what I replied—all I remember is that he suddenly lost his temper and kicked me in the chest.

I felt the ground give way under my feet and everything swirling around me. My father, who had never scolded me before in his life, had struck me. I was convinced I had acted for the good of the family, and my pride was hurt. I felt deeply humiliated. I cried for the first time in memory. And while the tears were streaming down my face, I ran up to the roof and threw myself off.

The jump wasn't particularly dangerous, since our house was an elevated one-story and only about ten feet from the ground, which in any case was sandy and soft. Rather than an act of despair, my gesture was the expression of anger, a way to protest what I saw as unjust treatment. Not that the fall was entirely harmless: It had the lasting effect of a distortion in the spinal column which has given me chronic back problems.

I lost consciousness on landing. When I came to my senses, my mother, brothers, and sisters were hovering over me while waiting for the ambulance to take me to the British hospital, one of the best in Gaza. I immediately noticed that my father wasn't there. Nor did he come to visit me during the ten days I was in the hospital. My father was a profoundly good man and I knew how much he loved me, so his behavior seemed inexplicably harsh. It was only later that I understood. He was a man with deep feelings, but not very demonstrative—simultaneously sensitive and headstrong. He had been very upset at my seeming flaunting of tradition, which he saw as the honor and reputation of the family and thus more important than anything. On top of everything else, he interpreted my behavior as an insolent challenge to paternal authority, equally sacred to him.

When I got out of the hospital, he called a family council. He told me how distressed he had been and asked me to give up my job at the Al Kamal at once. My mother opened her purse and pulled out a bundle of bank notes, more money than I had ever seen. She said she had sold all her jewels and that we would live off the proceeds until I passed my baccalaureat. My uncles and cousins, who had also been called to the meeting, assured me that I could count on their support if I decided to continue my studies. I was touched by such solidarity, and announced on the spot that I would no longer work at the Al Kamal.

The year 1951 marked a turning point in my life. Three years after the exodus, I left Gaza for Cairo with the intention of enrolling in the university. As promised, the family took up a collection, each according to his means. Besides the blessing of my parents, I was given fifty Egyptian pounds to tide me over during the first months. My father had recommended me to one of his cousins, Sheikh Yusuf, who was studying theology at the Islamic university Al Azhar. Although he was blind, Sheikh Yusuf came to the railway station to meet me and offered to put me up at the university dormitory while I looked for a place of my own. I jumped at the offer, even though the dormitory—a vast, foul-smelling gallery where countless beds were lined up in long rows—was dirty and generally repugnant.

Before sleeping, I hung all my clothes—including the trousers in which I had stuffed the fifty pounds—on the hooks provided. When I opened my eyes the next morning, I noticed they had disappeared. Panic-stricken, I awakened Sheikh Yusuf and asked if he knew what had happened. He didn't, and it was clear my things had been stolen. My cousin chided me for my carelessness, informing me that he always kept his things under his mattress. The venerable religious institution of Al Azhar was obviously not the unimpeachably honest place one might expect.

Shattered, I scarcely left my bed for the next ten days. I didn't have a piaster for food or lodging. With all my clothing stolen, the only thing I had left was a *dishdasheh*, a traditional robe I wore only at home. My future seemed bleak. It was out of the question to continue my studies, as higher education was not yet free in Egypt. As if that weren't enough, the Arab League had just cut off student subsidies for Palestinians in an economy drive.

My father had given me the name of one of his relatives, a wealthy merchant from Sumeil who had emigrated a few months before us. Mr.

al-Kashaf lived with his family in a fine residential neighborhood of Cairo. The thought of going to see him flashed through my mind, but because of my pride I decided against it. I didn't want to visit him when I was down. Some years later, however, as a young teacher, I was to marry his daughter.

Sheikh Yusuf advised me to enroll in the Al Azhar university, which subsidized needy students, thanks to a fund provided by charitable institutions. He himself was lodged free of charge and received a monthly stipend of four pounds. I declined the suggestion politely, not telling him how horrified I was at the very idea of religious education.

I did let myself be talked into applying for a scholarship to Dar al-Ulum, a sort of teachers' college. It was a far cry from my secular ideal, being closely associated with Al Azhar, but at least it offered courses in academic fields other than theology, such as Arabic literature, philosophy, and psychology. The grant in question was a mere four pounds a month, but I thought I could survive while pursuing my studies.

However, one couldn't enter Dar al-Ulum just for the asking. I had to pass a competitive exam, reputed to be tough, which covered Arabic literature about which I knew virtually nothing. I decided to have a go at it anyway, presenting myself before the jury along with about 500 other candidates. When my turn came, the president of the jury, an Al Azhar sheikh, began by questioning me on two famous poets. I had to confess I had never even heard of them. The examiner was appalled. The situation seemed so hopeless that I decided to play all or nothing, and said: "You're perfectly free to fail me, but first let me tell you what I think of the Al Azhar university you represent on this jury!" I told him how my money and clothing had been robbed, and that I had nothing left to lose but the *dishdasheh* on my back.

My little tirade left the sheikh with his mouth hanging open. After a silence which seemed interminable, one of his two colleagues asked me kindly, on a note of complicity: "But I'm sure you know a great deal about Palestinian poetry . . ." I picked up the cue and started reciting, and then analyzing, the poems of Muein Bessisso, who was later to be recognized as one of the leading poets of the Palestinian Resistance.

I got into Dar al-Ulum, and a few days later I joyfully took leave of Sheikh Yusuf and Al Azhar's sinister domitory, throwing off my *dishdasheh* for a shirt and pair of trousers. My monthly stipend of four pounds didn't allow me to rent a room, but some Palestinian students invited me to share their apartment without paying. Solidarity is a very real thing among Palestinians of the exodus and exile. I lived with these friends—some of whom were to become Fatah militants—for two years since I wasn't receiving any money from home. Then one day in 1953 I got a money order from my father— a royal sum. He had found a job in Saudi Arabia and had sent me his entire first month's salary. His employer at the time was an important contractor, Hamid Abu Sittah, who today sits on the Executive Committee of the Palestine Liberation Organization (PLO).

The year 1951 wasn't important only because it was the first time I was on my own and the start of my student years. More importantly, it marked the beginning of the political activism which has been the focal point of my life ever since.

My membership in the Najjadeh "cubs" in Jaffa, although a form of political involvement, doesn't really count, given my age and the circumstances. In Gaza, I had taken a lively interest in the development of the Palestine question despite my preoccupation with family matters and financial problems. But in the aftermath of the Arab collapse and the despair it engendered, the national movement was virtually finished. Only a handful of the traditional (and completely anachronistic) leaders tried in vain to revive it, most often under the auspices of the Arab League—a fossilized institution manipulated by reactionary Arab regimes tied to imperialism and little disposed to support the Palestinian cause. At the time I was burning with contempt and anger, and eager to rebel against the established order.

In the fall of 1951, the Arab League decided to cut off allocations for needy Palestinian students, which triggered a wave of indignation. I jumped into the fray feet first, participating in the demonstration organized at the League headquarters. We occupied the League and stormed and ransacked the office of Ahmad al-Shukeiry, at the time assistant secretary general of the League in charge of Palestinian Affairs. Our action was successful since the student subsidies were immediately reinstated. However, the police arrested the ringleaders, including myself, and packed us off to the Abdin prison near King Farouk's palace. I was released after forty-nine days.

It was during this period that I met Yasir Arafat for the first time. The man who was to gain international fame fifteen years later under the code name Abu Ammar was then a twenty-two-year-old engineering student. He was four years older than myself and I was immediately taken by his energy, enthusiasm, and enterprising spirit. Yasir was in charge of training the engineering students who wanted to participate in anti-British guerrilla activities in the Suez Canal Zone. He was also ac-

tive in the Palestinian Student Union (where I met him), a sort of umbrella organization grouping Palestinian students of various political
stripes—Muslim Brothers, Communists, Baathists, Arab Nationalists
(the party founded by George Habash), and others.

Palestinians in general took a passionate interest in the pan-Arab parties, whether rightist or leftist, and pinned all their hopes on them in
the absence of a strictly national group devoted to the liberation of Palestine. Consciously or unconsciously, they saw the various ideologies
they adopted merely as vehicles which they hoped would ultimately
lead to the common goal.

Like Yasir Arafat, I hadn't joined any political party. It's true that I
had a certain sympathy for the Muslim Brotherhood which I'd seen in
action in Gaza. They had preachers who, unlike the traditional *ulema*,
used a militant, impassioned language readily accessible to ordinary people. They called the faithful to the struggle and lifted the morale of the
masses when they needed it most. At the time the Muslim Brothers
were being persecuted and arrested by the Egyptian authorities, which
only added to their appeal. They knew how to die for their ideal, and a
number of them were killed between 1950 and 1952 while waging guerrilla activities against the British occupying forces along the Suez Canal.

Despite all this, I didn't join. My grandfather had been a sheikh and
my father was a good practicing Muslim, but the deep-seated tolerance
and open-mindedness of my circle had made the Brotherhood's ideology
foreign to me. Furthermore, my natural inclinations drew me toward a
secular nationalism which had yet to be defined.

Yasir Arafat and I didn't have any well-defined ideas on the subject,
but we knew what was damaging to the Palestinian cause. We were convinced, for example, that the Palestinians could expect nothing from the
Arab regimes, for the most part corrupt or tied to imperialism, and that
they were wrong to bank on any of the political parties in the region.
We believed that the Palestinians could rely only on themselves. In
1952 we decided to test the appeal of this fundamental idea by running
for the executive committee of the Palestinian Student Union on this
platform. As the only Palestinian organization which held democratic
elections, the PSU was the only group which could pretend to represent
any sector of Palestinian opinion.

The success of our undertaking was by no means assured. Most of the
students were either members or sympathizers of the various political
parties. Since we didn't belong to any of them and in fact outright
rejected them, in a way we were challenging the parties themselves, all

represented by candidates. These candidates, moreover, benefited in varying degrees from the prestige and material resources of their party.

On the other hand, we had our advantages. Yasir Arafat and I had succeeded in establishing good relations with the students irrespective of their political affiliations. We didn't present ourselves as being against the parties, but rather as being for the Student Union, the name we gave our ticket for the nine seats on the executive committee. Six of them, including Arafat and myself, belonged to our group. We gave three seats to members of other parties—to a Muslim Brother, a Baathist, and a Communist—to show our democratic and unitary attitude.

Our calculations turned out to be correct. Our ticket was elected with an overwhelming majority, showing that the students put their desire for unified Palestinian action before their party preferences. Yasir Arafat became president of the PSU and remained in that position until finishing his studies in 1956, at which point I succeeded him as head of the organization after having been his vice-president for four years.

In November 1952, two months after the elections, the Arab League once again cut off the subsidies for Palestinian students. As in the previous autumn, we declared a general strike and some of us occupied the League headquarters. This time the authorities didn't give in, and the police dislodged us with considerable force. I managed to escape with most of the others, but nineteen were arrested. Shortly thereafter, the security police headquarters notified the PSU that the students would not be released unless I turned myself in, which I did on the advice of Yasir Arafat at whose apartment I was hiding in the Cairo suburb of Heliopolis. The security police tried to humiliate the hothead they saw in me by locking me up in the prostitute section of the Abdin prison. I was released thirty-five days later on the personal intervention of Ahmad al-Shukeiry of the Arab League. He tried to win me over by arranging an interview for me with Salah Salem, one of the members of the Revolutionary Council that had seized power in Cairo four months earlier, but the meeting in no way lessened my fighting spirit.

The authorities, meanwhile, seemed to bear me a particular grudge which sometimes took the form of sheer pettiness. For example, I was a member of a delegation led by Yasir Arafat which was supposed to attend an international student festival in Warsaw, Poland, in July 1954. A few hours before our plane was to take off, I was arrested on the grounds that I was "too dangerous" to be allowed to leave the country. Numerous Palestinian students demonstrated noisily against this arbitrary action, demanding that my visa be returned, but to no avail. It was not until thirty-seven days later, after the delegation had returned to Cairo, that I was released.

At the time I had little sympathy for Gamal Abdel Nasser, sharing the distrust the Muslim Brotherhood and the Communists had for him in the early stages of his regime. I was especially critical of the fact that he did nothing for the Palestinian cause. The Israeli raid on Gaza on February 28, 1955, which claimed more than three dozen lives, gave rise to a surge of anger among Palestinians, indignant at the Egyptian army's passivity and inability to defend the population or counterattack on the same scale. Throngs of demonstrators swarmed through the streets of Gaza demanding arms. Palestinian students in Cairo organized strikes and demonstrations, publicly calling for the downfall of the regime.

While holding a sit-in and hunger strike at the PSU headquarters, we presented three demands to the Egyptian authorities: the abolition of the visa system imposed on Palestinians entering and leaving Gaza; the resumption of train services between Cairo and Gaza (interrupted when the demonstrations broke out); and the introduction of obligatory military training for Palestinians to enable them to defend themselves against Israeli attacks. We further demanded that Nasser visit us in person to discuss our grievances.

After two days of the strike, we were informed that Nasser was prepared to receive a delegation of our choosing. We rejected the offer, explaining that the meeting must be held in the presence of all 200 strikers or not at all. Nasser gave in and invited us to his office at the Ministerial Council. An imposing security guard was waiting at the entrance of the building and diligently searched us before we were admitted.

Nasser began by assuring us that he recognized the justice of all our demands, which he said he'd satisfy fully. Indeed, he gave orders that same day to lift all restrictions on Palestinian movements between Egypt and Gaza and to open camps for training fedayeen, or commandos. (On this last point, he did not always keep his word in practice, as we were to discover as years passed.) The atmosphere became relaxed and the conversation took on a cordial tone. At the end of the meeting, just as we were leaving, Nasser said he'd like to continue the discussion with four of us.

Abdel Hamid al-Tayeh (a Baathist), Izzat Auda (Communist), Fuad Ahmad (Arab Nationalist), and I were designated to carry on the second dialogue. With Nasser were Lutfi Waked, one of his closest associates,

Kamal el-Din Hussein, a minister many times over, and the future prime minister Ali Sabri.

The Egyptian president wanted to know more about the Palestinian Student Union, our feelings and aspirations. His first question—whether or not we belonged to any political parties—was somewhat indiscreet, not to say potentially dangerous in a country where all political formations had been banned and replaced by a single party. He realized his error when we replied innocently that we were nothing but Palestinian students. A lively discussion developed and we soon fell under the immense charm of the man, who seemed a great patriot. It was during this conversation that he revealed his intention of getting around the selective arms embargo imposed on him by the Western powers by going elsewhere, "to the devil himself if necessary," to assure Egypt's defense against Israeli aggression. Indeed, a few months later he roused great popular enthusiasm by concluding an arms deal with Czechoslovakia acting down the gauntlet to England and France. These two powers, through of our support, even though some of us didn't trust him completely.

The real turning point took place in July 1956 when Nasser announced the nationalization of the Suez Canal Company. An explosion of joy erupted among the Palestinians, who from then on saw Nasser as the champion of the anti-imperialist struggle. Like all Arabs from the Atlantic to the Gulf, we were deeply impressed by Nasser's daring in throwing down the gauntlet to England and France. These two powers, through their control of the Canal, had been violating Egypt's sovereignty and exploiting it in the most shameless fashion. In nationalizing the Company, Nasser restored an inalienable right to his people while giving all the Arabs—and in fact all the peoples of the Third World—a sense of dignity and self-confidence. Everything seemed possible, even the liberation of Palestine.

Three months later, Israel, Britain, and France invaded Egypt. Enthusiasm ran high as we mobilized to resist the aggression. We formed a Palestinian commando battalion to fight alongside Egyptian volunteers. Yasir Arafat, who was a reserve officer at the time, was sent to Port Said as part of the engineering corps to participate in mine-sweeping operations. I enlisted in the popular resistance forces but was unable to fight since the authorities didn't grant me authorization to go to the Suez front. I had to be satisfied with defensive tasks which included, among other things, mounting the guard at Cairo's bridges.

Resistance to the Israeli occupier in Gaza was organized by a newly formed front of Muslim Brethren, Communists, Arab Nationalists, Baathists, and Nasserists who joined forces on the basis of a united action program. There had initially been some difficulty reaching agreement with the Communists, who wanted to include a clause providing for cooperation with Communist-led Israeli progressives opposed to the tripartite invasion. At the time, most people weren't ready for this kind of fraternization: The Israeli, whatever his ideology or political convictions, was perceived as the enemy. The Gaza Communists ended up by watering down their text so the agreement could be concluded.

We helped the Front within the limits of our modest possibilities, smuggling funds, a few arms, and numerous political tracts into the occupied city. Our efforts brought us more frustration than satisfaction, and it was during this period that we began to contemplate an idea which still seemed like a dream. The Algerian nationalists had built up a powerful organization which had been locked in bitter conflict with the French army for the past two years. Their heroic struggle, which we had been following closely, fascinated us and filled us with admiration. In the course of long evenings we asked ourselves if we, too, couldn't create a broadly based movement, a kind of front which would bring together Palestinians of all political persuasions with a view toward launching an armed struggle in Palestine.

There had in fact been a few commando raids against Israel during those years 1954–1955, but almost all of them had been set up by the intelligence services of the countries adjacent to Israel. Groups formed by the Egyptian Mokhabarat primarily for espionage missions operated in Gaza and Jordan under the leadership of Mustafa Hafez, subsequently killed by a letter bomb sent to him by Israel's intelligence service Mossad. The same situation applied in Syria. We didn't feel particularly concerned by ventures dictated by national interest rather than concern for the Palestinian cause. We were suspicious of all Arab regimes whether progressive or conservative, and believed that an armed struggle worthy of the name had to be prepared, organized, and carried to its conclusion by Palestinians with no ties other than the devotion linking them to their own people. Our distrust was based on experience. Our comrade Abu Jihad (Khalil al-Wazir), for example, one of the founders of Fatah and currently a member of its Central Committee, had organized a raid against Israel from Gaza in 1954, and was promptly arrested by Egyptian Security.

We were all agreed on the general principles which should guide the movement we dreamed of creating. While awaiting the occasion to develop and codify them, we decided to spread these principles around us while simultaneously recruiting cadres who could one day put them into practice. At the time—just after the Suez War of 1956—our ideas concerning the creation of a large popular movement, let alone an army of national liberation, were still nebulous, but they were to crystallize into specific objectives over the next two years.

We went our separate ways in the first months of 1957. Yasir Arafat and Abu Jihad took jobs in Kuwait, where they were later joined by Faruq Qaddumi (Abu Lutf), presently head of the PLO department and Central Commitee member of Fatah. Yusuf al-Najjar, Kamal Adwan, and Abu Mazen moved to Qatar. As for myself, I opted for Gaza. With a degree in philosophy and psychology from Dar al Ouloum and a teacher's certificate from Ain Shams University, I could easily apply for a teaching position there.

The Security Police must have understood that I had ulterior motives in applying for work in Gaza at a time when numerous officials there were trying desperately to improve their lot by getting transferred to Cairo or some other large Egyptian city. I was appointed to Gaza anyway, but to my astonishment it was as a teacher in a girls' school. This was an exceptional measure, generally applied as a sort of punishment, since it's very embarrassing for a man in a traditional Islamic society to work in a feminine environment.

I went to see the director of national education and pointed out that my nomination was contrary to the regulations, which stipulated that only married men could teach in girls' schools. He replied with a smile that there was an exception to every rule. It was clear that they were trying to prevent me from having any political activity by isolating me in a milieu where I would be treated like a pariah.

The school of Al Zahra, which means flower, wasn't disagreeable in itself, but I was given classes for girls who were repeating the year—often spoiled, capricious, and undisciplined daughters of wealthy and overindulgent parents. All the same I wasn't discouraged. I decided to "abuse" my position to devote myself openly to political agitation. After all, what was there to lose? Although I was teaching Arabic and psychology, I had my students form civic action groups called "patriotic committees" which were to lead debates during the class hours. Six months later, in the middle of the school year, the school principal abruptly informed me that I had been transferred to a secondary school for boys.

I was overjoyed even though the Khaled ben Walid school was neither attractive nor comfortable. Located in the open desert outside

Gaza, its students came from nearby Palestinian refugee camps. The classrooms were minuscule, desperately overcrowded with sixty to seventy pupils in each, and dilapidated. In the winter we shivered with cold while rain seeped through the fragile roof.

On the other hand, it was the perfect environment for the political activities I intended to engage in. My pupils were poor, living in pitiful conditions and suffering with their parents from the trauma of exile. They seemed to show above-average intelligence and sensitivity.

I remember an incident which touched me deeply. I had formed a support committee for the Algerian revolution and asked them to contribute what they could to a collection. Despite their poverty, every one of them responded as of the very next day. They filed past my desk with their little offerings, a piaster, two or three, paltry sums equivalent to a few cents but which constituted real sacrifices for them. One little boy, visibly embarrassed, put his shirt on my desk. "It could be used by an Algerian boy," he said simply.

About that time—it was in 1958—I wrote a play entitled *Glorious Days* centered on the 1948 exodus. The text was drawn mainly from my own memories, starting with the flight from Jaffa by boat and including, of course, the tragic end of the couple who threw themselves into the sea to recover their lost child. The play created a great stir, and played for months in all the refugee camps of Gaza before being staged in various Gulf countries.

Another play I wrote during the same period was considerably more risky, as it was meant to denounce the attitude of the Arab regimes— including Nasser's—toward the Palestinian cause. I chose as my central character a buffoonlike figure of the Iraqi regime which had just seized power in Baghdad, Abbas al-Mahdawi, who presided over the "peoples' court" charged with dispatching opponents to the gallows. In my text, the accused were the Arab heads of state, whose "crimes" were listed by Mahdawi in the spicy language for which he was famous. A satire, the play ridiculed Mahdawi while at the same time having him say truths to which the Palestinians would be sensitive.

I took a number of precautions to get the play past the ever-vigilant censors. I couldn't be accused of subversion since the words of my character were quotations taken directly from the real Mahdawi's tirades. I also asked the subprefect of Deir al-Balah (where my school was located) to direct the play. A great drama enthusiast, he jumped at the chance. Finally, I invited the military governor of Gaza to the opening night. All the ambiguities and double meanings soared completely over his head.

He was delighted with the play, to the point of sending me an official letter congratulating me on it three days later.

That same day I received an urgent summons from Colonel Kamal Hussein, chief of the local security police. He had seen the play too, but more perceptive and better informed on my opinions, he hadn't missed its militant nature and clearly wanted to make me pay for my insolence. I protested my good faith, and as a proof referred him to the participation of the subprefect, the praise of the military governor, and the censors' seal of approval. "Could they all be imbeciles?" I exclaimed with feigned indignation. Colonel Hussein gritted his teeth, then said coldly: "You may be clever, Salah, but I'll catch up with you, don't worry."

What the colonel didn't know was that my literary exercises were merely the tip of the iceberg. The bulk of my activities, besides teaching, were underground and consisted of recruiting and organizing groups of militants. I used the same methods as those applied by my comrades working in the Gulf countries. We chose candidates for our organization according to moral and political criteria we considered indispensable: They had to be politically independent with no ties to any party, and they had to have blameless conduct in their private lives. As a proof of their respectability and seriousness, we asked that they renounce alcohol. During a probationary period, we gave them a political formation and had them read various books and pamphlets.

For security reasons, we chose the "vertical" organizational model, with each of us linked to a single militant who in turn recruited another and so on. The resulting "chain" seemed to us less vulnerable than cells grouping three or more members all of whom knew each other. Our meetings were generally held in coffeehouses (my favorite was the Al Kamal) where we played backgammon or dominos while talking in low voices.

From time to time we drew up and printed political pamphlets denouncing this or that oppressive measure adopted by the Egyptian authorities. But in general we avoided attracting attention. The recruitment and training of cadres phase is inward-looking and calls for extreme prudence. As a precaution, we signed each tract with a different name: "The Generation of Reform" or "The Young Avengers," for example. As of early 1958, however, my comrades in the Gulf and I had decided to name the movement we intended to create Fatah (the Conquest). We had originally adopted the name Harakat Tahrir Filastin (Palestine Liberation Movement), but then reversed its initials to produce

Fatah. We decided against using the name until we had set up the movement's structures, statutes, and centralized leadership, a task we finally accomplished in October 1959.

At the beginning of 1959, Yasir Arafat asked me to seek a better-paying job in an Arab oil-producing country. My teacher's salary in Gaza barely enabled me to support myself, and the movement desperately needed money. Furthermore, we could operate more freely in the Gulf states where the security services were less developed and the rulers better disposed toward us than in the countries bordering on Israel.

So I filed an application for a position advertised by the Education Department in Qatar. But after receiving a favorable reply, I was brusquely informed that the position was not available after all. Abu Mazen, one of our comrades who had a high position in the department, looked into the matter and discovered that Egyptian Security had warned the Qatar authorities that I was a "dangerous Communist."

A little later, however, Kuwait's Director of Instruction, Abdel Aziz Hussein, came to Gaza at the head of a mission to recruit teachers. I had an interview with him and he hired me on the spot, ignoring the police report he had received about me similar to the one sent to Qatar.

Since I had recently gotten married, I decided to leave Gaza with my young wife. The day of our departure, a police officer appeared at the house and handcuffed me without explanation. Despite my protests, he stayed with us all the way to the Cairo airport, refusing to remove the handcuffs until I actually boarded the plane for Kuwait.

My old friend, Colonel Kamal Hussein, head of the Gaza security police, having failed to have me arrested or denied an exit visa, apparently wanted to remind me of his little warning.

3

The Tidal Wave

ON OCTOBER 10, 1959, a small group of us met in a discreet house in Kuwait to hammer out the organizational structures of Fatah. More meetings with other participants took place over the following days, always in the greatest secrecy. There were fewer than twenty of us in all, representatives of underground groups from various Arab countries and beyond, coming together to centralize our activities for the first time. This limited congress marked the formal creation of what was to become the most powerful national liberation movement Palestine had ever known. And yet, the total number of militants represented by those attending the restricted congress was under 500 persons.

A number of documents were drawn up and approved during those October meetings. These involved the movement's structures and statutes as well as the strategy and tactics, means of action and financing, of the revolution we intended to launch. The tasks of Fatah's various organs were spelled out as were the methods of recruitment and training of cadres. The political program per se, defining the guiding principles of the movement, had been finalized at the beginning of 1958. Drafted by a committee formed for that purpose, the document had been discussed, revised, and then approved through personal contacts or correspondence.

The program reflected the consensus we had reached in the course of countless discussions throughout the 1950's in Cairo or Gaza, but it was

also based on the experiences of our predecessors in the national movement.

Although at the time we hadn't undertaken a systematic study or collective reflection on the subject, each of us had drawn lessons from the
past through his own reading. The conclusions we reached were similar,
even though our perceptions and analyses of the events marking Palestine's history differed. Furthermore, our assessments were to evolve
and crystallize as time went on.

I don't think it would be fair to condemn totally the actions of those
who came before us. First of all, they didn't constitute a monolithic
bloc. There were among them members of the great families and men of
the people, patriots and traitors, those who saw clearly and those who
didn't. In any case, they can only be judged in the context of their time,
taking into consideration the prevailing mentality, the objective and
sometimes decisive difficulties they had to face without the necessary
experience to carry them through. Many of them made heavy sacrifices,
some paid with their lives for their miscalculations. But the failure of the
Palestinian movement cannot be attributed solely to an unfavorable international situation or the enemy's strength and cleverness. Serious
errors were committed. One of the tasks we set for ourselves was to pin-
point and analyze these errors so as to avoid repeating them.

There is no question that our predecessors failed to set up a strongly
structured organization. Until the creation of Fatah, the national movement was led by members of the great families, particularly the Hus-
saynis and the Nashashibis, more often than not pitted against one another in bitter rivalry or open conflict concerning the course of action to
follow. The organization, when indeed any existed, was improvised and
never rooted in the masses, so it fell apart as soon as the leader who
dominated it disappeared. Through the local committees which sprang
up spontaneously, various forms of struggle were waged, such as strikes
and demonstrations or even guerrilla warfare. The uprisings of 1919,
1922, 1928, 1933, and 1936–1939 testify to the fighting spirit of the population, but also to the sterility of a struggle which is not launched,
directed, and sustained by a central, structured, and permanent body.
This is why Fatah's founders attached such importance to the development of an authentically popular organization which would survive whatever the fate of any of its leaders.

Another error committed by our predecessors was that they underes-
timated the importance of integrating the Jewish population, or at least
part of it, into the national liberation movement. Before the Second

World War there was no question in the minds of the movement's leaders or the population at large that the struggle was being waged against the British occupier. They invariably demanded the withdrawal of British troops, the proclamation of independence, and the sovereignty of the Palestinian state. They accused, and rightly so, Britain of having provoked the conflict by issuing the Balfour Declaration in 1917, which promised the Jews a national home in Palestine, and of having fueled this same conflict through various means in order to justify and perpetuate its colonial power. It was clear that this policy could only be detrimental to the entire population, Arab and Jewish alike.

If for no other reason, Hajj Amin al-Hussayni, Mufti of Jerusalem and preeminent leader of the resistance between the two wars, deserves credit for obliterating any trace of religious antagonism among the Arabs. He managed to unite both Christian and Muslim Arabs in the same anti-imperialist struggle. But why hadn't he tried to convince the Palestinian Jews that their real interests lay in renouncing Zionist illusions and making peace with the Arabs? And why didn't the Palestinian trade unions form a common front with the Jewish workers? Of course it was difficult for the victims of Zionist colonization—particularly those who lost their lands and jobs to the new immigrants—to distinguish the Jews who tried to live with the Palestinians from their Zionist leaders. Still, the Palestinian leadership should have made a real effort to dissipate the ambiguities and misunderstandings that stood in the way of Jewish-Arab understanding.

From the very beginning, then, the founders of Fatah had foreseen the possibility of creating a democratic state on all Palestine in which Jews, Christians, and Muslims could live in harmony as equal citizens. In the early stages, however, various political factors prevented us from making public the proposal we were to offer the Israeli Jews in 1968.

Our predecessors also committed the grave error of placing the Palestinian national movement at the mercy of the Arab regimes, confusing the selfish motives of these last with the disinterested motives of the Arab people. Most of the Arab governments at the time were heavily influenced if not dominated by Great Britain, and thus could not, either by necessity or inclination, be sincere allies of a liberation movement struggling against the very imperialism to which they were tied. Sheikh Izz al-Din al-Qassam, a true freedom fighter who organized the peasants before taking to the maquis in 1932, died heroically in 1935 at the end of a battle doomed from the start because of the total lack of support from any "brother" country. It was the British who actually killed him, but responsibility for his death must be borne primarily by the Arab accomplices of the mandatory power.

Nor did any Arab regime help the Palestinian people during the great popular uprising of 1936. The general strikes—the first of which lasted six months—the demonstrations, the pitched battles that followed one after another in rapid succession up until the very eve of the Second World War, were all put down in blood. The Arab states stood by idly, neither trying to stop the carnage nor supplying the slightest material aid to a defenseless population confronting British cannons and tanks. As if that weren't enough, they issued an appeal to the Palestinian people inviting them to stop fighting against "our great ally, England." At the same time they tried to divert the revolution by designating the Jews as the enemy to attack.

After the war, while the Zionists were receiving huge quantities of arms with the complicity of the British, while the balance of power was tipping dangerously in the Zionists' favor, while Haganah in early 1948 was pursuing its conquest of territory, still the Arab states refused to give the Palestinians the means to defend themselves. For form, they sent a few hundred guns which had to suffice for the tens of thousands who could have been mobilized for the battle.

To justify their passivity, the Arab states said they had taken it upon themselves to liberate Palestine. The outcome of their miserable adventure is well known. Their armies, which poured into Palestine on May 15, 1948, were not even capable of retaining the area allotted to the Arabs under the partition plan adopted by the United Nations General Assembly in November 1947. And with good reason. King Abdallah of Jordan, casting a covetous eye on the West Bank, rushed to annex it, while King Farouk, more discreet, placed the Gaza strip under Egyptian administration. The Palestinian government set up in Gaza in September 1948 under the presidency of Ahmad Hilmi Pasha never even got off the ground, with no Arab capital willing to risk supporting it. In practice, the Arab states favored the consolidation of the fait accompli, enabling the new Israeli state to extend the territory allotted to it by the UN.

Countless examples could be given to illustrate the popular dictum that "all revolutions conceived in Palestine abort in the Arab capitals." Experience has shown that when the chips are down all the Arab regimes, whether progressive or reactionary, act in the same way, sacrificing the Palestinian cause to their own parochial interests.

So the founders of Fatah swore to resist all attempts to place the

Palestinian national movement under the tutelage of any Arab government, regardless of which one. It was only at this price that our undertaking could be lasting and succeed in the long run. This being the case, we were not, as we explained to our militants, separatists. Quite the contrary, we aspired to become the champions of Arab unity, especially since we were convinced that the Palestinians would not be able to liberate their country single-handedly as long as the local and international balance of power remained what it was. Our goal was to become the catalysts of a unitary and revolutionary Arab force, the spearhead of a wide front which alone would be capable of restoring Palestinian rights. Such was and remains our strategy. In the meantime, our stress on self-reliance in no way precludes agreements or tactical alliances with foreign governments, Arab or otherwise, whose interests coincide with ours.

This principle was falsely applied by Hajj Amin al-Husayni when he rallied to Nazi Germany during the Second World War, thereby committing an error which we vigorously condemn. However, his behavior must be placed in its true context. For obvious reasons, Zionist propaganda presents him as a Nazi sympathizer. Anyone who knew him personally, myself included, knows otherwise. Hajj Amin was a nationalist, a conservative to be sure, but sincere all the same. In his defense I must say that despite his mentality and the serious differences which separated us, he never publicly criticized Fatah and its leadership.

I saw him for the last time in 1974, three months before his death. When, during our conversation, I reproached him for having linked his fate to Germany, he explained why. Outraged by Britain's role and activities in Palestine, relentlessly hounded by the mandate authorities, he felt it was only natural that he should join the enemy camp. Like many other Arab nationalists, especially in Egypt and Iraq, he believed that the Axis powers would win the war and that they would grant Palestine its independence as a mark of appreciation toward those who supported them during the conflict. I told him that such calculations were a bit naive when one considers that Hitler placed the Arabs in fourteenth place, *after* the Jews, in the hierarchy of races on our planet. If Germany had won, it would have instituted a far crueler occupation than the one known under the British Mandate.

Hajj Amin in any case was not a Nazi, any more than the Palestinian leaders who supported Great Britain during the war were agents of imperialism. The pro-British faction was quite simply betting on an Allied victory and hoped through their support of Britain to wrest their country's independence, which after all was the primary and sacred goal of all the struggles waged by the Palestinian people since the First World War.

Those who have tried to promote the belief that the Palestinian nationalists were agents of Nazi Germany conveniently forget that thousands of our compatriots fought in the British army. Even today, Fatah's best military instructors were trained in the British forces. Ironically, General Wajih al-Madani, the first commander-in-chief of the Palestine Liberation Army constituted in 1965, was a classmate of General Moshe Dayan in a British military school in Palestine.

It wasn't only the experience and errors of our predecessors which helped guide our first steps. The guerrilla war in Algeria, launched five years before the creation of Fatah, had a profound influence on us. We were impressed by the Algerian nationalists' ability to form a solid front, wage war against an army a thousand times superior to their own, obtain many forms of aid from various Arab governments (often at odds with one another), and at the same time avoid becoming dependent on any of them. They symbolized the success we dreamed of.

At the time we didn't have any relations with representatives of the National Liberation Front (FLN), so we read everything we could get our hands on concerning the Algerian movement. My political culture was somewhat lacking in those days. As a philosophy student, I naturally had some familiarity with Hegel, Marx, and Lenin. But my personal readings were eclectic, ranging from Michel Aflaq (founder of the Baath party) and Sayed Kotb (one of the ideologues of the Muslim Brotherhood) to adventure stories and detective novels. It was only after my return to Gaza in 1957 that I developed a strong interest in revolutions, all revolutions.

I devoured the works of Lenin. I found his courage, his basic optimism, even while living as a political refugee abroad, exalting. The Bolsheviks' seizure of power and the difficulties they faced held many lessons of universal interest. But I personally felt closer to Mao Zedong, whose moral sense struck me as more akin to Islam than to the strict materialism of Lenin. More than anything, the Long March captured my imagination. In my mind's eye, I pictured the Palestinian people, armed, returning to their country to drive out the usurpers.

Frantz Fanon was one of my favorite authors. In his *Wretched of the Earth*, which I read and reread countless times, he said that only a people who doesn't fear the guns and tanks of the enemy is capable of fighting a revolution to the finish. By that he meant that the Algerian nationalists would never have started anything if they had taken into account the balance of power at the time they launched their insurrection. Later it became clear how right he was—from one end of the Third World to the other, entire peoples, deprived of everything, took up arms to gain their freedom and independence.

The founders of Fatah were well aware of Israel's military superiority, the means at its disposal and the power of its allies, but still they set as their main objective the launching of the armed struggle. Not that we harbored any illusions regarding our ability to overcome the Zionist state. But we believed that it was the only way to impose the Palestinian cause on world opinion, and especially the only way to rally our masses to the peoples' movement we were trying to create.

In this regard, we took two factors into account: the mood of the Palestinians and their dispersal among various Arab political parties. As for the parties, we couldn't compete with them on ideological grounds. We didn't have anything better to offer than the Muslim Brethren, the Communists, the Arab Nationalists, or the Baathists in their respective domains. In truth, we believed that these formations were negative in that they divided the Palestinians and relegated the liberation of Palestine to the background.

Only armed struggle would be capable of transcending ideological differences and thus become the catalyst of unity. Indeed, we had noticed that many of our compatriots, saturated with the speeches and promises of Arab parties and politicians, began to tire of this sterile verbosity and to ask themselves if pan-Islamism, pan-Arabism, or Communism weren't really tedious detours or, worse still, substitutes for the goal most important to them, the recovery of their country.

We exposed our doctrine to the public through a monthly magazine called *Filastinuna* (*Our Palestine*), edited anonymously in Beirut as of 1959. It appeared irregularly, in keeping with our means and possibilities, and included news coverage and items, editorials, and articles signed by pseudonyms. In it, using simple language understandable to everyone, we outlined our basic theses which could be summarized as follows: revolutionary violence is the only way to liberate the homeland; it should be carried out, at least in a first stage, by the Palestinian masses themselves and led independently of parties and states; although the active support of the Arab world is indispensable for its success, the Palestinian people must retain the power of decision and the role of vanguard.

Fatah, running counter to the Arab nationalist theses which held sway at the time, also proclaimed that "Arab unity will be achieved through the liberation of Palestine" rather than the reverse. These were daring positions at a time when Nasserism was at its peak and when the birth of the United Arab Republic grouping Egypt and Syria seemed to herald a tidal wave that would submerge the state of Israel.

Our primary task during that autumn of 1959 was not to win over large sectors of public opinion, but rather to set up an organization which would enable us to launch the armed struggle and become a mass movement. We conceived two branches, one military and the other political, to be built on a pyramidal model. Cells at the base, sectional and regional committees, and a revolutionary council were to function under the supreme control of a central committee. The committee would draw its authority from a national congress, a sort of parliament grouping representatives of all segments of the Palestinian population—merchants, functionaries, manual laborers, members of the liberal professions, and intellectuals—among whom our members would lobby as independents.

During the phase devoted to the training of cadres, which lasted from 1959 to 1964, we created hundreds of cells, not only in the areas bordering on Israel (the West Bank, Gaza, refugee camps of Syria and Lebanon) but also within Palestinian communities in the other Arab countries, Africa, Europe, and even North and South America. Our militants, without revealing their membership in Fatah, succeeded in getting elected to leadership positions in trade unions, clubs, cooperative associations, and municipal councils. Those who possessed particular talents were even entrusted with high positions in a number of Arab governments.

Absolute secrecy was the cardinal rule dominating all our activities. Each cell consisted of a maximum of three members who knew each other only by code names which were changed from time to time for additional security. The cells generally met in public places in full view of everyone. Telephone or postal contacts were strictly forbidden, and all messages were delivered orally even if the leadership had to send emissaries to other countries for this purpose.

In keeping with our determination to safeguard our independence, we refrained from asking the slightest financial aid from any Arab country during this period. But our needs were great. Not only did we have to assure the operation and development of Fatah, we also had to pump money into various funds, including one for arms purchases. We had to ask heavy sacrifices on the part of our militants, who turned a large share—sometimes over half—of their salary or wages over to Fatah. Our funds were further increased by generous donations from Palestinians of the diaspora, who either belonged to Fatah or sympathized with our cause. Over the years, our fund raisers set up a vast network of contributors, integrated or not into the official support committees.

Fatah really began to take off in 1964. Two events contributed to swelling its ranks. The first was our success in unifying most of the thirty-five to forty Palestinian organizations which had spontaneously come into being in Kuwait. It's true that many of them had a very tenuous existence, with only a small number of enthusiasts. But their absorption into Fatah ended a wasteful scattering of goodwill and effort, and in some cases brought us dynamic and competent elements. Still more important was the merger we negotiated with the organizations in Qatar and Saudi Arabia led by three men who were to play major roles in the future: Yusuf al-Najjar and Kamal Adwan (both killed by an Israeli commando in Beirut in April 1973), and Abu Mazen, presently a member of Fatah's central committee. Their ideas were very close to ours, so the merger agreement was concluded without difficulty.

But it was really the breakup of the United Arab Republic in September 1961 which marked the beginning of our transformation into a mass movement. The letdown following the collapse of the Syrian-Egyptian union was commensurate with the immense hope raised when it was proclaimed under Nasser three years earlier. Bitterly disappointed, numerous Palestinians left their respective parties to join Fatah.

It would be difficult to empathize with the Palestinians' impatience to recover their land without some idea of the extent of the hardships they endured. Exile in itself is a painful experience that can only be understood by those who have gone through it. The grief of losing one's home and country is even greater when compounded by separation from one's loved ones. Rare is the Palestinian family (which is traditionally close-knit) that was able to stay together, and not be scattered by the force of events throughout various Arab countries and parts of the world as far away as the United States or South America.

The situation of my family is not unusual in this regard. My older brother Abdallah was a mechanic in Saudi Arabia before becoming an air-conditioning technician in Kuwait. My young brother Ahmad is a professor of English literature in Qatar, but before that lived in Pakistan, Egypt, and England. My two sisters, Salwa and Insaf, are both in Saudi Arabia, but one teaches in Jiddah and the other lives in Riyadh where her husband works for the Defense Ministry. In a quarter of a

century we managed to get together only once, in 1977, when my
brother Abdallah underwent a serious operation in Kuwait. The only
one absent from this memorable family reunion was my father, who had
died the year before in Cairo.

When the Palestinians left their country in 1948, they thought they
would be welcomed like brothers in the Arab states. A big surprise was
in store for them. The lucky ones were treated like foreigners; more
often it was as undesirables. In Lebanon, a hospitable country if ever
there was one, they were admitted with solicitude, but the refugee
camps soon turned into ghettos which you couldn't leave or enter without permits. In Jordan there was free access to the camps, but the refugees were subjected to unremitting police surveillance: Any political
activity, the slightest hint of dissent, was punished by harsh
interrogations, arbitrary imprisonment, even torture. Everyday conditions were less severe in Syria, but on the other hand the authorities
demanded a total conformity and unconditional allegiance to the regime
of the moment, whether rightist or leftist, separatist or pan-Arab. The
employment problem was the same from one end of the Arab world to
the other: The local citizens had priority for the available positions, the
Palestinians having to accept the difficult and ill-paid subaltern jobs. In
any case, they had first to get clearance with the security police, who
thus had the power to condemn to unemployment any Palestinian
judged "disloyal" or suspected of "subversion."

Kuwait was one of the rare exceptions to the rule. Both the citizens
and the rulers of this minuscule state have always given us sympathy
and support. It's true that our people contributed immensely to the development and well-being of the country, even before the vastly increased oil revenues started pouring in. The Palestinian community,
which today represents about 20 percent of the population, includes
numerous teachers, engineers, doctors, and high government officials,
not to mention a large body of skilled workers.

It is not a coincidence that Fatah was founded in Kuwait. Many of us
had good positions in the country: Yasir Arafat was a respected engineer
at the Ministry of Public Works, Faruq al-Qaddumi (Abu Lutuf) headed
a department at the Ministry of Public Health, Khalid al-Hasan and Abd
al-Muhsin al-Qattan were part of the high government administration,
Khalil Ibrahim al-Wazir (Abu Jihad) and I were teachers in secondary
schools.

Compared to Palestinians living in other Arab countries, we were
privileged. Although vigorously pursuing underground activities, we

were neither hounded nor persecuted. I used the courses I taught in philosophy, psychology, and Arabic as a platform to expose Fatah's ideas, and never had any trouble. Moreover, I recruited excellent elements from among my students.

On the other hand, our movements were subjected to the same restrictions as those of Palestinians everywhere. Although we had travel documents delivered by this or that Arab state, we were obliged to obtain exit and entrance visas which were granted sparingly and only after repeated and time-consuming applications. No matter that we were Egyptian, Syrian, Jordanian, or Lebanese subjects, the authorities of our adopted countries continued to treat us like foreigners, and suspicious ones at that.

I had to travel quite frequently in connection with my political duties within Fatah. Added to the problems of getting visas and exit permits, I had to go through considerable administrative red tape to get time off during the school year. Due to my frequent absences, the educational authorities began to suspect that I was involved in troublesome activities, so I ended up avoiding trips that weren't absolutely necessary.

I remember a case in March 1963. My wife had just gotten word that her older brother, an engineer who worked in Cairo, had been killed in an accident. We had to go at once, and with some difficulty I got permission to leave. There were no direct flights to Egypt, so my wife, three-year-old daughter Imane, and I took a plane to Beirut, where we planned to spend the night before catching a connecting flight for Cairo. But the Lebanese authorities refused to give us a twenty-four-hour transit visa, and we were forced to remain at the Beirut airport. We were herded into a tiny room where we didn't even have space to lie down. I begged them to let my wife and little girl go to a hotel in town while I stayed at the airport, but the security officer was adamant.

At this juncture, a dog was ushered into the room where we were being sequestered. It hadn't been granted entrance into the country either since it didn't have valid vaccination papers. I began to console myself with the idea that no discrimination separated Palestinians from dogs, when someone came in to fetch the creature which in the meantime had received a special dispensation thanks to an "intercession from high quarters."

The incident, which struck me as symbolic of our fate, remains vivid in my memory. More than ten years later, in an effort to illustrate the sad plight of the Palestinian people and the sense of our struggle, I told this story to a prominent Lebanese who today has a high position in the

Falangist party. The Lebanese, after coldly looking me up and down, replied contemptuously: "Your so-called liberation movement hasn't attained any of its objectives. You will remain undesirable foreigners and you will never have free access to the Arab countries. The only concrete result of your presence here in Lebanon is that we have to pay our servants higher wages thanks to your salary demands." The Falangist's wife was unable to hide her indignation at such cynicism. "If I were Abu Iyad," she said to him, "I'd shoot you down right here."

He was right about one thing: Despite our struggles, despite our thousands of martyrs, our dead on the Arab battlefields, we are still treated like a plague-ridden people.

Another and equally revealing incident happened not so long ago. A certain Naji al-Astal, holder of a bona fide Egyptian travel document, was refused entry at the Cairo airport one day in 1976. The authorities packed him onto a plane for Damascus, whence he was sent to Kuwait. There, they put him on a plane for Amman, which similarly refused to let him in. He thus made a tour of various Arab countries for several weeks before being granted asylum thanks to countless interventions on his behalf. To my knowledge, Astal had never committed a reprehensible act. But a police report based on mere gossip is enough to incriminate a Palestinian.

A stateless people are a people without recourse, without defense. It is hardly surprising that we seek our identity, indeed our very existence, in symbols such as a passport or a flag.

At the beginning of the 1960's, then, discontent was rife among Palestinians faced with the indifference of the Arab regimes. Increasing numbers of my compatriots, inspired among other things by the campaign we were waging in the *Filastinuna* magazine, began to feel a pressing need for a purely Palestinian fighting organization. Various governments, taking note of the situation, believed that this "vacuum" should be filled by the creation of a movement that would channel the growing anger and make sure it didn't turn against them. But they needed a man capable of restoring Palestinian self-confidence and organizing them under Arab government sponsorship.

Egyptian President Nasser favored Ahmad Shukeiry, an eloquent lawyer and excellent orator who had gained experience in international politics as Saudi Arabia's representative to the United Nations. So in September 1963, Shukeiry was assigned the task of seeking ways to bring about a "Palestinian entity." To this end, he was supposed to consult with Arab governments and convene a Palestinian congress which would give rise to a representative organization.

Fatah's leadership immediately saw through the maneuver, and realized how threatening an institution formed, actuated, and controlled by the Arab regimes could be for the Palestinian national movement. Yasir Arafat and I had known Shukeiry well in the early fifties when we headed the Palestinian Student Union. We decided to try to persuade him to cooperate with us.

During a first meeting in Cairo, I told Shukeiry why we believed that an organization formed from above would be ineffective without the active support of the base. I proposed a secret coordination between his public activities and our underground activities. The Palestine Liberation Organization (PLO) he had been charged to set up by the first Arab summit in January 1964 would become, I told him, a legal front for the armed struggle to be waged by our militants. The liaison could be assured by certain of our cadres whom he could appoint as members of the PLO Executive Committee.

Ahmad Shukeiry—who still knew nothing of Fatah—listened very attentively and even, I thought, sympathetically. He asked for time to think it over. During his tour of Arab capitals, a number of comrades were instructed to talk to him along the same lines as I had. His final response, however, was negative. He informed me that his position, his relations with the Arab regimes, and his duty not to jeopardize Arab League strategy (which then consisted of preventing Israel's unilateral diversion of the Jordan headwaters) made it impossible for him to conclude such an alliance with us. Several years later, when he was ousted from the PLO leadership, he tried to blame his negative attitude on Nasser and the other Arab leaders. His belated explanations were not very convincing. Since we had proposed secret relations, why did he feel the need to get the green light from the Arab chiefs of state? Far from helping us, as he promised, Shukeiry was to fight us tooth and nail.

The first Palestinian National Congress was convened for May 28, 1964, facing us with the dilemma of whether or not we should attend. On the one hand, a number of factors, including its sponsorship, composition, and real purpose, inclined us to boycott it. At the same time we didn't want to cut ourselves off from Palestinian politics. More importantly, the congress would enable us to infiltrate a rich and powerful organization and take advantage of the means at its disposal. In fact, it could be useful as a facade for our underground activities. So a number of our comrades—including Abu Jihad, Yusuf al-Najjar, and Kamal Adwan—attended the congress and used the opportunity to defend Fatah's main tenets, including the need for armed struggle.

At the time we were feverishly trying, within our limited means, to lay the groundwork for the guerrilla activity we planned to launch. Without financial support from any Arab government, we bought light weapons, often of inferior quality, on the open market. The toughest problem we faced was the training of our future fedayeen, more than a thousand of whom were already organized in cells. The actual training wasn't difficult: In a pinch we could make use of former soldiers who had served in the Arab armies or in the British forces during the Second World War. What we really needed was a secure place where they could be trained.

The only Arab regime favorable to us in 1964 was that of Ahmed Ben Bella, who had authorized us to open a representative office in Algiers. But Ben Bella was very close to Nasser and refused us any material assistance. It was only when Houari Boumedienne came to power in 1965 that Algeria sent us a first arms shipment—thanks to General Hafiz al-Asad, at the time Syria's air force commander-in-chief, with whom we had been on good terms since 1964.

Asad took consignment of the air-freighted arms and delivered them to us, unknown to his government and the Baath party to which he belonged. Indeed, while the Syrian government was hostile to us in those days, we enjoyed the complicity of two men occupying key positions: Asad and General Ahmad al-Sueidani, chief of military intelligence and subsequently chief of general staff. It was because of them that we were able to use two training camps in Syria as of early 1964. Other fedayeen underwent shooting exercises in desert regions, sometimes among the bedouins. Still others, without revealing their membership in Fatah, received training by enlisting in the Palestine Liberation Army (PLA) that Ahmad Shukeiry had begun to set up as an arm of the PLO.

The PLA was a paper tiger. It was not designed to fight Israel—which all the Arab regimes wanted to avoid at all costs—but rather to sidetrack the Palestinians, to keep them from waging an autonomous struggle. The calculation was not unfounded, and if we were going to thwart it we had to act fast.

The Fatah leadership held a meeting in Kuwait in early autumn 1964 to discuss the matter. The debate was heated and split between two divergent viewpoints. Certain of our comrades, subsequently referred to as the "reasonable faction," opposed what they considered a dangerously premature action. In their view, it was too early to launch guerrilla activities while we were still inadequately equipped and while we had only limited numbers of fighters. It would be wiser, they concluded, to wait for Fatah to become a mass movement with substantial forces before pluging into a venture which could set the entire Arab world against us.

A few of us took exactly the opposite position. To our minds, the situation was ripe for armed struggle. The Palestinian masses had not yet fallen under the intoxicating sway of Shukeiry's demagoguery and would be impressed by our dedication and will to act. Fatah would develop into a mass movement by actually practicing armed struggle, not the reverse. This argument earned us the epithet "the adventurers."

To break the resulting deadlock, we called a larger meeting in October to which we invited the leadership cadres in the areas adjacent to Israel, especially the West Bank and Gaza from where the first fedayeen raids would be launched. The assembly split along the same lines as the one in Kuwait, but this time after long debates a consensus was reached in favor of the "adventurers." Several days later, the date for the first military operation against Israel was set for December 31, 1964.

On that day, commando units from the West Bank, Gaza, and Lebanon were supposed to cross over into Israel and attack various military and economic targets, particularly installations for diverting the Jordan headwaters to Israel. The entire Gaza commando team, which had been infiltrated by two Nasserist agents, was arrested by Egyptian Security one week before the date of the operation. The secret was better kept in the West Bank and Lebanon, from which our fedayeen were able to successfully carry out their mission.

There were about ten attacks in all that day. They did not inflict important losses on the enemy, and that was not even their primary objective. Above all, we wanted to mount a spectacular operation that would arrest the attention of the Israelis, Palestinians, Arab regimes, and world public opinion. We wanted to signal our presence to the Israelis, reinforce the Palestinians' determination to fight on their own, challenge the Arab regimes, and remind the world of the fate of our people.

The December 31, 1964, operation was meticulously prepared. We gave the fedayeen strict instructions not to cause loss of life among the Israeli civilian population under any circumstances. This was our original intention. Unfortunately, the behavior of the Israeli authorities subsequently obliged us to make exceptions to this rule. Israel's punitive raids invariably claim numerous civilian victims—especially through Israeli aviation's savage and indiscriminate bombing of refugee camps—

and it's only natural that we fight back in such a way as to discourage the enemy from carrying on the massacre of innocents. The racist character of the Zionist doctrine is well known, and consists of justifying the extermination of dozens, even hundreds, of Palestinians and sometimes the total destruction of entire villages to compensate for the death of a single Israeli.

The Tel Aviv government was to all appearances surprised by our operation of December 31. From Beirut, I listened non-stop to the Israeli radio which broadcast confusing bulletins attributing the raids to organizations we had never even heard of. It was only after we issued our first military communiqué on January 1, 1965, signed "al-Asifah" ("the Storm") that the Zionist officials realized the nature and scope of the enterprise. To be on the safe side, we had chosen the name al-Asifah since we didn't want to compromise Fatah in the event the operation didn't succeed. It wasn't until much later that we made public the fact that al-Asifah was the military branch of our movement.

After a few days of silence, the Arab mass media unleashed a torrent of invective. For Egypt, we could only be fanatic Muslim Brothers in the pay of imperialism. The pro-Nasser daily *Al Anwar* in Beirut splashed its front page with headlines "revealing" that we were CIA agents. For the Saudis, on the contrary, we were agents of international communism, while Jordanian sources branded us as pan-Arab revolutionaries.

Palestinian nationalists not belonging to Fatah didn't spare us either. Patriots such as Ghassan Kanafani—who was to be killed by the Israelis in 1972—vehemently took us to task in the Beirut daily *Al Moharrer*, which carried my counterarguments under a pseudonym a few days later. Ahmad Shukeiry denounced us in the name of the PLO as enemies of the Palestinian liberation movement. To counterbalance us, he promptly set about creating more or less bogus fedayeen organizations and financing small groups like Ahmad Jibril's "Heroes of the Return."

In fact, Ahmad Shukeiry was nothing more than a tool of the Arab League, which was bent on destroying us. The Egyptian general Ali Ali Amir, at the time commander-in-chief of the Unified Arab Forces, sent a note to all Arab governments asking them to crush our activities so as "not to give Israel an excuse to attack the Arab countries." Jordan and Lebanon, among others, went so far as to prohibit the very mention of al-Asifah in the press. Certain newspapers got around the censor's dictates by printing declarations by Israeli civilian and military spokesmen who explicitly referred to al-Asifah and its actions.

On January 28, 1965, we published our first political manifesto, still under the name al-Asifah. In it, we proclaimed our attachment to the Arab world and its struggles and at the same time appealed to the Arabs for support in the armed struggle we had just launched to end the Israeli occupation. "We will not lay down our arms," we concluded, "until Palestine is liberated and has regained its rightful place at the heart of the Arab nation."

This appeal fell on deaf ears as far as the Arab regimes were concerned. In fact, they stepped up their repression. Ahmad Musa, our first martyr, fell under Jordanian bullets, shot down by King Hussein's soldiers while returning from a mission in Israel where he had escaped the vigilance of the Zionist forces. Police searches and roundups became commonplace in the Jordan valley. On the eve of the 1967 war, some 250 Palestinians suspected of being members or sympathizers of al-Asifah were languishing in Jordanian prisons. Similar repression, albeit less ferocious, was taking place in other Arab countries, where Palestinians were watched, hounded, imprisoned.

Fortunately for us, there were at least two exceptions to this rule. In Kuwait, the security police remained neutral in keeping with its traditions of prudence and tolerance, and also no doubt because it sympathized with a liberation movement which in no way threatened the authority and stability of the regime. In Syria, the situation was more complex. The government and ruling Baath party considered us separatists insofar as we didn't share their pan-Arab ideology, but numerous Baathist militants believed our struggle worthwhile and offered us help on an individual basis.

Without actually fighting us, the Damascus government maneuvered to keep us in check, indeed even to control us. Acting in cooperation with our opponents within the Fatah leadership—the "reasonable" faction—they attempted to infiltrate our organization with elements supporting their viewpoint. Such was the case of Yusuf al-Orabi and Muhammad Hikmet, Baathist-leaning Palestinians and trained soldiers who enlisted in al-Asifah. We thought they were fighters devoted to our cause when, at the end of February 1966, they were shot to death under mysterious circumstances which haven't been clarified to this very day.

The Baathist authorities suspected us of having liquidated them. The Fatah leaders who were in Damascus at the time—Yasir Arafat, Abu Jihad, Abu Ali Ayad, and Abu Sabri—were arrested along with seven cadres of lesser importance and charged with murder.

Faruq Qaddumi, Yusuf al-Najjar, and I left Kuwait in haste for Damascus to try and secure their release. Colonel Salah Jadid—the strong man of the regime which had just seized power after eliminating the Baath's rightist faction—listened to us with considerable courtesy. At the end of a long meeting we were given to understand that the matter was in the hands of Hafiz al-Asad, the newly appointed defense minister. Our success seemed assured. Although I had never met Assad, I knew he was on good terms with Yasir Arafat and Abu Jihad, so I was certain we wouldn't have any trouble convincing him of their innocence—especially since they had been on a hunger strike for almost a month by that time and their lives were in danger.

Our first surprise was that Hafiz al-Asad made us wait for three days before agreeing to see us. The second was that when he finally did receive us, he asked us coldly at the door of his office what we wanted. He cut me off in the middle of my explanation to tell us that our imprisoned comrades were guilty and that no one could convince him otherwise. Exasperated, I said, "Your attitude confirms our suspicions that your real aim is to crush the armed struggle we've launched before it gains momentum. Thank you for receiving us, but you have dealt a harsh blow to the Palestinian liberation movement and I hope you're prepared to assume responsibility in the eyes of history!"

Hafiz al-Asad fell silent. He invited us into his office. We talked for over three hours. He bombarded us with a thousand and one questions about Fatah, its ideology, objectives, and especially about Arafat (known at the time under the code name Rauf), whose personality intrigued him. Yet Yasir Arafat wasn't unknown to the Syrian authorities. He had already been arrested in Damascus on suspicion of involvement in the Tapline oil pipeline sabotage at the end of 1965, but had been released a few days later for lack of evidence.

Obviously satisfied, Asad ended the conversation by telling us to go straight to the Mezzeh prison to fetch our comrades. He promised to give orders for their immediate release, and kept his word for ten of them. The eleventh, a simple Fatah militant, is still in prison even though he is innocent of the crime he is accused of.

The Fatah leadership decided to "freeze" the activities of the released prisoners both as a goodwill gesture toward Damascus and because of the errors they had committed. Yasir Arafat reacted badly to what he saw as a sanction. His character in any case made him incapable of remaining inactive. He proposed a deal: If we would cancel the measure decided against him, he would undertake an important operation in Israel which could easily cost him his life if it failed, but which would be particularly beneficial to the movement if it succeeded. We accepted his offer.

With a group of fedayeen, Arafat set off for the Lebanese-Israeli border. As luck would have it, he was intercepted by the Beirut Security Police. One of the Deuxième Bureau officers who took turns interrogating him, Samir al-Khatib (presently commander-in-chief of the Arab Deterrent Force in Lebanon), suspected him of belonging to Nasser's secret service. Arafat, who can speak the Egyptian dialect perfectly, made no effort to dispel the error. He ended up by revealing his real name, but not that he was on the Central Committee of Fatah and commander-in-chief of al-Asifah. At the time there was a tight cooperation between the Syrian and Egyptian intelligence services, so Khatib's suspicions about Arafat seemed confirmed when the Syrian Deuxième Bureau, acting on our request, interceded in his favor. Meanwhile, we had notified the Beirut government that we would carry out a series of reprisals in Lebanon if Arafat and our companions weren't released. With the combined weight of our threat and Damascus' pressures, Arafat and the others were freed after being held for three weeks in the Sablons prison.

It was clear that we would have to normalize our relations with the Arab regimes if we wanted to pursue our activities effectively. We took a number of steps designed to reassure the Syrian government and charged Yasir Arafat and Faruq Qaddumi to make contact with the Egyptian authorities, whose influence—as we had learned—could be decisive in several states of the region.

Arafat and Qaddumi were received by Salah Nasr, the all-powerful chief of the Mokhabarat (the Egyptian secret police) in a manner not generally reserved for leaders of a national liberation movement. He started off by telephoning instructions that a suite be reserved for them at the Omar Khayyam Hotel, at the time one of the most luxurious in Cairo. Next, he asked his aides to remain at the disposal of his guests and to provide them with whatever they needed, including, he specified, "the most beautiful women in Cairo."

It seems that this sort of behavior was not unusual for Salah Nasr, who was tried for corruption and conspiracy against state security in the immediate wake of the 1967 defeat. But this didn't make it any less shocking. Faruq Qaddumi, outraged, exclaimed indignantly: "We are the representatives of a revolutionary movement on which the fate of an entire people depends! It isn't with favors and loose women that you can establish relations with us!"

Initially taken aback, Salah Nasr took another tack, blandly assuring them that this was far from his intention. He simply wanted to know beforehand exactly what our movement was all about. How did it operate? In which countries? How many members did it have? Who financed it and where did we buy arms? Finally, was it possible to have the names of Fatah's leaders?

Arafat and Qaddumi, totally disconcerted, refused to reply to any of these questions. It was clearly pointless to prolong the discussion. They left Cairo profoundly disappointed and thoroughly disgusted.

A few months later—I think it was in November or December 1966—we decided to renew efforts to establish relations with Nasser's regime, this time on specific bases. In a meeting with Egyptian Defense Minister Shams Badran (also imprisoned after the 1967 war), we proposed that the Egyptians help us set up fedayeen cells in the Negev aimed at harassing the Israeli army, particularly in peacetime but also in the event of war. We would take care of training and then installing some 200 to 300 guerrillas in the desert part of the Negev, while the Egyptians would supply logistical support.

Shams Badran listened to us with arrogant condescension. He declared, not without irony, that our project was "certainly most interesting" but that he didn't see how he could have any part of it without knowing anything about Fatah and its leaders beforehand. His attitude scarcely differed in substance from Salah Nasr's. It took the defeat of the Egyptian army in June 1967 and the purge of the regime which followed for a bridge to be built between the Palestinian movement and the most powerful Arab state.

Meanwhile, there had been developments on the internal front that ultimately increased Fatah's fighting power and cohesiveness. Immediately after our December 31, 1964, operation, the opponents of armed struggle within the leadership, the "reasonable faction," stepped up the pressure to neutralize the adventurers they still considered us. They stopped at nothing to demonstrate that our action had jeopardized the movement. A militant was arrested in Jordan? We were responsible. The press accused us of being CIA agents? We hadn't sufficiently prepared public opinion for the guerrilla activities we were launching. A raid carried out by our fedayeen had failed? It was our fault because we hadn't recruited professional soldiers. The Arab regimes reviled us? Yet another proof that our venture was premature.

The quarrel was at its peak when our opponents revealed their true colors. When Yasir Arafat and his companions were charged with the murder of the al-Asifah officers, the "reasonable" faction made the mistake of dissociating themselves from our imprisoned comrades. When these last were released, cleared of all accusation, the reasonable faction's days in the Fatah leadership were numbered. Shortly afterward they were obliged to withdraw, and we were once again a united group.

We were then in a position to pursue and develop our guerrilla activities. From 1965 to the eve of the Six Day War, our fedayeen carried out about 200 raids. It's true that most of them were limited in scope and not of the sort that could endanger Israeli state security or stability. But they contributed to increasing the tension between Israel and the Arab states, which were accused—irony of ironies!—of fomenting the fedayeen movement.

On June 5, 1967, I heard over the radio that Israel had launched a lightning air attack against Egypt. The school vacation had just begun, and I left Kuwait the same day for Damascus. One phase of my life as a militant was over, since from that time forward I became what is called a professional revolutionary. The war that was beginning also marked a turning point in the history of the Palestinian movement.

4

High Tide

JUNE 5, 1967. The little car into which five of us were crammed raced at top speed along the road from Kuwait to Baghdad. We had chosen the northern route, although it was longer, to avoid the road toward Jordan along which Israeli tank divisions were advancing. The stark splendor of the desert stretching as far as the eye could see, the suffocating heat and blinding light by day, the cold and impenetrable darkness which enveloped us at night, nothing touched us. We were obsessed with one idea: to reach Damascus as soon as possible. The "full-time" Fatah leaders— Yasir Arafat, Abu Jihad, Abu Ali Ayad, Abu Sabri—were already there, and we were to meet urgently to outline policy in the light of the war that had just erupted.

The road was long, difficult, and, at times, seemed to lose itself in the sand. More than once we lost our way. We took turns at the wheel, driving continuously day and night, hardly speaking. Our thoughts were elsewhere. My four companions—also Fatah militants—and I listened to the radio. At first we were intrigued by the discrepancies in the news bulletins broadcast from Cairo, Tel Aviv, and London. We had faith in the power of the Egyptian army. The firmness of Nasser's statements in the weeks leading up to the war, his impassioned speeches, his defiant actions—especially in closing the Gulf of Aqaba to Israeli navigation—all this led us to believe that far from fearing a confrontation, he actually wanted it.

Doubts began to creep in during the early hours of the fighting. The divergent versions of the battle became contradictory. The triumphant bombast of Radio Cairo contrasted sharply with the cool, measured tones emanating from Tel Aviv. The battles on the Egyptian, Syrian, and Jordanian fronts obviously weren't going in our favor. But what did it matter? The war was only beginning, and the Arab world hadn't yet had time to mobilize all its resources.

We arrived at our destination the night of June 6, about ten hours behind schedule. I was exhausted, but immediately rushed to the Fatah offices where I learned that none of the leaders was in Damascus. They had all gone to the Ilham base which the Syrians had turned into a training center for some 400 to 500 fedayeen. From there most of them, led by Yasir Arafat, had managed to infiltrate behind enemy lines where they were desperately trying to stem the advance of the Israeli forces.

Over the next two days, the reversals suffered by the Arab armies no longer seemed in question, and there were signs of a defeat. Still I wasn't prepared for the overwhelming, crushing, humiliating defeat that Nasser announced in his June 9 speech. The incredible was thus true: The Egyptian air force decimated on the ground during the first hours of the conflict; the infantry in full stampede in the Sinai; the Jewish army camped along the Suez Canal. And Nasser had surrendered! Who could ever have imagined such a thing? The great leader of the Arab nation, the man sent by destiny, the hero who was going to help us recover at least part of our usurped country, had plunged headlong into an enterprise without so much as a minimum of preparation! Bitterness mixed with anger. The Arab armies, all the Arab armies put together, hadn't been capable of keeping the little Israeli army at bay. Worse, they had yielded yet more territory to the Israeli expansionists.

Yasir Arafat and the others had rushed back to Damascus in the meantime, and together we listened to that fateful speech of June 9 over the radio. When Nasser ended it by announcing his resignation, our despair reached its peak. It was as if we had suffered a double defeat, military and political—political because for us, despite everything, the fall of Nasser meant the end of all hope. Despite everything, Nasser symbolized the rejection of the fait accompli, the symbol of the resistance which to our mind must inevitably emerge.

Our reaction was not an isolated one. Massive demonstrations erupted spontaneously from one end of the Arab world to the other. Crowds shouted their pain and grief even while demanding that the man who had led them to the catastrophe remain at the helm. The explosion of joy with which the Israelis greeted the news of Nasser's resignation was the final straw needed to convince us that it was our duty to stand by him in adversity. Within a few hours the hatred we felt for him was transformed into a sort of defiance. Our determination to resist at his side was reinforced over the coming days as we noted how the Arab bourgeoisie and reactionary governments shared the Israelis' jubilation over the crumbling of the Egyptian regime.

As soon as Nasser withdrew his resignation, a Fatah conference opened on June 12 to discuss the timeliness of renewing the armed struggle. As in the autumn of 1964 when we were deciding on whether or not to launch guerrilla warfare, the assembly split into advocates and opponents of immediate action. In meeting after meeting, day after day, in a feverish climate reminiscent of the one prevailing at the 1964 meetings, we debated the options and their implications. Were we going to take up arms against the victors? Did we have even the slightest chance of holding in check Israeli military might? Didn't we risk unleashing terrible reprisals against the population of the occupied territories? And yet if we refrained from any action, wouldn't we be lumped together with the vanquished, despised, and scorned as much as they by the Palestinian masses? Both options carried grave dangers for our future. We decided to table the final decision for two months. In the meantime, we passed a series of capital measures:

1. A number of high-ranking cadres, including Yusuf al-Najjar, Abdel Fattah Hammud, and myself, were appointed to join the leadership on a full-time basis. We were to devote ourselves exclusively to the organization of the movement in the new phase which was unfolding.

2. All the militants were authorized to seek and collect abandoned weapons left on the battlefields or in depots by the Arab armies. At the same time, no efforts would be spared to purchase arms on the local and international markets through arms dealers, smugglers, and so on.

3. A huge fund-raising campaign was launched, primarily aimed at the rich Palestinians of the diaspora. Yusuf al-Najjar, Kamal Adwan, Abu Mazen, and Khalid al-Hasan were instructed to drum up funds among our sympathizers and friends. Others were charged with soliciting subsidies from the oil-producing countries. Given the weakened position of the Arab states in the wake of the June debacle, we believed they would be unable to impose conditions on the aid they furnished, so we no longer feared compromising the financial autonomy we had so jealously guarded until then.

4. A number of militants, led by Yasir Arafat, were to slip into the

newly occupied West Bank and Gaza to consolidate and extend Fatah's underground network with a view toward renewing guerrilla warfare. Those designated for this most delicate mission all came from these areas, so they could move around like "fish in water," to use Mao's famous dictum.

5. Measures were taken to establish commando bases around the cease-fire lines, particularly along the Jordan River and in South Lebanon.

6. Delegations were to be sent to four Arab countries—Egypt, Syria, Iraq, and Algeria—for consultations on the advisability of immediately resuming Palestinian guerrilla activities.

The definitive decision concerning the beginning of operations was to be made at a new conference to be convened at the end of the two-month period. By that time, we had reached most of the goals we had set for ourselves at the June 12 congress, sometimes beyond our expectations. The loosening of state authority in the "confrontation" countries facilitated the appropriation of large stocks of weapons which piled up in our arsenals. Financial contributions from rich sympathizers were many and generous, though inadequate for our needs which were too great for any but governments to meet.

Two large oil producers were approached for support: Saudi Arabia and Libya. King Faisal, who received Abu Jihad in Geneva, was sympathetic to the cause. He had learned of Fatah's existence in the early sixties from Zaki al-Yamani, the present oil minister, who was on friendly terms with one of our militants. Abu Jihad assured the king that Fatah had no ties with any party and that one of its principles was noninterference in the internal affairs of Arab countries. For his part, King Faisal said he adhered to the views of his father, King Abdel Aziz, who believed that Palestine could only be liberated by its own children, a conviction which had led him to disapprove of the Arab army intervention in 1948. In principle, then, the king was in favor of the Palestinians' receiving the financial and other support needed to pursue their struggle.

Faruq Qaddumi and I, charged with contacting the Libyan leaders, went to King Idris' residence in Beida. The old king, who rarely received visitors, referred us to his prime minister. Abdel Hamid Bakkush greeted us with hostility. We had scarcely entered his office when he bluntly announced that he was as suspicious of us as he was of our movement, that he didn't believe in the seriousness of the revolution we intended to launch, and that in any case it couldn't lead to anything worthwhile. "If I receive you today," he told us, "it's only because I can't do otherwise since you enjoy a large measure of popular sympathy. The Libyans, unfortunately, are a people of imbeciles . . ."

I was shocked. "Imbeciles?" I exclaimed. "Very well, Your Excellency, you may rest assured that this most curious evaluation of your people will be made known. There is no point in continuing this discussion." Faruq Qaddumi, as indignant as I, went on angrily: "You don't know anything about our cause and you scorn your own people, even though I understand you were a Communist militant during your university years. Everyone knows that you have been involved in dubious arms transactions. One day, your people will judge you . . ."

Abdel Hamid Bakkush immediately changed his tone and manner. He courteously invited us to sit down and join him for coffee. We had misunderstood, he explained. Of course he would support the Palestinian revolution, that went without saying. But it was still necessary to define the modalities of this aid. Would we be kind enough to come see him again, this time at his office in Tripoli?

We took advantage of the intervening few days to launch a fund-raising drive through the "popular committees" set up by our representatives in the early sixties. We had many Libyan sympathizers who had always helped us generously, especially rich merchants. The Benghazi committee gave us a particularly warm welcome. At the end of the meeting held in our honor by the committee there, the president of the group announced that 10,000 dinars had been collected to be divided equally between Fatah and al-Asifah. He was unaware, as was everyone else at the time, that these two organizations were in fact one and the same. I thanked him for the gift, explaining in all seriousness that Faruq Qaddumi was a member of al-Asifah while I represented Fatah.

Our meeting with the prime minister a few days later in Tripoli contrasted sharply with our initial reception in Beida. This time Abdel Hamid Bakkush was friendly, even warm, and promptly granted us everything we asked. We left Libya with some 30,000 dinars in our pockets, a considerable sum in relation to our finances at the time. We avoided raising the question of a renewal of the armed struggle. We didn't want to alarm him and, besides, it would have been premature since we hadn't concluded our talks with the other Arab countries.

Of the four countries we consulted as to whether or not to resume the armed struggle, two came out solidly in favor: Algeria, which isn't surprising in the light of its own experience, and Egypt. It's true that Gamal Abdal Nasser didn't see our representatives personally. Faruq Qaddumi and Khalid al-Hasan were met by Foreign Minister Mahmud Riad and Mohamed Hassanein Heikal, Nasser's confidant and editor-in-chief of the powerful newspaper *Al Ahram*. Although Heikal came out in favor of Fatah's proposed action, he didn't hide his reservations regarding us. "We know very little about you," he said. "Our intelligence file on al-Asifah is virtually empty. Your mystery intrigues us, and in the last analysis your capacity for dissimulation is no doubt an indication of your seriousness."

The Iraqis weren't much help. The chief of state, Abdul Rahman Aref, concluded his meeting with our representatives by declaring: "We are neither for nor against your project. Frankly, we don't know what to think and it's up to you to make what you feel is the wisest decision." Syria's President Nureddin al-Atassi, on the other hand, was categorical. He warned us emphatically against launching an anti-Israeli guerrilla action: "You will lose and drag us all along with you in the catastrophe. Give us time to catch our breath."

Meanwhile, we had received reports from Yasir Arafat who had been in the occupied territories since mid-July. To his great delight he had found that the populations of the West Bank and Gaza, far from being demoralized by the Arab defeat, were in favor of waging the struggle through all available means. Although hiding his true identity, Arafat was lodged, protected, and received everywhere with open arms. Like his companions charged with the same mission, who reported similar findings, he had no difficulty moving from village to village and was even able to slip several times into Jerusalem, his native city, and into Tel Aviv.

With a mandate from our people, we could forge ahead despite the Arab states' mixed attitudes toward us. When we met on August 20 to come to a final decision, Arafat was still in the occupied territories. He rushed back at our request to participate in the debates, which were heated since some of our comrades were still opposed to an action they considered premature. The meeting nonetheless ended with a consensus and a firm decision: Guerrilla activity was to resume on August 31.

Our operations in the occupied territories took various forms, including ambushes, bomb or grenade attacks, bazooka and rocket launchings, and the laying of mines. Our objectives were modest, and at no time were we naive enough to think that we could endanger the security of the Israeli state. We wanted to raise the morale of the Arab masses, harass the enemy and oblige it to remain constantly on the alert, and to perturb the Israeli economy. It was the Arab and sometimes international mass media which blew our operations way out of proportion, thereby giving rise to the dangerous illusion that we would be able to liberate Palestine. I personally believe that in some cases these exaggerations were intentional, designed to hurt our cause. After building up expectations, our "powerlessness" was to be cited at the right moment as a failure in order to discredit us with our people and the Arab masses.

The Israelis countered our activities with a vigorous repression. Waves of arrests deprived us of hundreds of militants and sympathizers. Our losses could be attributed to at least two factors: the efficiency of the Israeli secret service and the carelessness of our fighters. Their enthusiasm and lack of experience led them to defy the occupying authorities too openly, to take useless risks. They were all the easier to track down in that Israeli intelligence had taken over both the files and the stool pigeons of the former Jordanian administration.

Something clearly had to be done. We created a counterespionage service which Faruq Qaddumi initially headed until I took it over at the end of 1967. Cadres were hand-picked to receive accelerated training in Egypt and elsewhere before being disseminated in the occupied territories or neighboring Arab countries.

A number of informers who had worked for the Israeli police came over to us wanting to make up for their past deeds. After intensive interrogations, we generally gave them the chance to redeem themselves either by joining our special services or by carrying out particularly dangerous operations. Before they left on the mission, we had them write and sign a declaration telling of their past activities for Israel and explaining the reasons for their about-face. We reserved the right to publish the document in the event that they turned out to be double agents (which never happened) or if they didn't come back alive.

From the very beginning, we adopted the rule not to punish treason by death. We executed only those whose collaboration with the enemy led to the loss of human lives within our ranks. Such cases were relatively rare, and in ten years only about twenty stool pigeons have been shot.

As for collaborators on the order of Sheikh Jaabari, the ex-mayor of Hebron, we generally don't take any action regarding them. We believe that it's preferable to neutralize them by isolating them from the population politically. Certain of our friends in the Third World have sometimes reproached us for not physically liquidating our adversaries, claiming that this contributes to maintaining the division and confusion within the Palestinian national movement. But the Fatah leaders have always believed that democratic dialogue is the only valid and effective way to settle differences in the long run.

During the first months following the 1967 war, we were the only ones braving the enemy with arms in hand. The other Palestinian organizations, including those which were to form the "Rejection Front" a few years later, had not yet appeared on the scene or at least hadn't yet decided to wage armed struggle. Fatah was much better prepared than they to launch guerrilla activities on short notice: In addition to the experience acquired since our first operation on December 31, 1964, we enjoyed logistical support from Syria and Algeria, which had agreed in 1966 to provide military training for our fighters.

The Six Day War opened new prospects for our development. The Jordanian regime was too weak to oppose us. King Hussein released the Palestinian patriots he had locked up in the years preceding the conflict. More importantly, he closed his eyes to the bases we were establishing along the Jordan River to serve as launching points for the fedayeen. We also got help from the local population and the Jordanian armed forces, with which we established excellent relations. The same East Bank officers who two years later were to massacre the Palestinians facilitated our task greatly in those days. The same held true for the Iraqi units which had reached the front too late to participate in the June 1967 fighting but which were still stationed in Jordan near the cease-fire lines. Iraqi officers gave Yasir Arafat and me false papers which enabled us to circulate freely. We felt even more secure in Jordan after setting up fedayeen bases near the Palestinian refugee camps, which offered an ideal protection for our activities. We installed our operational headquarters at our base near the village of Karameh, strategically located in a hilly area about four miles from the Jordan River.

At the beginning of March 1968, we received a message from a high-ranking officer of the Jordanian Deuxième Bureau, al-Hajj Arabiyat, requesting a meeting with some Fatah leaders. Yasir Arafat and I hesitated: We had never met a representative of the Jordanian regime and in our political inexperience feared that such a contact could in itself be compromising—not to say unworthy—of a revolutionary movement. Our curiosity got the better of us, however, and we agreed to meet him in a house in Karameh on March 10. There, Arabiyat gave us information that had been passed on to Jordan by the American CIA: Israel was going to launch a large-scale attack against our bases along the Jordan River. He advised us in an unofficial capacity to be careful and told us that the chief of staff, General Amer Khammash, wished to speak to us on the matter in Amman.

We met General Khammash on Monday, March 18. He was firm and straight to the point. The Israeli offensive would begin within the next three days, he announced, and the fedayeen would be wise to withdraw to the interior of Jordanian territory to avoid a confrontation. In any case, he insisted, the Fatah leadership would be making a big mistake if it exposed itself to the enemy's attack, and shouldn't waste any time getting to safety.

Logically speaking, General Khammash was right. Guerrillas by definition do not give battle to a regular army. Their effectiveness depends to a large extent on their mobility. However, political considerations inclined us to the opposite view. We explained to the general that the Palestinians, and more generally the Arabs, would never understand if once again we left the field open to the Israelis. Our duty was to set an example, to prove that the Arabs are capable of courage and dignity. We would hold our ground; if possible, we would explode the myth of the Jewish army's invincibility. Realizing that he couldn't convince us, he suggested that we ask for an audience with the king. We politely declined on the grounds that we needed every minute to prepare our bases along the Jordan.

We got back to Karameh the same day and called together all our military officers in the region. We informed them of the imminent Israeli attack and asked them whether or not we should avoid the confrontation. Not wanting to influence their decision, Arafat and I didn't tell them what we had said to General Khammash. The debate was brief and ended with the unanimous agreement that the fedayeen shouldn't shrink before the enemy under any circumstances. They did think, however, that the leaders should vacate the area as a security measure. Arafat, Faruq Qaddumi, Abu Sabri, and I nonetheless decided to stay and take part in the fighting. We dispersed to various sectors of Karameh, each taking position in caves on the hillsides.

On March 21, exactly three days after General Khammash's warning, I was awakened at dawn by one of the fedayeen who announced that the Israeli offensive had begun. In the distance tank columns of the Jewish army, followed by infantry units, could already be discerned crossing the Jordan. The artillery went into action while helicopters dropped parachutists behind our lines. Some 15,000 men stormed our bases along a front about eighty kilometers long. The main attack was clearly directed against Karameh, which we had to defend with fewer than 300 men. Without waiting for instructions from his high command, Mashur Haditha—the Jordanian general in charge of the region—gave orders for the Jordanian artillery to fire back.

The Israeli tanks descending upon Karameh were greeted by a hail of hand grenades and heavy gunfire. Fedayeen poured down from the surrounding hills to take part in the battle, sometimes fighting in hand-to-hand combat. Some demonstrated suicidal heroism. I saw one of our young commandos, for instance, destroy a tank by throwing himself under its treads with a belt full of explosives.

I personally had two close calls that day. One of the fedayeen under my command, a young man named George, left the cave where I was sheltered to get more ammunition. I don't know what premonition suddenly pushed me to leave, but I rushed out of the cave and took cover behind a boulder a hundred or so meters above. A few minutes later I saw George—his hands high—going toward the cave with a group of Israeli soldiers at his back. After tossing a tear-gas bomb into the place I had just vacated, they stormed it.

Because of my back problems, I wasn't able to follow my men who scaled the hill to occupy more secure positions. Still behind my boulder, I saw another group of Israeli soldiers coming in my direction, their fingers on the triggers of their submachine guns and obviously itching for a target. I remained absolutely still until they were only a few meters from the boulder. I slowly drew my revolver, ready to fire. Then the soldiers abruptly changed direction, leaving me behind. A little later, some fedayeen came to fetch me and helped me climb the hill where I could take shelter in a less exposed area.

The fighting continued until twilight, after which the Israeli forces began to gather their dead and wounded before withdrawing. They had destroyed three quarters of the buildings of Karameh, but in reality they left empty-handed. Their losses were high: Some thirty killed and about a hundred wounded according to their figures, more according to ours. But more importantly, they hadn't succeeded in crushing the fierce resistance of a small group of men determined to die rather than surrender.

The battle of Karameh, which means dignity in Arabic, was hailed as a stunning victory throughout the Arab world. Legends were woven around it. Tens of thousands of people, including the highest civilian and military officials of the Jordanian regime, descended on the town to pay their respects to the mortal remains of our martyrs, some hundred of whom were laid out in a shed.

For the Palestinian masses, jeered at and humiliated for decades, the Karameh victory gave rise to an immense pride and hope, marking what they saw as the beginning of their liberation. By the thousands, by the tens of thousands, young and old flocked to join Fatah. High school and university students abandoned their studies to swell our ranks. Our absorption capacity was limited, however, and we were obliged to make a strict selection. Out of the 5,000 candidates who tried to enlist in the forty-eight hours following the battle of Karameh, for instance, we recruited only 900.

The fedayeen movement witnessed an unprecedented growth. With the active sympathy of the population in the occupied territories, our comrades stepped up their operations. These increased from a monthly average of 12 in 1967 to 52 in 1968, 199 in 1969, and 279 in the first eight months of 1970. Fatah militants gave no respite to the occupying authorities, placing bombs in Israeli supermarkets and at bus stops, firing rockets on border settlements, engaging in skirmishes along the cease-fire lines, attacking Jewish army barracks.

Many women joined the Resistance. Their daring and self-sacrifice won the admiration of everyone, even those who generally looked down on them. Schoolgirls were the first to join violent demonstrations, the first to fight back when the police attacked. Many women were charged with delicate missions, such as carrying secret messages and transporting arms. Those who were arrested behaved with a courage which surprised even their jailers. One of them, who gave birth in prison, stoically endured separation from her child. Another, who refused to confess, was raped by her captors in a Gaza prison. Many Palestinian men offered to marry her. This unprecedented occurrence, virtually unheard-of given the prevailing mentality in a conservative society such as ours, was repeated several times in similar cases. One of the side effects of the Resistance was to promote the emancipation of women, and as a corollary, men's liberation from fossilized traditions.

Fatah's extraordinary expansion gave rise to organizational problems which we tried to resolve, as was our custom, in collective fashion. This wasn't always easy since the Central Committee members were often scattered in various countries, and there was one occasion when I had to make an urgent decision without consulting any of the others.

On April 15, 1968, about three weeks after the Karameh battle, I received a secret report in my capacity as Fatah intelligence chief indicating that one of our members was about to proclaim himself commander-in-chief of al-Asifah, Fatah's military branch. This would have caused a crisis within the movement and a dangerous confusion in public opinion, especially since the composition of Fatah's leadership at that time remained secret and anyone could have pretended to be part of it. The imposter in question was supposed to issue a proclamation within the coming hours. I was in Damascus and had no way of reaching my comrades of the Central Committee (most of whom were in Cairo, Amman, or Beirut) in time, so I had to take immediate action to thwart the move. I drew up a communiqué announcing that Yasir Arafat had been named spokesman of Fatah, and consequently of al-Asifah, and that as such he was the only one authorized to speak in the name of the movement. I distributed it to the press along with a short declaration, purportedly from Arafat, in which he accepted his new responsibilities while adding that the Fatah leadership remained collective.

Arafat heard the communiqué and the statement signed in his name over the radio and was completely taken by surprise. A modest man, he protested his nomination at a meeting held in Damascus shortly thereafter, stating that others deserved the position more than he. But as I had anticipated, all the other members of the leadership approved my choice. Arafat was one of the earliest militants of the movement, and all of us without exception respected and liked him. More important, Fatah was clearly entering a new phase and would need a spokesman worthy of representing it before public opinion and international bodies.

Thanks to the upsurge in guerrilla activities, our prestige was at a peak. Even Jordan's King Hussein, for whom we represented a rival force and a revolutionary alternative to his regime, had been obliged to publicly declare two days after the Karameh battle: "We are all fedayeen!" We decided to take advantage of this goodwill to develop tight relations with all the Arab regimes ready to help us.

To this end, we undertook a systematic tour of the main Arab countries, starting with the largest, Egypt. Remembering our disappointing experience with Nasser's Mokhabarat, Faruq Qaddumi and I requested an interview with Mohamed Hassanein Heikal, who readily received us. Nasser's influential confidant initially made a bad impression on me. Clothed with studied elegance, a fat cigar in his mouth, radiating assurance, he struck me as speaking to us with condescension. This man, I said to myself while listening to him, is incapable of feeling the slightest sympathy for the Palestinian cause. It wasn't long before I discovered that I had misjudged him. Moreover, he became one of the best friends of the Resistance.

The meeting with Heikal was relatively brief. After complimenting us on our movement's activities, he assured us that the Egyptian regime hoped to establish relations with Fatah "at the highest level." He proposed taking us to meet Ali Sabri, secretary general of Egypt's single party, the Arab Socialist Union (ASU). He drove us there himself, and on the way he asked suddenly: "Are you armed?" He apparently wasn't satisfied with our negative reply, because he reiterated the question. We soon understood his concern, for to our amazement we saw that we were approaching not the ASU headquarters but Nasser's residence. Heikal, who is fond of theatrical effects, had in fact set up an appointment with the Egyptian president.

Nasser greeted us in Arab fashion by embracing us. As soon as we were seated, he gestured toward Qaddumi's briefcase and asked: "Is it true that you are carrying explosives to kill me?" After a pause he added: "Rest assured, I am joking. A few hours ago I got a report from the Mokhabarat warning me that you were going to make an attempt on my life. I tore up the foolish report and opposed Heikal's suggestion to have you searched at the door."

I seized the occasion to criticize the Mokhabarat which had hounded us during the fifties (Nasser didn't recall the discussion we had just after the Israeli raid on Gaza, when I was still a student). I also told him how the intelligence chief had tried to corrupt our representatives in 1966. Nasser replied that he had totally reshuffled the Mokhabarat just after the Six Day War, and while analyzing the causes of the defeat hinted that on the eve of the conflict he was no longer in control of the main wheels of government, particularly the army. This is why, he added, he had let himself be dragged into a war he had hoped to avoid. Still, he insisted on declaring that despite everything he assumed total responsibility for the catastrophe.

His frankness encouraged us to speak very freely about Fatah. For over two hours he pumped us with questions about its creation, ideology, sources of financing, and activities. He wanted to know how we could hold our own against the Israelis at Karameh, about the technical merits of our RPG guns, etc. After listening with great interest, he asked about our political orientation, an issue which seemed to worry him. Was it true that many Fatah members were Muslim Brothers, the movement he feared above all others? Weren't we hostile to Nasserism? Reassured by our replies, he asked us about the personality of Yasir Arafat. We explained that Arafat—who wanted to meet Nasser personally—was part of a strictly collective leadership.

The meeting led to concrete results. Since Nasser said he wanted to establish direct relations with Fatah without having to go through the Mokhabarat (which we didn't want either), we agreed to contact Heikal for any political problems and General Sadek, chief of the Deuxième Bureau, for questions pertaining to the military. Nasser promised to send us arms and to help with the training of fedayeen. Egypt, he added, was not in a position to supply us with financial assistance. He suggested that we see King Faisal of Saudi Arabia, which we had intended to do in any case.

The Saudi monarch received me the same day I arrived in Saudi Arabia. I had been there before as a member of a Palestinian Student Union delegation in October 1952. King Saud had received us warmly and as we were leaving had given us the equivalent of $30,000 to finance PSU activities. King Faisal showed the same lively sympathy for the Palestinian movement during our four-hour meeting, even though he spoke at length about how leftist and Marxist elements had "infiltrated" the fedayeen and how unhappy this made him. A man of great finesse and delicacy, he refrained from mentioning names or criticizing this or that Arab regime. It was clear, however, that he was not at ease about the Syrian government, then controlled by Salah Jadid, and that he had no great affection for Nasser either.

King Faisal believed that we should avoid being identified with any Arab regime. As a result, Saudi Arabia would help us as discreetly as possible. "We don't expect either praise or criticism from you," he told me. On my suggestion, he agreed to authorize the creation of "support committees" in the kingdom to collect donations and to automatically deduct up to 7 percent of the wages of Palestinians working in Saudi Arabia, with the money to be used to finance Fatah. He graciously offered to match the total sum collected.

My trip to the Sudan—the third leg of my tour that summer of 1968—was equally fruitful. Faruq Qaddumi and Abu Saleh were with me, and we were all extremely impressed by the democratic spirit, tolerance, and generosity of the Sudanese people. The day after we arrived, the opposition parties—including the Communists and Muslim Brethren—organized a large rally at the entrance of the hotel where we were staying. The speakers sharply criticized Prime Minister Muhammad Mahjub, who was standing right next to us, saying among other things that he financially supported the PLO (still controlled by the Arab League) rather than Fatah. The crowd chanted "Mahjub, traitor! Mahjub, traitor!" I was extremely embarrassed. I took the floor to announce that negotiations were in progress and that I was certain the prime minister would not withhold assistance from the movement.

That same evening, a reception was given in our honor. The prime minister and the leaders of the opposition—the same ones who had been so vigorously denouncing him a few hours earlier—were there, and I was amazed to see them engaged in cordial, even friendly, conversation. Even the Muslim Brothers and the Communists seemed on good terms. The Communists scrupulously respected the religious beliefs of their compatriots, to the point that they interrupted their talks with our delegation to direct us to the mosque at prayer time! Thus, I was deeply shocked by the civil war which broke out in the Sudan exactly three years later, and ended with the execution of the major Communist party leaders.

Something else struck me during that same trip to the Sudan. At a public meeting organized by the Women's Union, the militant in charge of collecting woolen clothing for the fedayeen stood up and asked, "Don't you think these clothes will be unnecessary next winter if it's true you will have liberated Palestine by then?" This question gave me some idea about the extent of the myth created by the Arab press regarding our possibilities. It seemed inappropriate that day to publicly go into the weaknesses and failings—not to say betrayals—of certain Arab regimes regarding the Palestinian cause. How could I explain that our natural allies were purposely maintaining the balance of power in Israel's favor? I said something vague to the effect that one should never despair of an early victory, and let it go at that.

Now that we had improved our relations with the Arab regimes, we could turn our attention to the PLO. Ahmad Shukeiry had resigned, grudgingly, as president of the organization in December 1967 and had been replaced on an interim basis by Yahya Hammuda. Earlier that year, in June and August, Shukeiry had had two meetings with Fatah leaders. He tried to convince us that he had been betrayed by King Hussein, who, he said, had deliberately handed the West Bank over to Israel. He told us that he hoped to gain renewed confidence from the Arab chiefs of state, who were to meet at the summit conference planned for the end of August in Khartoum. But his hopes were deceived: Violently taken to task by many of the Arab leaders, he was left to his fate by Nasser whose protégé he had been until then.

From then on Nasser began pushing for the integration of the fedayeen movements into the PLO, which to his mind would kill two birds with one stone. On the one hand, it would end the duality of power (the formal power of the PLO versus the legitimate power we represented), and on the other, it would establish an appropriate framework for the unification of the Resistance. Indeed, a number of rival Resistance organizations had emerged since the 1967 war. Although they were a minority, they still constituted forces which should be grouped in one way or another.

At the beginning, we weren't unanimous in wanting to take over the leadership of the PLO. Some of us feared that the movement would become bureaucratized, that its revolutionary purity would be diluted. We set a number of conditions on our cooperation, including one we considered indispensable: The fedayeen organizations would have to have the majority of seats in the Palestinian National Council (PNC), a kind of PLO parliament. By mid-June of 1968, following arduous negotiations, we had succeeded in obtaining about half the seats. The fourth PNC, held in Cairo the next month, did not change the composition of the Executive Committee (the supreme body of the PLO) but it did adopt resolutions reflecting our policy. The National Charter, which had been passed in Jerusalem by the first council in 1964, was revised to stipulate that "armed struggle is the only road to the liberation of Palestine."

By the time the fifth session of the PNC met in February 1969, the various fedayeen organizations had gained the absolute majority of seats and the Resistance took over full control of the PLO. The newly elected Executive Committee designated as its president Yasir Arafat, who wept from emotion at the enormous responsibilities he would have from then on. It was during this same session that the PNC adopted Fatah's strategic objective (the one I had outlined at a press conference on October 10, 1968) of creating a democratic society in Palestine where Muslims, Christians, and Jews would live together in complete equality.

All the Arab countries, including those which were—and still are—suspicious of the extreme leftist fedayeen groups, greeted the PLO's takeover by the Resistance with satisfaction. This was because Fatah, which most of them trust, made sure of getting the overriding influence both within the PNC and on the PLO Executive Committee.

We could now concentrate on initiatives aimed at giving us an international base. Considering the hostility or indifference of the Western powers and their satellites in the Third World, our efforts were inevitably directed toward the socialist countries. The prejudices we harbored against Marxism and socialist countries in the early 1950's had gradually disappeared over the years, largely due to our everyday experiences rather than through readings. It's true that our relations with the Soviet

Union remained distant and marked by suspicion. The Soviet leaders were slow to grasp the sense of our struggle, perhaps under the influence of the Arab Communist parties which by and large continued to denounce our "adventurism," accusing us of being Muslim Brethren and reactionaries.

As for the People's Republic of China, Yasir Arafat had already been to Peking twice, in 1964 and 1966. The first visit had led to nothing, but the second ended with promises of aid which materialized after the Six Day War. As of 1968 a number of fedayeen groups were sent to Chinese camps for military training, but we still needed to develop and consolidate these relations. We were thus delighted when at the beginning of 1970 we received invitations to visit China and Vietnam, and Yasir Arafat and I set off for Peking that February.

The trip was kept secret for political and security reasons. To avoid arousing suspicion, we each followed a different itinerary to Pakistan, from where we were to take the same plane. We tried to pass unnoticed. Arafat, for example, dressed in a conservative business suit and traded his usual head covering, the kaffiyeh and agal, for a respectable felt hat. Our precautions were in vain. No sooner had we boarded the plane when we ran smack into Abdal Salam Jallud, the number-two man of the Libyan regime which had overthrown the monarchy on September 1, 1969. He clearly wasn't very happy to see us, either. Head down, visibly embarrassed, he greeted us halfheartedly and didn't say a word for the entire journey. We learned later that he, too, was on a secret visit to China, the first since the revolution.

We were given a warm official and popular welcome at the Peking airport, just as we had been during the stopover in Shanghai. We were lodged in an old palace which had once belonged to the French Embassy, and given tours of various factories and people's institutions. One day, we unexpectedly asked to visit a commune. At the time there was a massive campaign in the world press against this form of collectivization, and we were curious to see how it really worked. Our hosts immediately and graciously complied, putting an airplane at our disposal which flew us to a commune in the country's interior within six hours. An exhaustive tour of the facilities and long conversations with the workers and leaders convinced us of the positive role communes played in the country's development.

I was extremely impressed by the Chinese people's dedication. They seemed totally devoted to labor—manual or intellectual—and spent their leisure time in simple and healthy activities. Their life-style seemed characterized by a puritanism worthy of the most fundamentalist Islam. "The Prophet Muhammad couldn't have done better than Mao Zedong," I remarked to Arafat.

Zhou Enlai, with whom we had long and friendly meetings, charmed us with his lively intelligence, finesse, and vast culture. The questions he asked revealed not only his profound sympathy for the Palestinian people, but also his extraordinary knowledge of the problem in its regional and international context. Endowed with a remarkable memory, he could recall in detail how other Palestinian visitors had replied to the same questions he asked us.

Broaching the delicate subject of our attitude toward the Soviet Union, we explained that we would like to establish friendly relations with Moscow and hoped this would not jeopardize our cooperation with China. Judging from the slogans and posters on walls all over Peking, the regime was mobilizing the population against Soviet "social imperialism."

Chou Enlai listened to us, unruffled, and to our great surprise replied that he understood our preoccupations perfectly. "You represent a national liberation movement," he said, "and it is normal that you should try to get help wherever you can find it."

He promised China's full support and asked us to specify our needs. He also arranged an appointment for us the following day at the defense ministry, where we were informed that all our requests for military and civil assistance had been granted.

We left for North Vietnam on board a Chinese military aircraft. I was moved by the first contact I was to have with a people whose tenacity and heroism I so admired. Everything I had read and heard about the Vietnamese resistance, first to the French occupation and then to the American aggression, filled me with a sense of hope. The Palestinian people, I said to myself, also small in number and poor in resources, would be able to stand up to the powerful of the world and win their right to freedom and independence. Everything I was to see in North Vietnam was a source of enrichment and inspiration for me.

The Hanoi airport wasn't much to look at. With its modest size and desolate air, it testified to a country at war: bristling with antiaircraft guns, most of the runways were occupied by helicopters, MIG-17s and MIG-19s. We were met by members of the Politbureau of the Workers' party (Communist) and ushered into an airport reception room where we talked for three hours. When I expressed surprise at this long wait, they answered without a trace of embarrassment that the authorities were still looking for a place we could stay and a car to drive us there. During our entire two-week visit, we didn't see more than fifteen private cars.

I noticed that in certain respects the Vietnamese people suffered greater hardships than the Palestinians. Living conditions in Hanoi were worse than those in the refugee camps. Most of the buildings were in an advanced state of deterioration. The population stoically endured countless daily deprivations and difficulties, including shortages of the most vital foodstuffs as well as bombings.

I was struck by the role played by Vietnamese women. They were active everywhere, in factories and offices, in schools and on construction sites, even on the battlefields. All the launching ramps of SAM missiles I visited were manned by young girls, whose seeming fragility and delicacy never ceased to amaze me. The emancipation of Vietnamese women is all the more impressive when one thinks that for centuries, and until very recently, they were subjected to a cruel system of discrimination and oppression. For example, it was considered "normal" for a father to sell his daughters to the highest bidder to provide for the rest of the family.

Our visits to military bases and training camps were extremely useful, giving us the opportunity to see how they organized and trained their guerrilla fighters. Many of their methods could be adapted to our own training of fedayeen. We noted with interest the presence of political commissars similar to our own, whose task was not only to stiffen the fighters' motivation but also to act as liaison between the party and the army.

General Vo Nguyen Giap made a powerful impression on us, not only because of his total command of military affairs and wide political culture, but also for his modesty and discretion. He opened our first meeting by quoting a verse from the Koran to the effect that force is indispensable when confronting the enemy. He went on to warn us against the illusions that could arise from such current notions as "people's war" or "power comes from the barrel of a gun." "Things are not so easy," he told us, referring to the Vietnamese experience. "Certainly guns are important, but they aren't enough to assure a victory. You also have to have cannons, missiles, tanks, fighter bombers, and the whole range of weaponry the aggressor has.

"The Vietnamese and Palestinian people have much in common," he went on, "just like two people suffering from the same illness. But our struggle has certain advantages which yours lacks. Unlike the Palestinians, who live in a hostile environment, we have a friendly hinterland, the Chinese continent, which gives us an inestimable strategic depth. We also receive many forms of assistance from the socialist countries." He concluded that three other ingredients were absolutely necessary for the success of a guerrilla war: sophisticated weaponry, an ideology that mobilizes the masses, and an organization capable of uniting and leading them.

On this last point, General Giap explained how the Workers' party had managed to set up and actuate the National Front, which embraced almost all layers of society, not only peasants and workers, but also Buddhists, Christians, and Muslims, and—to our great astonishment— the middle classes: craftsmen, merchants, and industrialists whose interests had suffered because of American imperialism. We read the National Front's program while we were there, and at first glance were disappointed. Written in disarmingly simple terms, the objectives of the movement as set down in the program struck us as obvious, even summary: national union, the liberation of the fatherland, democracy, and so on. After thinking about it, however, we realized that this text was conceived to meet the needs of the entire population without exception.

Seeing this, I couldn't prevent myself from reflecting on the sterile verbosity that reigns in the Arab world—on the thousand-and-one slogans we launch without being capable of implementing any of them, on the demagogic outbidding which in the last analysis alienates even the best intentioned. Arab parties and political movements, I said to myself, have a great deal to learn from the discretion, modesty, and realism of the Vietnamese leaders.

Our discussions with the members of the Workers' party Politbureau gave us much food for thought concerning the nature of our own program. Our ultimate strategic objective was to set up a unitary democratic state on all Palestine. But we hadn't provided for any intermediary stage, or any provisional compromise. Without ever referring explicitly to Fatah or the PLO, the Politbureau members gave a long exposé of the various stages in the Vietnamese people's struggle, explaining why they had had to resign themselves to various concessions, sometimes important ones such as the division of the country into two separate, independent states.

We had another occasion to observe their realistic revolutionary spirit while drafting the joint communiqué to be published at the end of our visit. I was a member of the committee formed to write the text, and I noticed their hesitations when we proposed including a harsh denunciation of Israel and Zionism. One of them, a member of the Politbureau, explained that they would prefer to use moderate, even vague, terms so as not to offend the American Jews, many of whom were active in the antiwar movement. I complimented him on his frankness and especially his prudence, and immediately agreed to the watered-down version of the passage concerning Israel they showed me. The communiqué did, however, proclaim Vietnam's support for the Palestinian people's right to self-determination. There again, I thought, we had much to learn from our Vietnamese comrades, who don't hesitate to sacrifice the detail so as to preserve the essential.

Our hosts also granted us important facilities in their camps for the training of our commandos. Knowing their limited means, we hadn't asked them for any other assistance.

In the spring of 1970, shortly after my return from Vietnam, I received an invitation to go to Cuba for the July celebrations marking the eleventh anniversary of Fidel Castro's revolution. Preoccupied by the situation in the Middle East, particularly in Jordan where tension between King Hussein and the fedayeen was mounting, I didn't agree to go until a few days before the festivities began. In fact, the main reason I went was to avoid attending the ceremonies organized the same week in Egypt to commemorate the eighteenth anniversary of the overthrow of the monarchy. According to confidential information I had received, Nasser intended to use this occasion to announce his acceptance of the Rogers plan for an Israeli-Arab settlement. Needless to say, we were resolutely opposed to the U.S. plan and I preferred not to be present for the event. Despite Mohamed Hassanein Heikal's urging, which I found somewhat suspect, I declined the invitation on the grounds that it would be impossible to turn down Castro's.

The trip from Cairo to Havana via Madrid was absolutely exhausting. After an interminable wait at the Madrid airport, where the other members of the Palestinian delegation and I were looked after by Cuban bodyguards, we boarded a modest plane of the Cuban national air company. The flight lasted fifteen hours, and the traveling conditions reminded me of those in trains of the Egyptian provinces. Crammed full of passengers, who far outnumbered the available seats, suitcases and bundles blocking the aisles, the aircraft seemed to limp along.

I sat next to Amin al-Howeidi, the head of the Egyptian Mokhabarat, who was clearly suffering as much as I from the cramped quarters and the heat. "So!" he said to me while mopping his brow, "you are planning to fight the Rogers plan and Nasser?" I explained that we were against any undertaking that ignored Palestinian national rights. He replied that we should trust Nasser, his patriotism, and his loyalty to the Palestinian cause.

I was met at the Havana airport by my counterpart in the Cuban intelligence, a warm, wonderfully humorous man who became a friend. Once settled in the simple, comfortable house they put at my disposal, I was handed a schedule of interviews which seemed unduly heavy. In addition to the meetings set up with representatives of national liberation movements from Asia, Africa, and Latin America, I was also to receive delegates of the countless rival organizations in each Latin American country. The divisions within the PLO seemed insignificant compared to the fragmentation that apparently characterized these movements. Putting aside propriety and at the risk of offending a number of minor groups, I asked my hosts to limit my meetings to the major formations within each country.

I used the time thus gained for other activities. I attended a meeting held in my honor by the Palestinian community, some fifty families who had emigrated long ago. The young people, born in Cuba, spoke only Spanish and in some cases English, while the old ones spoke a rather broken Arabic. The meeting was nonetheless very moving. While I was outlining the goals of the struggle we were waging, I saw tears running down many faces.

Another day Fidel Castro invited me to visit some sugar plantations with him. It was during this excursion through the countryside, with Castro himself at the wheel, that I got to know this veritable force of nature, this plain-speaking man, earthy and vibrant. In the course of our political conversations, he showed a profound knowledge of the Middle East conflict and especially the Palestinian cause. He considered Israel a pawn of U.S. imperialism. But like the Vietnamese leaders, he said he wanted to avoid strong language regarding the Zionist state in our joint communiqué. Cuba had relations with influential Jewish business circles for its foreign trade, he explained, and still maintained diplomatic ties with Israel which he didn't want to compromise. "But trust me," he added, "when the time comes I'll do what's necessary."

In September 1973, a little more than three years after our conversation, Castro was as good as his word. Speaking at the Nonaligned Conference in Algiers, he made his spectacular announcement that he was breaking with Israel. I was among the first to hug him in congratulations. His verbal prudence in July 1970 hadn't offended me in the least—especially since he gave me the freedom to express myself as I saw fit, seeing to it that I had ample space in the newspapers and giving me virtually free access to the Cuban radio and television. I used this opportunity to the fullest, giving countless declarations and interviews.

It was a fruitful visit in other ways as well. Fidel Castro showed his support for the Palestinian people's armed struggle by granting us military aid, especially in supplies and training facilities for our fedayeen in Cuba. There was never any question of sending Cuban volunteers to the Middle East, since we have no shortage of fighters.

The speech Castro gave on July 26, 1970, in front of hundreds of thousands of people, was one of the most extraordinary spectacles I have ever seen. The Cuban president is without doubt one of the most powerful orators of our time. For six straight hours, he held his audience. He spoke sometimes with anger, sometimes with irony, illustrating his points with dates and figures cited off the top of his head. His voice was as fascinating as his speech. Often he had his audience, which cheered and applauded wildly, almost in a delirium.

Taking his foreign guests, one at a time, by the hand and raising it in Cuban fashion, he had each of us acclaimed in turn. I felt a lump in my throat as I heard the crowd roar in unison: "Palestine! Palestine!" I was proud, happy, deeply moved.

The name of my country chanted by hundreds of thousands of Cubans was still ringing in my ears as I boarded the plane—this time of the Moroccan national airlines—for the Middle East. Little did I know that scarcely two months later King Hussein of Jordan would try to wipe Palestine, already struck from the map, from the language as well.

5

Ebb Tide

THE BATTLE OF JERASH AND AJLUN sounded the death knell for the Palestinian Resistance in Jordan. For five whole days, from July 13 to 17, 1971, some 3,000 fedayeen entrenched in the forests and wooded hills around these two villages in northern Jordan fought to the last cartridge, with incredible heroism, against the forces unleashed by King Hussein. The Jordanian soldiers showed no mercy, obviously bent on liquidating the last knot of guerrillas remaining after the September 1970 massacres.

The local commander, Abu Ali Ayad, a member of Fatah's Central Committee, refused to surrender. Captured following a gigantic man hunt, he was savagely tortured, mutilated, and finally executed. Some 700 fedayeen were massacred and about 2,000 were taken prisoner and subsequently turned over to the Damascus authorities. Some 100 men managed to take refuge in Syria or, the supreme humiliation, in the occupied West Bank where the Israelis granted them asylum.

Thus ended one of the bloodiest chapters in the history of the Resistance. Thus, again, ended the Palestinian movement's golden period, one of the high points of which was incontestably the Karameh victory in March 1968. A little more than three years had passed since King Hussein, impressed by this exploit, had exclaimed: "We are all fedayeen!" How did we reach this point? What had gone wrong?

It goes without saying that the Jordanian king had never lost much love on us. Despite his pretty words, we knew full well that he never ceased his intrigues to engineer our downfall. But I must say we did help him immeasurably in his task by our repeated errors of judgment, our blunders and excesses, and our provocations. By the very nature of things the confrontation was inevitable.

King Hussein was a man corroded by suspicion. Despite our repeated assurances, he wrongly believed that we were trying to wrest his power from him. Certain members of his entourage, and sometimes even foreign dignitaries, nurtured his anxiety, intentionally or otherwise. Hassan II of Morocco, for instance, told him one day that it was only natural for the fedayeen to seize power in Amman. Shocked by these words, Hussein called in Yasir Arafat to ask if it were true that he coveted his position. All this despite our tireless reiteration that one of Fatah's principles from the very beginning had been noninterference in the internal affairs of host countries. We also pleaded that his support of the Palestinian movement would make him a hero in the eyes of the Arab nation. Half convinced of our sincerity, King Hussein vacillated between skepticism and disbelief.

Our relations began to deteriorate in mid-October 1968 after the funeral we organized in Amman for Abdel Fattah Hammud, one of Fatah's first members. Abdel Fattah had been a very close friend of mine since the early fifties, when he was elected to the PSU leadership along with Arafat and myself. His political involvement had never flagged. After Cairo, he worked for the cause in Qatar where he had an important position as an engineer. Even though he had seven children to support, right after the June 1967 war he gave up his extremely well-paid job to devote himself to the movement full time. The day of his death he was to meet Arafat and me in a Jordanian village near the Syrian border. Knowing how prompt he always was, I started to worry when he didn't show up at the appointed time. A few minutes later we heard that a serious automobile accident had taken place not far away. With a terrible premonition and afraid to witness something that would be unbearable for me, I asked Arafat to go to the scene alone. He came back in tears, and before he even said anything I knew that Abdel Fattah Hammud, scarcely thirty-five years old, had been killed at the wheel of his car.

We decided to hold the funeral in Amman, where we appeared in force for the first time. Tens of thousands of people turned out to pay him homage. I delivered a speech exalting his action and that of the Resistance. King Hussein took umbrage at this first public demonstration in his capital, and it was from that time forward that he began to implement the plan which was to lead, less than two years later, to the bloody conflict of September 1970.

In November 1968, a month after Abdel Fattah Hammud's funeral, an officer of the Royal Jordanian Guard was kidnapped by members of an underground organization claiming to be Palestinian. None of us had ever heard of it, and much later we learned that the group in question had been formed, financed, and armed by Jordan's secret service. King Hussein placed his army in a state of alert and threatened to storm the refugee camps to capture the kidnappers and free the hostage. To dissuade him, a group of leaders of various organizations—including Yasir Arafat, Yahya Hammuda, Bahjat Abu Garbiyya, Hamid Abu Sittah, and I—requested an audience.

That was the first time I ever met the king personally, and I remained silent throughout so I could observe him more closely. In retrospect, he must be commended on his extraordinary acting talent. Although, as the instigator of the kidnapping, he knew better than anyone that we had nothing to do with it, he gave a majestic performance. With perfect self-possession, he expressed his displeasure, flew into rages, and at one point even appeared on the verge of physical violence. We had a great deal of difficulty calming him down. We protested our innocence, explaining that we knew nothing of the organization claiming the kidnapping and that we vigorously condemned the act. We assured him once again of our determination to maintain good relations with the Jordanian authorities. Finally, the king gave in and ordered his troops to lift the siege of the refugee camps.

King Hussein acted with a great deal of skill and cunning. Systematically, patiently, he prepared public opinion, and especially his army, for the confrontation he was leading up to. He kept tensions running high, he provoked crises not only through the pseudoresistance groups created by his intelligence services, but also through agents provocateurs infiltrated into the fedayeen organizations.

As we later discovered, some of Hussein's agents occupied responsible positions in the Resistance. In June 1970, for instance, I was called into the office of Abdel Moneim Rifai, who had just formed a new government. Rifai, a man of unquestioned integrity, had me listen to a tape of a speech made the previous night by Abul Raed, a member of the politbureau of George Habash's Popular Front for the Liberation of Palestine (PFLP). In his speech, Abul Raed heaped obscenities not only on the king, but on his wife and mother as well. The language was so utterly foul that I couldn't bear to hear the tape to the end.

Prime Minister Rifai then showed me a letter from the king instructing him to have the PFLP offices closed down within forty-eight hours, failing which the army would see to the matter. I immediately rushed to the Royal Palace to explain to Hussein that whatever the revulsion we felt toward Abul Raed, we were obliged to defend the PFLP's right to exist and to protect the Palestinian masses against a potential police assault. Once again, the king gave in. Much later, Abul Raed was unmasked as a Jordanian intelligence agent and expelled from the PFLP.

The divisions within the Resistance similarly served the king's designs. A few months after the Six Day War, a number of fedayeen organizations sprang up, more often than not with the sole objective of wresting the movement's leadership from Fatah. Some of them were nothing but puppets of various Arab regimes, transposing the inter-Arab rivalries and struggles to the Palestinian scene.

Demagogic statements and outbidding became inevitable. Each group tried to appear more "revolutionary," more intransigent than the next. I remember that at working sessions with Hussein, representatives of certain organizations struck the table with their fists and insulted members of the royal family (for instance, accusing Sharif Nasser, the king's uncle, of trafficking in drugs). In such cases, I did what I could to recall my comrades to reason, pointing out that such behavior could only play into the hands of our enemies, especially Hussein's.

Sometimes it was difficult to distinguish between political extremism and provocations carried out by paid agents. The proliferation of leftist slogans—such as the one inviting the masses to give "all power to the Resistance"—the distribution of Lenin's portraits in the streets of Amman and even in the mosques, the calls for revolution and the establishment of a socialist regime—all this attested to a criminal obliviousness. The extremists jumbled together the fight for national liberation (which Fatah advocated exclusively) with the class struggle.

It's true that our own behavior wasn't terribly consistent either. Although we tried to appeal to the entire population without regard to national origin, we tended to neglect the Jordanians in favor of the Palestinians. Proud of their force and exploits, the fedayeen often displayed a sense of superiority, sometimes even arrogance, without taking into consideration the sensibilities or interests of the native Jordanians.

Still more serious was their attitude toward the Jordanian army, which they treated more as an enemy than as a potential ally. It's true that King Hussein went to great lengths to drive a wedge between the fedayeen and the royal forces, first by provoking bloody clashes and then by granting collective leaves after these confrontations to the officers and soldiers who participated. These last, back in their homes, ran up against the hostility—all the same understandable—of our fighters. Insulted, bullied, humiliated, sometimes even detained, the king's men grew more eager to get on with it daily. Commenting on these incidents which were becoming more and more frequent during the first months of 1970, the king explained his apparent passivity to a member of his entourage: "I'm giving them more rope so they can hang themselves."

Tension had reached a peak in July 1970, when we called an extraordinary session of the Resistance Central Council (RCC), made up of representatives from some dozen organizations. I asked my comrades two questions straight off: "Do you want to seize power in Amman? And if so, do you think the balance of power will enable us to win?" The vast majority said no to both questions. On the one hand, they believed the Resistance should avoid getting bogged down in government responsibilities and red tape, and on the other they were convinced of the crushing superiority of the royal forces.

This confirmed my conviction that for most members of the Central Council, tactics took the place of strategy. Hence the dangerous ambiguity of their policy, which in my opinion was leading us straight to disaster. I told them the king would not stand for the dual power we had established in his country much longer. We had to make a clear choice, I said, in keeping with our analysis and strategy. If it were true that we didn't want to overthrow the monarchy—which in any case was invincible for the time being—I argued that our most pressing duty was to normalize relations with Hussein before it was too late.

When I finished speaking, I started toward the door, saying: "Those of you who have the interests of the Palestinian people at heart, follow me! We'll all go to the palace together and negotiate a modus vivendi with the king!" The majority remained frozen in place, while only a handful of delegates from organizations other than Fatah left with me.

The supreme obliviousness of most of the RCC members would be incomprehensible if I didn't explain that they were convinced that King Hussein would never dare attack the fedayeen, scattered as they were in the capital and throughout the country, for fear of triggering a massacre within the population. Some of them were still laboring under the illusion that the royal army, or at least a good part of it, would rebel if ordered to fire into the crowd.

I personally was convinced of the contrary. The king had secured the loyalty of his officers by showering them with material privileges. The soldiers, including the Palestinians who constituted about a third of the royal forces (and not 60 percent as has often been written), had been mobilized against the fedayeen movement through an extremely clever propaganda campaign. We were presented as atheists, enemies of God, Communists cooperating closely with shadowy international forces including Jews of the extreme left. We were seeking not to defend the interests of the Palestinian people but to seize power on behalf of foreign powers. Despite the effectiveness of his propaganda, Hussein took the precaution of excluding Palestinians from the elite units, especially the tank and artillery divisions which he used heavily during the September 1970 fighting and the Jerash and Ajlun battles of July 1971.

By the end of August 1970 I was even more worried, especially since King Hussein appeared so sure of himself. He had good reason. Like Nasser, he had subscribed to the Rogers plan for a settlement with Israel and consequently enjoyed powerful support on the international scene, particularly in the Arab world. Even Iraqi president Ahmad Hasan al-Bakr and Libya's chief of state Muammar al-Qaddafi publicly expressed their sympathy for him while criticizing the "errors" of the Palestinian Resistance.

Two weeks after the cease-fire on the Israeli-Egyptian front took effect, bringing to an end the war of attrition between the two countries, Hussein flew to Alexandria where he was warmly greeted by Nasser. Once the king was back in Amman, the Jordanian authorities spread the rumor that the Egyptian president had given the green light to crush the Palestinian movement, which had unanimously opposed the Rogers plan and the UN Security Council resolution on which it was based.

The Resistance Central Council was divided on what stance to take concerning Nasser. The majority thought we should have a showdown with him. Fatah, supported by the pro-Syrian organization Saiqah and a few independents, was on the contrary convinced that such a move at this time would be sheer madness. Tactically, it would be suicidal to attack Nasser while we risked being stabbed in the back by Hussein. Strategically, we couldn't afford to break with the most powerful Arab country whose regional and international support was so precious to us. Finally, we still believed in Nasser's patriotism. We were sure he wouldn't betray us since he had already publicly declared that he understood perfectly why the Resistance rejected Resolution 242, which in no way met the aspirations of the Palestinian people. We decided to send emissaries to Nasser to try to work things out.

The delegation that flew to Alexandria included Yasir Arafat, Faruq Qaddumi, Hayel Abdel Hamid, and myself (all representing Fatah's Central Committee), Daffi Gamassan (of Saiqah), and Ibrahim Bakr (an independent). Nasser greeted us with a certain coldness. "I've been walking around my garden for the last hour to get my anger under control before seeing you," he said by way of introduction. He had been furious at the attacks on him in Fatah publications and showed us samples lying on his desk. We had no right to criticize him before learning the reasons that pushed him to accept the Rogers plan, he continued.

During the meeting, which lasted over seven hours, he said there was one chance in a thousand that the American peace project would be realized, since he knew in advance that Israel had absolutely no intention of respecting its commitments and returning all the occupied territories. He nonetheless would pursue his efforts to reach a peaceful settlement. In the meantime, he had to gain time to prepare himself for war, which he believed inevitable as a first stage. He told us that during his recent trip to Moscow he had gotten the Soviets (after threatening to resign) to agree to deliver SAM missiles to Egypt. "We are taking advantage of the cease-fire now in effect to install them along the canal secretly," he confided.

The Soviet leaders, he went on, had at first been astonished when he agreed to rally to the American plan, and had proposed as an alternative a plan that could be presented jointly by Moscow and Washington. He had rejected the offer, explaining that he hoped to "corner" the United States, which for the first time since the June 1967 war had committed itself to obtaining Israel's evacuation from almost all the occupied territories. The advantage of Resolution 242, he added, was that it gave the Arabs an internationally recognized legal basis for recovering their lost territories.

Turning to Yasir Arafat, Nasser asked sarcastically: "In your opinion, how many years do you need to destroy the Zionist state and build a new unified and democratic state on the whole of liberated Palestine?" He criticized us for an "unrealistic" policy and pointed out that a ministate in the West Bank and Gaza was better than nothing.

After the initial coolness, the meeting, for the most part, was cordial, later even friendly. Over dinner, Nasser shared his worries over the situation in Jordan. "I know that the Hashemite special services have been spreading rumors that I encouraged Hussein to strike. But the opposite is true. During his trip to Egypt I warned him against such an undertaking twice, once when we were alone and a second time in the presence of his prime minister, Abdel Moneim Rifai."

We left Alexandria only half reassured. King Hussein did not seem to have taken Nasser's warnings very seriously, since he was in the process of pounding Resistance positions. The sporadic fighting, which took place almost daily, coupled with the persistent incertitude and tension, had ended up by tiring public opinion. Part of the population directed its bad temper against the fedayeen, held responsible for the clashes. It was in this atmosphere of crisis that the PFLP chose, on September 6, to hijack four airplanes and to hold them on a landing strip in Jordan, which they called the "airport of the revolution." This was another slap in the face for King Hussein.

The operation struck us as highly suspect, as indeed did the decision of the PFLP's president, Dr. George Habash, to leave Amman a month earlier, when the crisis was already in full swing, for a "friendly visit" to North Korea. The hijackings put the entire Resistance in the dock and gave Hussein the chance he was waiting for. Even Iraq, theoretically on our side, sent a sort of ultimatum to Fatah demanding the arrest of the hijackers and the release of the hostages. They overestimated our power. Yasir Arafat succeeded merely in having the PFLP "suspended" from the PLO Central Committee, but the measure seemed pathetically benign after the planes were blown up and when one considers the dozens of passengers, including women and children, being held.

The fighting spread throughout northern Jordan, where our offices were systematically bombarded by the royal artillery. We had to act fast. We had nowhere to turn for outside help, even though some months earlier the Iraqis had actually made a concrete proposal encouraging us to seize power. While on an official visit to Amman the previous May, an Iraqi delegation composed of three of the regime's most influential members (Abdel Khalek al-Samarai and Zeid Haydar, both of the Baath Party leadership, and Mahdi Ammash, the interior minister) met Yasir Arafat and me at the Habbanieh base. "Organize a coup d'etat," they told us, "and the Iraqi units stationed in Jordan will help you overthrow the monarchy and set up a people's government." According to the plan, the Iraqis would occupy Zarqa and Irbid in the north, while the fedayeen would seize Amman.

Even at the time, Arafat and I didn't take the idea very seriously. We suggested that the Iraqis get Syria's approval and possibly even its participation. Given the rivalries between the two countries, we knew agreement between them was virtually excluded. Our skepticism turned out to be well founded, since the Iraqis remained totally passive throughout the entire war which erupted several days later between the fedayeen and the royal forces.

We tried everything during the first half of September to avoid a confrontation. Difficult negotiations dragged on under an Arab League mediator, the Sudanese ex-Minister Amin al-Shibli. We had been reluctant to agree to a compromise accord which seemed draconian, when on September 14 I received a telephone call from Abdel Moneim Rifai. His voice on the other end of the line was nervous, filled with anguish. "Sign the agreement, whatever the cost!" the prime minister said, and abruptly hung up.

We trusted Rifai, whose loyalty to the king in no way detracted from his indulgence for the Resistance. He was clearly trying to get across the message that if we didn't come to an immediate agreement with the king, general hostilities would be unleashed. Without wasting a second, I rushed to the palace, signed the protocol agreement as it stood, and informed Rifai, who immediately had the text broadcast over Radio Amman. We thought we had avoided the worst.

We were mistaken. The next day, the king dismissed the Rifai government and appointed General Muhammad Daud (of Palestinian origin) to form a war cabinet composed exclusively of the military. The same day the mass media, particularly the radio and television, launched a virulent campaign against the Resistance. On September 16, Yasir Arafat sent an urgent appeal for help to all the Arab heads of state. But it was too late. The following day the royal forces unleashed their general offensive against the fedayeen, indiscriminately bombing all the neighborhoods of Amman in the process.

Curious as it may seem, we were totally unprepared for the ordeal even though it had been months in the making. Up to the very last minute, a number of Resistance leaders persisted in the conviction that King Hussein wouldn't dare. It was only a few hours before large-scale fighting broke out that the various guerrilla organizations formed a unified command. The headquarters of Fatah's military command were occupied by the king's army in a matter of minutes. We had set it up on Jebel Hussein, a particularly vulnerable part of town, whereas we could have installed it in Ashrafieh, which was virtually impregnable.

I hurried to the military operations center, which was also on Jebel Hussein but hadn't yet fallen to the enemy forces. Yasir Arafat was there, desperately trying to reach the king by telephone while mortar shells were exploding all around. "Hang up!" I told him. "It's useless. No one's going to so much as speak to you!" I was right. He had asked to speak to the king and several members of his entourage, but each of them, he was told, was saying his morning prayers and couldn't be disturbed.

We were much less organized than we had been at the time of the Karameh fighting. We hadn't prepared a battle plan; we hadn't managed to get in touch with certain military commanders; we hadn't provided for hiding places for members of the leadership. Five of us were at the military operations center that morning. We had to disperse without losing another moment. I suggested that Arafat entrench himself at Jebel al-Webda, while I took off with Faruq Qaddumi, Ibrahim Bakr, and Bahjat Abu Gharbia to try to get to the Resistance's general intelligence headquarters.

We had hardly reached the other end of the street when a number of tanks of the royal army turned a corner and started coming straight toward us, firing in all directions. We rushed to the nearest house, where a Jordanian judge, a Christian, took us in. We ended up spending five dramatic days in his company.

We soon learned that the entire quarter was under siege by Hussein's forces and that an around-the-clock curfew had been imposed on all Amman. We worked out a number of escape plans, but the surveillance was so tight that we had to drop all of them. Finally, the security forces started a systematic search of the entire neighborhood. A peremptory voice, amplified over a loudspeaker, ordered all the inhabitants outside for an identification check. We slipped our pistols under a mattress and went down to the street.

Heavily armed soldiers, eyes narrowed with suspicion, interrogated and searched everyone, even smelling the palms of hands for the odor of powder to detect those who had been handling firearms. A young major started coming toward us, staring at us hard. From his face it was clear that he had recognized us. "What are you doing here?" he asked ambiguously. The judge at whose house we had taken refuge courageously answered for us: "They are my guests, some friends from Kuwait." To our great astonishment, the officer said that would be all and told us we could go. So we had friends within the royal forces after all!

But just as we were starting back to the house, a soldier shouted: "That guy's a fedayeen leader! I recognize him!" He made a dive for Ibrahim Bakr and started slapping him around. Caught off guard, the officer made a quiet gesture for us to leave discreetly while Ibrahim was being handcuffed and led away.

The web was tightening around us. That same night we decided to make a break for it, come what may. At about two-thirty in the morning, Faruq Qaddumi climbed out the window and started letting himself down by a rope. Before I could follow, I noticed in the darkness that he had suddenly begun scaling up it again. He reappeared, out of breath, and explained that before reaching the street level his foot had come upon a solid mass, which turned out to be a tank parked right under our window.

The next morning we were relieved to hear over the radio that the curfew would be lifted for an hour the following day to enable the population to buy provisions. We saw this as the ideal chance: We could lose ourselves in the crowd and then join our fighters in one way or another. But at dawn of the appointed day we were awakened by a loud din. Additional forces, including tanks and armored cars, were in the process of surrounding our block of houses. Once this was completed, a loud-speaker reverberated: "Abu Iyad! We know you're in one of those houses. Give yourself up or we'll shell the whole neighborhood!"

I sensed that the most excruciating hours of my life were at hand. Bahjat Abu Gharbia thought we should comply with the orders to avoid risking innocent lives. Faruq Qaddumi and I were reluctant. We had trouble resigning ourselves to a humiliating capitulation. Our host didn't say a word, but he was clearly terrified. The neighbors, who had guessed who we were after Ibrahim Bakr's arrest, came one after another to beg us to surrender. One of them, a distant relative of Qaddumi's who had recognized him, subjected him to ignoble pressures. The throbbing voice of the loudspeaker became more and more menacing.

At about ten o'clock, or four hours after the first warning, volleys of machine-gun fire crackled through the air, followed by terrifying explosions. Several houses in the neighborhood were hit. Women's shrieks and children's crying could be heard above the noise of bullets, some of which lodged themselves in the venetian blinds of our windows. Neighbors sent their children to knock on our door and beg us to go away. One of our neighbors even gave us three white flags that he had cut from a sheet. But I tore them to ribbons, furious.

The shooting stopped as abruptly as it had begun. We took advantage of the lull to convince our neighbors to be patient until noon when the curfew was to be lifted. We could then leave the house without having to raise our hands in surrender. Our honor would be safe.

A few minutes after the truce became effective, we left the house. No sooner had we stepped into the deserted street than a soldier stopped us and led us to his superior, who asked for our papers. Bahjat Abu Ghar-bia and Faruq Qaddumi had passports under their real names stating that they were employed in Kuwait. I had no document to show. Qad-dumi marshaled all his talents as an actor and humorist to disarm the officer's suspicions, but to no avail. Perhaps he had recognized us, for he insisted on having us taken to the Tabarbour military camp about five kilometers from Amman, which was being used as a detention center. We were herded into the back of a truck where about a dozen suspects were being beaten around by soldiers. The officer ordered our guards not to touch us before we got to the camp.

Unluckily, the intelligence officer they led us to recognized me at once. Or perhaps it was lucky. Mustafa al-Eskandarani embraced me warmly, reminding me that I had rescued him one day from some fedayeen who where holding him hostage. He spared us the tortures inflicted on those being held at Tabarbour—we could hear their screams—by having us immediately transferred to the central head-quarters of the special services, which had been alerted to our arrest.

The welcome we got wasn't very encouraging. They took away our shoes and all our personal effects before leading us underground where they locked us in adjoining cells. Mine was about two meters long and a meter wide, humid and foul-smelling. I felt nauseated. The twelve or so hours spent there, in total darkness, without eating or drinking, plunged me into a depression. Not only because I was sure we would be killed, but also because of the dishonor our enemies would try to inflict on us after we were put to death. I was certain that our arrest—like Ibrahim Bakr's—would be presented as a cowardly surrender with the intention of demoralizing our troops.

Late that night, I was pulled from my cell to undergo my first inter-rogation. The examining officer was courteous, even kind, and offered me a cigarette, which I refused even though I'm a heavy smoker. I was worried about what was happening to Abu Gharbia and Qaddumi, and refused to answer his questions until they were at my side. The officer insisted: Couldn't I at least tell him the location of Radio Asifah's secret transmitter (which obviously irritated the royal power immeasurably)? I replied that I knew nothing, which was true, and that even if I did, I would never divulge it. I even threatened him, saying that after peace was restored the fedayeen would know how to settle accounts with over-zealous officers like himself.

He didn't press the point and had Abu Gharbia and Qaddumi brought in. Playing his part, Faruq was bristling with indignation, insisting that

he had never been so offended in his life, he whose duties within the
PLO were on a par with those of a minister! We were laughing to ourselves when the chief of special services, al-Nazil Rashid, came in and
hugged us in Arab fashion to wish us welcome. General Rashid was a
former opponent of the Jordanian regime and had spent years as a political refugee in Egypt before rallying once more to King Hussein. He
came across like a staunch Arab nationalist, put an end to the interrogation, and gave orders that we get preferential treatment. He realized it
was useless to pressure us and thought the wisest course would be to
preserve our lives. This opinion was not shared by his predecessor,
General Rassul al-Kilani, one of the king's intimates. When Qaddumi
and I met him at the end of the fighting, he told me: "The biggest mistake we made was sparing you. We would have won the war if we had
executed you on the spot!"

The day after our meeting with the head of the special services, a
large room was put at our disposal for discussions with the series of ministers, important officials, and high-ranking intelligence officers who
came to see us. The political talks were very lively, but seemed so
sterile that they ended by tiring us. The following day the war of nerves
began. The guard officers would tell us "confidentially" that Yasir Arafat
had surrendered, or that he had been killed, or else that the U.S.
marines were about to land to help the royal forces.

These bits of information left us confused. We didn't know then that
Syrian units had crossed the border to help the fedayeen, or that the Soviets and Egyptians, anxious to avoid an Israeli-American military intervention, were pressuring Damascus to withdraw its troops. Later we
were to learn that the Syrian army had had to withdraw four days after it
entered Jordan. As for the Iraqi contingent, just as we had predicted, it
didn't budge. While I was being held, a Jordanian intelligence officer
had me listen to a taped conversation between King Hussein and the
Iraqi defense minister General Hardan al-Takriti. Takriti said distinctly:
"In accordance with our commitments, our troops won't move . . ." Indeed, the Iraqi army units were withdrawn from Jordan shortly after the
September 1970 fighting. Several months later, President Bakr explained to me that Baghdad had feared an American intervention which
might have endangered the Baathist regime.

In short, the news that reached us from the outside wasn't terribly encouraging. One night three highly placed Jordanians, including the chief
of staff and the head of the special services, came to talk to us. I outlined
a plan for a cease-fire agreement which I said could become effective

only after Yasir Arafat and the other members of the leadership approved it. Overriding the protests of Faruq Qaddumi and Ibrahim Bakr, I had insisted that the draft agreement be transmitted to King Hussein on my exclusive responsibility. I figured that if the fedayeen were on the point of being defeated, it would help offer an honorable way out. If, on the other hand, the military situation was in our favor, I would be the only one compromised by the initiative.

The draft agreement, which I drew up in the presence of the three Jordanians, covered four points: the return of the royal army to its barracks; the fedayeen's evacuation from Amman; the opening of negotiations with the PLO as the sole legitimate representative of the Palestinian people; and the establishment of fedayeen bases along the demarcation lines of the territories occupied by Israel. On the suggestion of the Jordanians, I read the text of the draft accord aloud, which unknown to me was recorded and transmitted to the king. It was agreed that my comrades and I would be escorted to the Egyptian Embassy, where we would contact Arafat by radio to get his approval. But the king violated the agreed-upon terms on the very next day. On September 23, he had my proposals, purportedly coming from the Fatah leadership, broadcast over Radio Amman along with his own acceptance of them, this despite the fact that I had clearly specified that as a prisoner I was in no position to negotiate—much less to decide—in the name of my organization.

Unaware of how my proposal had been misused, that same day Qaddumi, Bakr, and I (Abu Gharbia was sick) started off for the Egyptian Embassy as had been agreed. The fighting was so intense that the armored car we were being driven in could barely advance a few dozen meters. After several vain attempts, the heavy shooting and exploding mortar shells forced us to turn back. But this relatively brief foray had been enough to show me that the fedayeen, far from being beaten, were still controlling several sectors of the capital. There was no way I could have known that the Resistance forces had liberated the Irbid-Ramtha-Jerash triangle that very day and that they now controlled these three northern cities.

Shortly after, I was called from the prison to the Homar Palace, where I was awaited by the king and members of the delegation the Arab chiefs of state had sent from Cairo to mediate an end to the fighting. The delegation, headed by Sudan's president, General Jaafar Numeiry, included Tunisian prime minister Bahi Ladgham, Kuwaiti defense minister Sheikh Saad Abdallah, and the head of Egypt's Deuxième Bureau, General Sadek. General Sadek had preceded the rest of the delegation to Amman with orders from Nasser to ask the king for Qaddumi's and my release. He rejected the offer to visit us in prison and insisted that we be brought to the palace.

A few minutes after our arrival in front of the royal residence, Hussein came to wish us welcome. After embracing me warmly, he said in a reproachful voice: "Well, are you satisfied with the tragedy we're living?" "Your Majesty," I replied, "we did everything we could to avoid this catastrophe, as you well know. But are you aware of how your troops are acting? That they are massacring the population? That your men are torturing young patriots at the Tabarbour military camp not far from your palace?" Taking me by the arm, the king guided me into the palace while assuring me that he would open an inquiry into the matter.

Our talks with the members of the Arab delegation, in Hussein's presence, revolved around how to contact Arafat and initiate a cease-fire as soon as possible. The atmosphere was tense, and I withdrew to the ground floor of the palace along with a few members of the royal entourage. While I was talking with former prime minister Ahmad Tuqan, I asked for something to drink. A young aide who was standing next to us shot me an insult, adding that he'd rather see me "die of thirst." Tuqan went to inform the king of the incident, and a few minutes later the king himself appeared with a glass of water in his hand.

I learned that day that we had friends even within the royal walls. While we were waiting for the deliberations to end, a Jordanian superior officer got me aside and told me that the army had received the order to shell Irbid as of five o'clock that afternoon. I immediately rushed upstairs and in front of the Arab delegation asked Hussein to countermand the order to prevent new massacres.

The king, caught off guard, was furious. His first reaction was to deny it. "Who supplied you with this false information? I demand to be told!" he cried angrily. Obviously, I refused to reveal my source. Pressed by the Arab delegation, the monarch went to the room that served as a communications center and returned a few minutes later to announce that the general staff had assured him that "Irbid will not be shelled."

The Arab delegation decided to return to Cairo that same night. King Hussein agreed to release my three companions, but insisted on keeping me in Amman, where, he said, I would be more useful. General Sadek held his ground, however, firmly repeating that Nasser had ordered him not to leave Amman without me. In the end the king gave in.

It wasn't until we were actually flying to Cairo that I learned, from

President Numeiry's own mouth, of the dirty trick he had played on us. Before leaving Amman, Numeiry had broadcast over Radio Amman a cease-fire agreement he had negotiated with Hussein, but which was attributed to my three companions and myself. I flew into a rage, and when the Sudanese president handed me the text of the agreement I threw it on the floor and said it was worthless. Indeed, the Fatah leadership issued a communiqué to that effect, pointing out that we couldn't have approved the accord since as prisoners we weren't in a position to exercise our will freely.

Gamal Abdel Nasser was waiting for us at the Cairo airport. He embraced us warmly, obviously happy to find us safe and sound. He took us in his car to the Kubbeh Palace on the outskirts of Cairo, where the Arab heads of state had been in session for a number of days and were now awaiting the results of the mission to Amman.

I described to them the situation in Jordan, the brutality of the royal forces, and the terrible destruction I had glimpsed in the streets of the capital. I emphasized the human losses inflicted on the civilian population and King Hussein's determination to liquidate the Palestinian Resistance. Even while I was talking, I was struck by the lack of sensitivity on the part of most of my listeners. With impassive faces, looking at me in an indifferent or absent manner, they listened politely, to be sure, but with a detachment which sent shivers up my spine. Were these the leaders of the Arab nation, indignant over the frightful tragedy the Jordanian and Palestinian people were going through?

When I finished talking, Nasser drove Qaddumi and me to the Hilton Hotel in Cairo where he had been staying while the summit was in progress. He took us to the presidential suite, where Hussein al-Shafei, vice-president of the republic, and Ali Sabri, a former prime minister, were waiting. "What do you want me to do to help you?" Nasser asked. His face was tired, his expression filled with sadness. He seemed very moved, and I thought I detected a touch of guilt in his attitude toward us. Explaining why it had taken him so long (about five days) to intervene in effort to end the fighting, he told us: "I was at my residence at Marsa Matruh, far from my sources of information, which is why I thought at first that the confrontation was of minor importance, the same as all the others . . ."

He tried to make up for it. "Would you like to use Radio Cairo again?" he asked. (He had deprived us of the radio three months earlier as a reprisal for our criticism of the Rogers plan.) I replied that we had to attend to more urgent matters first, and find a way to get Yasir Arafat

out of Amman. King Hussein, I said, wouldn't halt the fighting as long
as the PLO president was still in Jordan, and the war had to be stopped
as soon as possible. According to our information, the royal army's offensive against the Ashrafieh sector where Arafat had established his headquarters was gaining momentum while our fighters were beginning to
run low on ammunition. Despite my reservations about the way Sudanese president Numeiry had carried out his mission, I suggested that he
return to Amman to deliver Arafat.

Our meeting with Nasser lasted all night. By morning he had agreed
to my suggestion. General Sadek, he told me, would be in charge of
working out Arafat's escape plan. The only thing left for me to do was to
convince the other Arab leaders about the new mission. King Faisal of
Saudi Arabia chose his advisor Rashad Pharaon as a member of the delegation. The Emir of Kuwait immediately named his defense minister.
Abu Gharbia and Qaddumi were to go to Syria to rally President Atassi,
who hadn't attended the Cairo meeting, while Ibrahim Bakr would ac-
company the Arab mission to Amman. Nasser was firmly opposed to my
participation in the delegation on the grounds that I could be detained
once again.

To my surprise, General Numeiry refused to lead the delegation. He
considered his mission terminated and said he never wanted to set foot
in Amman again. But Nasser, whom he venerated, insisted and he finally gave in.

General Sadek's plan to get Yasir Arafat out of Cairo was implemented
as soon as the Arab ambassadors arrived in Amman. They asked to be
taken to the Egyptian Embassy where they entered into contact with
the PLO chief by radio. Using a code unknown to the Jordanian authorities, they set up a meeting in a sector controlled by the Resistance.
While part of the delegation was negotiating with King Hussein, others
went to meet Arafat. They provided him with Kuwaiti bedouin robes,
and using this disguise he was able to leave Jordanian territory for Cairo
on the same plane as the delegation.

Until then, King Hussein had refused to attend the Arab summit on
various pretexts. But when he learned in a telegram from Nasser that
Arafat had managed to escape, he flew to Cairo at once. As I had predicted, a cease-fire agreement approved by the two parties was immediately proclaimed, and this time applied by the Jordanian army under the
supervision of the Arab officers dispatched to Amman.

On September 28, the day after the Arafat-Hussein agreement was
signed in Cairo, Faruq Qaddumi and I were at some friends' house

when the radio suddenly and inexplicably began to broadcast verses from the Koran. This sign of mourning filled us with a terrible foreboding that something had happened to Nasser. Friends from the press confirmed it: Nasser, after rescuing us from our ordeal, had just died of a heart attack. Overcome with sadness, I sent a message of condolences in the name of Fatah to Anwar Sadat in his capacity as vice-president of the republic. I wrote the text spontaneously, from the heart, certain that each word expressed the profound feelings of all Palestinians. I said something to the effect that Nasser, who incarnated the aspirations and dreams of the entire Arab nation, had fallen on the field of honor, but that his ideas would remain engraved in the memories of generations to come of the Palestinian people, to whom he restored, as to all the Arab peoples, their dignity and cause for hope.

Yasir Arafat, Abu Jihad, and Abu Mazen, who were in Damascus that night, heard the news along with my telegram over their car radio. All three burst into tears. Arafat immediately rushed back to Cairo, and his eyes were still wet when I saw him.

Some people could be surprised at the extent of our sorrow, given the differences and sometimes even clashes we had had with Nasser. They could also have trouble understanding the affliction of the Egyptian people, who turned out for his funeral by the millions to shout their grief, just as they had demonstrated on June 9 and 10, 1967, after the disaster of the Six Day War. But Nasser was for all of us a father and a guide, even if he was sometimes wrong. As a patriot, he served the Egyptian people; as an Arab nationalist, he gave inestimable assistance to the Palestinian people. He cared for us sincerely.

Nasser was true to the commitments he had made on our first official meeting in 1968. He received us often, giving us unstintingly of his time. Our conversations were always frank, and always led to concrete results. I remember a meeting Arafat and I had with him in November 1969 in the presence of Anwar Sadat. When we got up to leave, Nasser insisted on accompanying us to the front porch of his residence, following us with his eyes as we continued to our car. I noticed his gaze, beaming with satisfaction and paternal affection. Sadat, who was walking beside us, whispered: "The president respects you both very much, and it always makes him happy to see you together, united in the struggle. Stand by him without faltering, he needs it."

It's true that Nasser held off reacting to King Hussein's offensive against the fedayeen in September 1970. Certain people, crediting the rumor spread by the Jordanian secret services, believe that Nasser gave the king the green light to eliminate the fedayeen. But in my view this thesis has no grounding in fact. If Nasser had really wished our destruction, why would he have gone to so much trouble to halt the fighting, to save the leaders of the Resistance? The reasons he gave me to explain his passivity during the first few days of the fighting struck me as sincere. Even if they weren't, the worst hypothesis that could be made to stand is that he wanted to teach us a lesson, to remind us of our limits at a time when we were trying to obstruct a peace settlement based on the Rogers plan.

In any case, I am convinced that Hussein would never have dared carry out his plan to eliminate the fedayeen from Jordan if Nasser had still been alive. The massacres of Jerash and Ajlun, which constituted the culmination of this strategy, would have been impossible. It was thanks to Nasser and his preponderant influence in the Arab world that Hussein was obliged to agree to the cease-fire at the end of September 1970. Isolated, he had to conclude the October 13 agreement with the PLO. He signed it, but he had no intention of carrying it out—as I was later told by Wasfi al-Tal, appointed prime minister and military governor of Jordan on October 28. Under the terms of the agreement, we would retain considerable freedom of action and our militants were authorized to remain in the cities. One clause in particular was intolerable to the king: the one whereby he recognized the PLO as the sole legitimate representative of the Palestinian people. Indeed, one of the principal objectives of the September war was precisely to restore to the Hashemite throne the right to negotiate the future of the occupied Palestinian territories.

The first thing I did upon returning to Amman at the end of October was to visit the judge who had so courageously hidden my three comrades and me during the fighting. Needless to say, I had kept our secret, and the security police hadn't managed to track him down. Seated around a well-laid table, we laughed while remembering certain episodes of our common ordeal.

I had several more meetings with Hussein and Wasfi al-Tal to work out a framework for our future relations. I had absolutely no confidence in al-Tal, whom I had known for some time. I had nicknamed him the "ideological agent." He had no interest in money, but he was of an incredible docility when it came to executing London's policy at the time when England was the power to be reckoned with in Jordan. He had adopted a similar attitude toward American imperialism, whose arm, the CIA, reached to the very heart of the royal palace.

Known for his pitiless brutality, al-Tal was also a man of consummate skill. He flirted with Jordan's Arab nationalist circles, trying—and sometimes succeeding—to manipulate them. During our meetings in the fall of 1970, he was kind, attentive, warm in his dealings with me. To listen to him, his greatest desire was to breathe new life into the fedayeen movement. He only wanted to help us, he said. All I had to do was tell him what we wanted. But I wasn't taken in, especially since I had observed at close range his maneuvers which were to lead to our destruction scarcely nine months later.

All through November and December, Wasfi al-Tal set up gendarmerie posts near each of our positions, ostensibly for routine purposes but actually to serve as bases for the royal army. By January, shooting incidents and clashes began to break out mysteriously between the fedayeen and the police. Al-Tal then informed us that he could not tolerate the anarchic situation created by a movement that didn't know how to control its own men. He demanded that the guerrillas evacuate all the cities in the kingdom and that our militias be disarmed. Our fighters, he said, should be concentrated in Jerash and Ajlun where they could better combat the Israeli enemy. At the end of January, our representatives—thinking that they would be able to elude the vigilance of the authorities—actually agreed to conclude an accord providing for our disarmament.

I was in Kuwait at the time and rushed back to Amman the minute I heard the news. I was convinced that we had just committed a serious blunder that would cost us dearly. Unfortunately, the events were to prove me right. Wasfi al-Tal began by promulgating a law imposing the death penalty on anyone found in possession of a firearm. The army then proceeded to search every house, neighborhood by neighborhood, discovering our arms caches with remarkable ease. It was clear that the security police had been well informed of our underground activities. We later conducted investigations enabling us to unmask a number of their agents, who for the most part had passed themselves off as fanatic militants advocating maximalist positions. This only served to reinforce my conviction that the diehard extremists are either imbeciles or traitors.

When the plot appeared to be taking shape, I requested an audience with the king. This time I was unable to maintain the courtesy I had always shown him. My exact words to him were: "If you strike the fedayeen in their last holdouts in Jerash and Ajlun, I'll follow you to the end of the earth, to my dying breath, to give you the punishment you deserve!" Taken aback, the king's only reply was a murmured: "God forbid . . ." I never saw him again.

Measures against the fedayeen increased drastically over the next two months. The army occupied most of the refugee camps, repression was stepped up, armed incidents provoked by the government became commonplace. There was no question in my mind that the final showdown was at hand. I decided to fight in the open. I called a public meeting at the Wehdate refugee camp in Amman for May 15.

"Impossible!" my comrades told me. "People are too frightened to take part in any public demonstration." No Resistance leader had addressed the people since the September 1970 war, and I believed in the courage of my countrymen. I asked that the assembly be held in a stadium which could hold over 10,000 people. However, the night before the meeting I was informed that the army had encircled the stadium and was installing machine guns on the roofs of the surrounding buildings. "What difference does it make?" I asked. "The meeting will go on anyway."

The next day, at 3:45 in the afternoon, or fifteen minutes before the demonstration was scheduled to begin, the organizers came to tell me that the stadium was still empty. I set off for the Wehdate camp anyway, arriving at four o'clock sharp. It was as if a miracle had taken place: The sports stadium was not only packed, it was overflowing with a dense crowd, mainly women (many of whom carried babies), children, and old men. The women were decked out for the occasion in the national costume—long dresses richly decorated with multicolored embroidery. I later learned that word had gone out to the various refugee camps to come to the meeting at the last minute so the police force would not be able to stop the enormous wave of people converging on Wehdate.

As I was mounting the speaker's platform, I noticed the soldiers in battle dress posted on the rooftops, the barrels of their machine guns pointing toward the crowd which appeared to ignore them. Taking the microphone, I began by addressing the soldiers: "Do you really think you can intimidate us by this show of strength? Nothing can make the Palestinians draw back. The Palestinians are not afraid of blows or bullets, and strive only to liberate their country. I would be ashamed if I were you. Instead of being on the front to fight the Israeli army, you are obliged to hold in check women and children with neither weapons nor defenses!"

I had hardly finished this short tirade when one after another the soldiers began sheepishly turning away the barrels of their machine guns to the wild applause of the audience. During my speech, many of them abandoned their positions to mingle with the crowd. I spoke with brutal frankness. Reviewing Palestinian relations with the Jordainian government, I denounced the duplicity of Wasfi al-Tal and King Hussein. Both had systematically lied to us; they had signed agreements without the slightest intention of respecting them; they had violated their commitments by occupying the refugee camps, by expelling the fedayeen from the cities. They had promised, I went on, to spare our guerrillas concentrated in Jerash and Ajlun, but according to our information new massacres were being prepared. I ended my speech with the words: "This may be the last time you'll see me among you. Be strong! The future is yours!"

The crowd, immobile and silent, suddenly went wild. Women raised their babies above their heads, shouting: "We are all fedayeen!" The entire assembly started chanting slogans expressing their will to resist, their determination to pursue the struggle until victory.

Two months later to the day, on the morning of July 15, I rushed to the Egyptian seaside resort of Marsa Matruh where Sadat, Qaddafi, Syrian prime minister Mahmud al-Ayubi, and a member of the Sudanese Revolutionary Council were meeting to examine the crisis in Morocco. I had come to ask them to intervene urgently to stop the massacres the Jordanian army had been carrying out for the past two days in Jerash and Ajlun. They knew I was coming and why, but still they made me wait no less than ten hours before receiving me. They would have made me wait even longer if they hadn't learned that I had lost my patience and had started toward my car to drive back to Cairo.

After listening to me, Colonel Qaddafi suggested that the Egyptian air force intervene to break the siege of the Jerash-Ajlun region. He further advised that the Syrian border—closed since the September fighting— be reopened for fedayeen and for the arms Algeria had sent to the Palestinians via the port of Latakia, which Damascus had been blocking for weeks. Sadat turned to me and said: "What do you think of that idea?" I replied: "Do you really believe, Mr. President, that my requests would be more modest than Colonel Qaddafi's? The essential is that you do something, anything, to stop the carnage!"

Embarrassed, Sadat and Ayubi didn't say a word. Luckily for Premier Ayubi, he was called to the telephone. He returned, beaming, to announce that Damascus had just informed him that a Syrian-Palestinian delegation was negotiating a cease-fire in Amman. An agreement was believed to be imminent, so we could take our leave reassured.

Two days later, the crime was consummated. Nothing could be done now for the some 3,000 fedayeen killed, wounded, arrested, or in flight. On July 18, Adnan Abu Odeh, the Jordanian minister of information (who had been one of my most frequent visitors when I was being held in Amman), announced to a group of journalists that the October 13, 1970, agreements between the king and the Resistance could henceforth be considered "lapsed." A chapter in our history was closed.

There was nothing left to do but to count our losses, analyze where we had gone wrong, and plan the future in the light of the lessons drawn from this experience. When, in September 1971, the leadership held its first plenary meeting since the events in Jordan, my comrades already had a better understanding of why I had proposed a cease-fire to the king a year earlier. That action, taken freely without any external pressure, was aimed at ending futile bloodshed and preventing an all-out civil war. The meeting also roundly condemned the extremism of the diehard maximalists and George Habash's PFLP, which had carried out the fateful hijackings on the eve of the conflict.

At the practical level, the leadership decided to create an underground apparatus in Jordan to work for the downfall of the regime. I was designated as the head of the organization. At the same time, instructions were issued to reinforce our bases in Lebanon, quantitatively and qualitatively, so as to launch anti-Israeli guerrilla activities from the south. Finally, an extraordinary congress was to be convened in October of the following year to chart a course of action designed to give the movement a new impetus.

The Fatah Congress of October 1972 turned out to be one of the most important in the history of our organization. The principles of democratic centralism were implemented: For the first time, the delegates of the congress (about three hundred) as well as the members of the leadership (nine) were chosen by vote. My reelection to the Central Committee by an overwhelming majority attested to the fact that I had maintained the confidence of the rank and file. The internal statutes were amended and a new policy adopted. One of its most important clauses was that guerrilla warfare constituted one of the means (and no longer the only means) at our disposal to wage our struggle for liberation.

Meanwhile, we had been up against a major problem ever since the tragic outcome of the Jerash and Ajlun battles. The initial despair of our militants had given way to a thirst for vengeance. Casualty figures for the "Black September" 1970 fighting had reached some seven to eight thousand, not counting the victims of July 1971 in northern Jordan. Fatah's young men didn't forget their dead comrades. Unable to wage classic guerrilla warfare across Israel's borders, they insisted on carrying out a revolutionary violence of another kind, commonly known elsewhere as "terrorism." They wanted to wreak vengeance not only on the Zionist enemy, but also on the Arab murderers and traitors who had made themselves Israel's accomplices. To keep the violence from taking an individualistic and anarchic form, there was no other way than to channel the wave of anger, to structure it and give it a political content.

6

The Shadow War

ON THE AFTERNOON OF NOVEMBER 28, 1971, Wasfi al-Tal, flanked by his aides and bodyguards, briskly climbed the wide staircase leading to Cairo's Sheraton Hotel. Two young men approached him. The crack of bullets sounded. The Jordanian prime minister crumpled in a pool of blood. Justice was done. One of the butchers of the Palestinian people was thus executed. Black September, the underground organization set up early that autumn, had just carried out its first operation.

A number of assassination plots had been conceived and then abandoned at the last minute in Amman as well as Cairo, where al-Tal was attending an Arab League Defense Council meeting. The two young men who carried out the mission were backed up by two others posted inside the hotel with orders to gun him down in the lobby if he managed to get through the door alive. The element of surprise played in their favor: In fact, they had waited two days, the time needed for the police surveillance to slacken, before attempting the operation. Wasfi al-Tal, symbol of betrayal of the Palestinian cause, was shot down under the very eyes of various Arab ministers, who hit the ground during the shooting. This was a fringe benefit of the operation, since the commandos had wanted to issue a warning precisely to those in the Arab world who might be tempted to sacrifice the rights or interests of the Palestinian people.

By nature as well as by conviction, I am resolutely opposed to political assassinations and, more generally, to terrorism. But unlike many people, I do not confuse revolutionary violence, which is a political act, with terrorism, which is not. I reject the individual act committed outside the context of an organization or strategic vision. I reject the act dictated by subjective motives which claims to take the place of mass struggle. Revolutionary violence, on the other hand, is part of a large, structured movement. It serves as a supplementary force and contributes, during a period of regrouping or defeat, to giving the movement a new impetus. It becomes superfluous when the grass-roots movement scores political successes on the local or international scene.

Black September was never a terrorist organization. It acted as an auxiliary of the Resistance, when the Resistance was no longer in a position to fully assume its military and political tasks. Its members always insisted that they had no organic tie with Fatah or the PLO. But I knew a number of them and I can assure you that most of them belonged to various fedayeen organizations. Coming out of the ranks, they accurately reflected the profound feelings of frustration and indignation shared by the entire Palestinian people regarding the Jordanian massacres and the complicities that made them possible. That this is true is clear from the spontaneous expressions of joy which greeted the news of Wasfi al-Tal's execution. Bowing to the popular will, the Egyptian authorities wasted little time in releasing the commandos responsible for the operation.

A little more than two weeks after al-Tal's execution, Black September struck another of Hussein's minions: Zaid Rifai, then ambassador to London. Rifai, a member of a leading Jordanian family, had been one of Hussein's closest advisors during the September 1970 fighting. Refined, passing himself off as a conciliator, Rifai exercised a far more deadly role than the rough bedouins who gravitated around the king. On December 15, while Rifai was returning to his residence at the embassy, his elegant car was caught in machine-gun fire. Instinctively he threw himself on the floor of the vehicle and escaped with nothing more serious than a slightly wounded hand. The young Black September commando dropped his machine gun and ran, diving into the first house along his way. The tenant was a very old woman who, suspecting nothing, offered him hospitality for a few hours. Using a second passport, false as was his first, he left England from a provincial airport the next day without encountering any difficulties. It's true that the British authorities, like those of other European countries, avoid complications by not going to great lengths to apprehend Palestinian commandos.

The struggle against the Jordanian regime took a variety of forms. One was to harass it continually, to weaken it by making it give in to force. Black September developed an ambitious plan, requiring several months of careful preparation, aimed at securing the release of hundreds of political prisoners in Jordanian jails. Two groups of tried militants were to be sent to Amman. One was to storm the U.S. Embassy and seize the ambassador and his staff as hostages to be exchanged against Palestinian prisoners. If something went wrong, the second group was to occupy the building housing the prime minister's offices and sequester the cabinet members for the same purpose.

The man chosen to head this extremely delicate mission was my friend Abu Daud, well known within the Resistance for his exceptional devotion and courage. As a commanding officer of the militia in Jordan before the expulsion of the fedayeen, he distinguished himself during the battle of Amman in September 1970. Endowed with a phenomenal memory, he is capable of naming the martyrs one by one, giving their family origins and past histories. Since he was a familiar figure in the Jordanian capital, both with the population and the security police, he took great risks in agreeing to return there secretly. He prepared himself for months in advance, letting his beard grow and keeping a very low profile in Beirut and Damascus, his usual places of residence.

Black September instructed three of its members in Amman to rent three apartments using false names for the fifteen or so fedayeen participating in the operation. Meanwhile, Abu Daud and the young militant who would be posing as his wife would stay in the apartment of a close friend of his named Mustafa. Although Mustafa didn't belong to the organization, he was known as a man worthy of confidence and had shown an unconditional and passionate devotion to the Resistance. He was about thirty-five years old, and had spent seven years in prison for communist activities before starting to work for the Resistance in 1968. His job as an official at the Jordanian ministry of information gave him a respectability which was perfectly suited to the role assigned him by the Black September commando.

On February 13, 1973, Abu Daud—disguised to perfection as a rich businessman from the Gulf with a flowing, gold-bordered abaya and traditional head covering—left Kuwait at the wheel of a luxurious American car. He was accompanied by his "wife," also dressed in traditional Arab garb. He drove first to Baghdad, from where he took the road for Amman, arriving at Mustafa's the next day. He informed Mustafa of the plan of operation, which was to take place the following afternoon, and asked him to transmit it to the respective leaders of the two groups charged with carrying it out. To this end, Mustafa was given the address of one of the three apartments and the password. The militant posing as Abu Daud's wife, who in reality was the wife of one of the fifteen fedayeen, went along to dissipate any reservations they might have about Mustafa as an outsider.

One of the two commando leaders (whose code name was Ben Bella) returned with them to get additional precisions from Abu Daud in person. That same night Abu Daud and his companion left for Damascus. According to the plan, two other militants—a young couple who knew nothing either about the operation or the true identity of Abu Daud— were to follow them by car to the Syrian border to make sure they crossed safely before informing Abu Ihab, the head of Black September, who was following the affair from another Arab capital.

Abu Ihab waited all night and all the next day without hearing a word. The attack on the American Embassy hadn't taken place, so it was clear that something had gone wrong. It wasn't until two days later that a Black September member in Amman informed him of the catastrophe: Abu Daud, his companion, the young couple assigned to follow them to the border, and the commandos had all been arrested. The police raids on the three apartments where the fedayeen were staying had been made simultaneously, at the same time that Abu Daud's car had been intercepted in a street of Amman. It was only too clear that there had been a stool pigeon, and equally clear that the stool pigeon was Mustafa—the only one who hadn't been arrested and the only one, besides Abu Daud and his "wife," who had an overall knowledge of the plan.

Abu Ihab telephoned him and in coded language innocently asked news of the commando. Mustafa told him about the arrests but assured him that Abu Daud was all right (in fact, he was subjected to inhuman tortures, as we were to learn later). Determined to punish the traitor, Abu Ihab decided to lure him into a trap. He sent him a message telling him of his intention to mount a new large-scale operation to obtain the release of Abu Daud and his companions. He asked Mustafa to come to Cairo to discuss the project.

The bait was attractive, especially for Mustafa's superiors. Abu Ihab's letter was analyzed and discussed at a meeting attended by al-Nazil Rashid, chief of intelligence, Prince Hassan, the king's brother (in his capacity as head of Jordanian security), and Adnan Abu Odeh, minister of information. Abu Odeh, sensing a trap, was the only one opposed to Mustafa's trip. Mustafa left for Cairo anyway, armed with a leave permit from the ministry. When he arrived, he learned to his surprise that Abu

Ihab was waiting for him in another Arab capital, where, he was told, he had been detained on important business. In fact, Cairo didn't lend itself very well to the Black September chief's plan, so he had chosen a country sufficiently accommodating to enable him to settle scores with someone who had very probably betrayed the organization's confidence.

Mustafa raised the question of his leave permit, valid for only five days and only for Egypt. His contacts at the airport proposed a false travel document enabling him to make the trip under another name, a solution which suited them perfectly since for their own reasons they didn't want him to leave any traces. Still suspecting nothing, Mustafa agreed to their proposal and left for the Arab capital in question. A car was waiting at the airport to take him to Abu Ihab, who had rented a discreet house for the occasion.

The confrontation was dramatic. Abu Ihab greeted Mustafa icily. He refused to shake his hand and after ordering him to sit down and keep quiet, launched into the indictment containing all the proofs of guilt he had been able to assemble. Mustafa burst into sobs and confessed everything.

Mustafa's story didn't surprise Abu Ihab much. He had known a number of other former militants who, like Mustafa, had been recruited by Jordanian intelligence during their prison years. In fact, Mustafa had followed the same path as Adnan Abu Odeh, minister of information and one of the king's inner circle, who had been a communist militant before going over to the police. As could be expected, Mustafa flaunted ultraradical opinions enabling him to infiltrate George Habash's Popular Front for the Liberation of Palestine, where he could carry out his activities as a provocateur and informer without much risk of being exposed, thanks to the prevailing atmosphere of extremism.

The Black September operation had been a veritable windfall for Mustafa. He alerted the security police to Abu Daud's forthcoming arrival, but at that point was unable to inform them of the nature of the operation or the date set for its execution. He supplied the details as soon as he had them: While accompanying Abu Daud's "wife" to see the fedayeen, he had slipped away for half an hour on the pretext of an urgent errand and rejoined the Black September group after making his report. Informed of the time set for Abu Daud's departure, the police had only to cast their nets and gather in all the members of the commando.

Mustafa's interrogation lasted several months, during which he gave precious information including the names of Jordanian agents within the

Palestinian movement. Abu Ihab succeeded in catching six of them, who to this day are interned in an Arab country friendly to the Resistance. As for Mustafa, since his past activities had cost human lives, he was condemned to death, although he was not executed until after a last confrontation with Abu Daud, released seven months after his arrest.

The story leading up to Abu Daud's release is worth recounting. When he was arrested on February 15, he was given the death penalty along with his fifteen companions. On the 28th of the same month, Black September decided to take action to force Hussein to back down. On March 1, a commando of eight fedayeen stormed the Saudi Arabian Embassy in Khartoum, Sudan, where about forty members of the diplomatic corps were attending a reception. The commando seized as hostages five diplomats—the Saudi and U.S. ambassadors and the American, Belgian, and Jordanian chargés d'affaires—and demanded among other things the release of Abu Daud and his companions.

Public opinion at the time didn't understand why Black September had chosen to attack the embassy of a country reputedly friendly to the Resistance, any more than it understood the choice of diplomats held. According to what I heard from the commandos later, chance played an important role in the operation. Convinced that Hussein wouldn't give in even if half the Jordanian people were to perish, they had decided to exert pressure through the United States, whose influence on the king needs no elaboration. Their target was the American chargé d'affaires, who had been stationed in Amman prior to the 1970 war and bore a heavy responsibility for its preparation. He was to leave his post in Khartoum on March 2, and the reception given in his honor at the Saudi Arabian Embassy was the last before his departure for Washington.

The commandos who carried out the operation had no intention of executing their hostages. After King Hussein refused to satisfy their demands—moreover on the express recommendation of President Richard Nixon—they asked for an aircraft to take the hostages to Washington where they wanted to open negotiations and plead their cause before the American people. Again on Nixon's instigation, President Numeiry rejected the demand and on the night of March 2 had his army storm the embassy. The Black September fedayeen were thus forced to execute three of their hostages—the two Americans and the Belgian chargé d'affaires whose active sympathy for Israel was notorious. The Saudi ambassador, who acted as mediator, and the Jordanian chargé d'affaires, whose wife was close to the Resistance, were quite naturally spared. After difficult negotiations, the commandos surrendered on March 4. A few hours later, King Hussein ratified the death sentence for Abu Daud and his comrades. However, under pressure from a number of Arab leaders—including presidents Sadat and Boumedienne and the Emir of Kuwait—the king first postponed the execution, and then on March 14 commuted it to life imprisonment. Finally, Abu Daud and his comrades were released under a general amnesty decreed in September 1973, three weeks before the October war broke out.

The epilogue of the Abu Daud affair took place not in Amman but, curiously enough, in Paris. More than three years later, in January 1977, the French secret police arrested him, accusing him of being an organizer of the September 1972 Munich Olympics operation. What is strange about this is that the accusation was based solely on Israeli allegations never confirmed by any evidence or other testimony. Furthermore, Abu Daud, a Fatah official who had been pardoned in Jordan and received by the king after his release, had come to Paris many times without encountering the least difficulty. It's true that his passport was delivered under a false name, as are those of all Resistance officials for security reasons, but the authorities knew his true identity. In fact, he had an appointment at the Quai d'Orsay at the time of his arrest.

A number of questions regarding the reason for his arrest and the motives of those who carried it out remain unanswered. The Ben Barka affair had already shown that there are elements disloyal to France within the country's special services. I personally am convinced that the American CIA and Israel's Mossad were not foreign to this initiative taken by certain members of the police. The main objective of the action was clearly to discredit President Valéry Giscard d'Estaing's Middle East policy.

What is certain is that the French police do not show a similar zeal when it comes to pursuing Israeli terrorists. Dozens of operations against Palestinian offices have been carried out, and at least four Resistance figures have been killed in Paris by Mossad agents without one arrest being made.

The cases of Mahmud Hamshari and Bassel Kubeisy are the best known. Hamshari, the official representative of the PLO in Paris, was killed by a remote-controlled explosive device. He was a politician and all his activities were public. Married to a Frenchwoman, he led a quiet life and abhorred any form of fanaticism or violence. The same applied to Bassel Kubeisy, a professor at the University of Baghdad who was pumped full of bullets near the Church of the Madeleine in the very heart of Paris.

The list of crimes committed by Zionist terrorists is too long to enumerate. Suffice it to say that many of the targets singled out by the Israeli hit squads were in no way connected, even remotely, to the Resistance's violent activities. Among the better known are Ghassan Kanafani, a writer and ideologue killed in Beirut in July 1972; Bassam Abu Sherif, head of the Popular Front's information services, and Dr. Anis Sayigh, historian and director of the Palestinian Research Center, both permanently disfigured by letter bombs sent them in Beirut in July 1972; and Wael Zuaiter, PLO representative in Italy, shot down in October of that same year while entering his modest Roman apartment with a loaf of bread and some books under his arm. Zuaiter was a leftist, close to the Italian Socialist and Communist parties, and energetically opposed any form of terrorism on ideological and political grounds.

It was as if the Israelis were seeking to suppress not the advocates of violence but rather the moderates, the politicians whose aim was to explain the justice of our cause before world opinion. Engaged as they were in civilian activities, these men were unarmed and had no way of defending themselves.

But in the last analysis, these assassinations are far less shocking than the massacres organized by the Israeli army. The random bombings of Palestinian-populated areas and refugee camps, the indiscriminate killing of hundreds, indeed thousands of innocent civilians including children, women, and old people, have unfortunately rarely moved world opinion, so quick to react indignantly to a hijacking threatening the lives of a few dozen people.

I can express this opinion all the more comfortably since I myself am firmly opposed to hijackings, as is the entire Fatah leadership, both on humanitarian and political grounds. With two exceptions, my organization has condemned every hijacking operation carried out by various Palestinian groups over the past ten years or so. The two cases which seemed to us justified (one in 1969, the other in 1972) directly concerned the Israelis and therefore could be considered to fall within the category of legitimate acts of war. As much as we are repelled by the idea of endangering the lives of innocent people whose countries are not directly implicated in the Israeli-Arab conflict, we have no scruples about attacking Israeli military men and officials, who fight and oppress the Palestinian people.

The plight of thousands of Palestinians languishing in Israeli jails is one of our major preoccupations. Total arbitrariness reigns in the occupied territories. People are arrested on the basis of mere presumption or a simple denunciation. The military courts in the occupied territories apply three repressive sets of laws according to their whim or interest of the moment—British, inherited from the Mandate era; Jordanian, introduced in the 1950s after King Abdallah annexed the West Bank; and Israeli, since the 1967 conquest—not to mention the Egyptian laws which remain in force in the Gaza zone.

The Israeli authorities try to pass off their decision not to apply the death penalty to fedayeen as a humane and civilized act. Given the treatment inflicted on the prisoners, however, death could seem preferable. The resisters are generally condemned to heavy prison sentences—10, 15, or 20 years—often cumulative to reach 50, 100, even 200 years. Those who manage to serve out their sentences are promptly slapped with "administrative internment" in keeping with a law promulgated under the British mandate. When they enter prison, they know they'll be there for the rest of their days unless there is a final settlement of the conflict—which is unlikely. What could be more disheartening for men who are also suffering from constant bullying, lamentable prison conditions (according to the admission of the Israeli officials themselves), and, on occasion, torture? And again, what could be more demoralizing, especially for Resistance fighters, who know in advance what is in store for them if they are captured?

This psychological factor posed, and still poses, an inextricable problem for the Resistance leaders. They had to act to secure the release of at least some of the prisoners, to show that Israeli high-handedness had limits. Everything was tried to this end, but in vain. All the escape attempts failed. International interventions of all kinds had no result. Israel had remained resolutely insensitive and indifferent to the discreet efforts and appeals of humanitarian organizations such as the Red Cross, not to mention the Pope, various religious institutions, the United Nations, and foreign powers great and small—hence the recourse to force and hijackings by certain Palestinian groups.

This ultimate and desperate weapon also proved ineffective. Aside from the first hijacking in 1969, which caught Israel off guard, the Zionist authorities have systematically refused any compromise with the hijackers. Worse still, they have maneuvered to bring about a bloody end to each confrontation so as to set world opinion against the fedayeen. It soon became obvious that far from serving our cause, hijackings actually seriously compromised the very meaning of our struggle.

It was for this same reason that Fatah vigorously condemned various other operations, such as the completely senseless exploit in September

1973 when a commando occupied the Saudi Arabian Embassy in Paris and seized diplomats as hostages, or the operation—much more suspect—of the adventurer "Carlos," who attacked the OPEC head-quarters in Vienna in December 1975, probably on behalf of shadowy forces on the world petroleum scene. Colonel Qaddafi, whose reputation as a superterrorist was totally fabricated by the international press, is frequently mentioned in connection with these events. But I know what I'm talking about when I say that the Libyan president has had nothing to do with the vast majority of violent operations organized during re-cent years.

On the other hand, Fatah did not denounce the Black September operation at the Munich Olympics in September 1972. This attitude could appear inconsistent at first glance, especially without knowing the motives, objectives, and behavior of the commandos or the events which led up to the operation's bloody conclusion. I knew the commando team's two leaders (who used the code names Mussalha and Che Gue-vara) very well, and later was able to closely question the three survivors of the mission, which puts me in a good position to give as detailed an account as possible within the limits of security regulations.

At the beginning of 1972, the PLO sent an official letter to the Olym-pics committee proposing that a team of Palestinian athletes participate in the games. Since no reply was received, a second letter was sent, which also evoked nothing more than a scornful silence. It was clear that for this honorable institution which claims to be apolitical, we didn't exist or, worse, didn't deserve to exist.

This affront, coming scarcely six months after the annihilation of the last fedayeen in Jerash and Ajlun, gave rise to indignation and rage among our young fighters. The Black September leaders decided to take the matter in hand. They formulated a plan with three objectives: to af-firm the existence of the Palestinian people; to give our cause resound-ing coverage—positive or negative, it mattered little—by taking advan-tage of the extraordinary concentration of mass media at Munich; and, finally, to force Israel to release fedayeen in a number initially fixed at 200.

We were obliged to note, with considerable sadness, that a large seg-ment of world opinion was far more concerned about the twenty-four-hour interruption in the grand spectacle of the Olympic Games than it was about the dramatic plight endured by the Palestinian people for the past twenty-four years or the atrocious end of the commandos and their hostages.

The operation was meticulously planned. The two commando leaders, chosen eight months beforehand, were tried militants who had fought in Amman in September 1970 and at the battle of Jerash and Ajlun in July 1971. Mussalha, twenty-seven years old, was from a poor peasant family who had fled Haifa for the West Bank when he was still a child. With an advanced degree in geology, impressive for his height and intelligence, he chose to join the ranks of Fatah where he became a political commissar. Since he was also fluent in German, he was perfectly suited to lead the team. His friend "Che Guevara," experienced in guerrilla warfare despite his youth (twenty-five years) and his years as a law student in Paris, was equally well suited as the group's military head.

Mussalha and Che were assigned four specific tasks in keeping with the three political objectives set for the mission: Work out a detailed plan of the operation itself; choose six other fedayeen to help them carry it out; procure the necessary weapons and get them into the Olympic village; and, finally, take charge of all aspects of implementing the operation including the negotiations for the exchange of Palestinian prisoners against Israeli hostages. Needless to say, Mussalha and Che could call on a host of backup men and accomplices to bring the operation off.

It wasn't easy to choose the members of the commando team. In a first stage, some fifty young fedayeen from seventeen to twenty years of age were selected to undergo intensive training. They all came from refugee camps in Lebanon, Syria, and especially Jordan, and all came from poor families. Most of them were motivated by the determination to bring about the release of members of their families locked up in Israeli prisons. They knew nothing of the operation that some of them would ultimately be selected to carry out, but all burned with impatience to be among the lucky ones chosen. The final selection triggered a number of dramas. One of the fedayeen, an adolescent, was excluded because two of his brothers had already died fighting for the cause. The young man was furious, protested, begged, burst into tears. He threatened to commit suicide if he weren't included in the commando. Finally, those in charge gave in. He was one of the first to fall in Munich under the bullets of the German security forces.

Before the six fedayeen dispersed in European countries where they were to familiarize themselves with the Western life-style, Mussalha and Che arrived in Munich as scouts. Mussalha got himself hired as a waiter at the cafeteria of the Olympic village, where preparations for the sporting event were already underway. He took advantage of his employment to systematically inspect the entire village, noting the layout of the pa-

vilions, especially the one assigned to the Israelis, as well as potential
exits. He was also able to collect a mass of useful information through
the friendly relations he established with numerous employees, German
and otherwise, as well as with a young Asian girl who had become
enamored of him. He transmitted information as he received it to Che,
who had set up headquarters in a nearby country. This phase lasted for
four months, and resulted in a detailed and coherent plan of action.

There was an extremely tense moment getting the weapons into Germany and the operation barely missed being torpedoed. The day the
weapons were to be flown in—there wasn't enough time for any other
means of transport—German police surveillance was suddenly greatly
reinforced on the border posts, along highways, at train stations, and
especially at the airports. The couple who brought them into the
country—a Black September member passing himself off as a well-
traveled businessman and a militant posing as his wife—escaped detec-
tion by bravado and sheer luck: The customs inspector opened only one
of their three trunks, and it was the one containing women's clothing.
The trunks filled with weapons were exchanged at the Bonn airport for
identical but empty ones and transported by other fedayeen to Munich.
There, the weapons—including machine guns and hand grenades—were
placed in lockers at the railway station on August 25, or about ten days
before the Olympics began. The Munich commando members were able
to pick them up, each with his own key.

The day of the operation, Mussalha and Che entered the main gate of
the Olympic village thanks to two entrance tickets procured by Mussalha's Asian friend. Their six comrades were to enter by scaling the
two-meter wall surrounding the compound. A man was specifically assigned to take them to a predetermined spot and help hoist them over.
Shortly before they arrived, an attractive young female militant struck
up a conversation with the German security officer who was mounting
the guard. While he was being distracted, the commandos jumped over
the wall without being seen. A few hours later, the young woman and
the "guide" were on a plane out of Germany.

The pavilion where the Israeli athletes were staying was about fifty
meters from the wall. The commando had received strict orders not to
cause any bloodshed except in the case of legitimate defense. Unfortunately, they were violently resisted by two of the team's trainers and in
the scuffle which followed they killed them. The nine athletes taken hostage were well treated, even comforted. During the twenty-one hours
the building was under siege by the German police, long and cordial

conversations took place between the fedayeen and their captives. The Israeli athletes ranged from eighteen to thirty years old, and for the most part were new immigrants to Israel from the United States, the Soviet Union, Rumania, Poland, and Libya, as was reported in the international press. Several of them were reserve officers in the Israeli army. Mussalha and Che told them they would be exchanged for Palestinian prisoners. The fedayeen explained that Palestine's place at the Olympics had been unjustly given to Israel, which in any case should have been excluded from the Games on the same grounds as South Africa and Southern Rhodesia.

Mussalha, one of whose close relatives had married a Jew, assured the Israeli athletes that the Palestinians bore no grudge against the Jews, nor even against the Israelis who, in a different way from the Palestinians, were also victims of the Zionist adventure. Although directly concerned by the discussion, the hostages insisted that politics was not among their primary preoccupations.

The negotiations with the German authorities—acting as mediators between the fedayeen and Israel—turned out to be difficult, which was understandable. Less understandable was the intransigence of Israeli Prime Minister Golda Meir, who showed absolutely no determination to save the lives of the hostages.

The guerrillas, instructed not to kill their captives, extended the deadline of the ultimatum from hour to hour in the hope that some compromise formula would be proposed. They knew from the outset that there was no chance of obtaining the liberation of all 200 Palestinian prisoners on the list (which had been established to reflect the geographical distribution and political tendencies of the some 10,000 Palestinian prisoners in Israeli jails). In practice, the commandos were prepared to exchange their nine hostages against fifty, twenty, or even nine Palestinian prisoners. However, to their great disappointment, the Israeli-German negotiators didn't make any counterproposal except to offer them an unlimited sum of money (a "blank check"), as if they were common criminals, and safe conduct for the eight revolutionaries in exchange for releasing the hostages.

Just as the negotiations had reached a dangerous impasse, an Arab embassy got a proposal through to Mussalha which could possibly serve as the basis for a secret agreement: The Israeli hostages would be freed and replaced by German volunteers, who would be taken by the fedayeen to an Arab country. Two or three months later, Israel would discreetly release some fifty prisoners. A number of countries would guarantee that Israel would honor its commitments. The formula was tempting, and had the advantage of satisfying the Palestinian side while being face-saving for the Zionist leaders.

As a disciplined militant, Mussalha decided to submit this proposal to his superiors since it hadn't been anticipated in their plan. For cases of this sort, he was to check with a man code-named Talal whose telephone number in Tunis had been given him before the operation was launched. Unfortunately for everyone concerned, the Talal in question had been detained at the Tunis airport, having failed to procure a visa in advance. By what seemed to be an extraordinary coincidence, the one who answered the telephone in Tunis was also named Talal. He was the son of a Jordanian ex-ambassador, Farhan Shebeilat, who had moved to Tunis after being fired from the diplomatic service on account of his sympathies for the Resistance. The ambassador's son, a friend of the Palestinian militant, didn't even know his friend was coming, much less that he had adopted the code name Talal for the occasion.

An incredible misunderstanding took place when Mussalha telephoned. The ambassador's son couldn't understand why someone was calling from Munich to speak in riddles. Meanwhile, Mussalha was astonished to fall upon a Talal he didn't know and who had no idea of the agreed-upon code. Knowing that the telephone made available by the German authorities was bugged, the commando chief merely said he'd call back in an hour. When he called again, the militant still hadn't reached the Shebeilat residence. Mussalha gave up and told the ones who had proposed the formula that he rejected it.

I have no idea whether or not Israel would have agreed to the plan. But according to the militant Talal, whom I questioned, the Black September leadership would have accepted it without hesitation as an honorable way out of the deadlock. No one will ever know. If "Talal" had arrived at the ex-ambassador's house on time, or if one of his numerous attempts to telephone Mussalha later had worked, perhaps the commandos and their hostages would still be alive today.

Whatever the case, the mishap led to a diplomatic crisis. The West German ambassador to Tunisia, armed with the tapes of the telephone conversations, lodged a strong protest with the Tunisian government demanding that the Black September members in Tunis be extradited. After long negotiations, it was agreed to keep the affair quiet. But ex-ambassador Shebeilat, who had the status of refugee, was expelled from Tunisia along with his entire family.

Up against Israel's intransigence, Mussalha could only fall back on the last-resort compromise provided under the plan he was charged with carrying out. At the last minute he proposed that the fedayeen and their captives leave for Cairo, a solution designed to avoid killing the hostages while not compromising Black September's credibility. Egypt never would have tolerated a violation of its sovereignty on its own territory. The Israeli athletes would have been detained as citizens of an enemy country and released only if the Zionist authorities resigned themselves to an exchange. In the worst of possibilities, the athletes' fate wouldn't have been any different from that of the Palestinian resisters incarcerated in Israel.

But Chancellor Willy Brandt wanted to get a better deal. He telephoned Egyptian prime minister Aziz Sidqi to inform him of Mussalha's latest proposal and asked him to see to it that the Israeli athletes were released and expelled the minute they arrived in Cairo. He also asked that the fedayeen be arrested. Needless to say, Aziz Sidqi—who repeated the conversation to me word for word—rejected the chancellor's suggestions on the grounds that it would be dishonorable for his government to betray the confidence of the fedayeen.

I don't know whether or not Chancellor Brandt knew that at the very moment he was talking to Sidqi, his police—in close cooperation with Israeli Security—were in the process of preparing the assassination of the fedayeen. Several plans were formulated before it was decided to lay the ambush at the military airport of Fürstenfeldbrück, where the commandos and their hostages were to board a Lufthansa plane for Cairo.

The tragic outcome of the story, caused by the sinister duplicity of the German government, is well known. Violating the agreement concluded and their own word, the Germans ordered their sharpshooters to open fire on the members of the commando. Mussalha and Che, who after inspecting the Lufthansa aircraft were on their way toward the helicopters in which the hostages were waiting, were the first ones hit. They fired back before collapsing in pools of blood. With their last strength they crawled toward each other and clasped hands in a fraternal salute. A third fighter who had been keeping guard was also killed. It was only after the death of the commando leaders and after the shooting died down that the helicopters blew up. The two fedayeen who were guarding the Israeli athletes, one in each helicopter, only resigned themselves to killing the hostages and themselves when it was clear that there was no hope left. The three wounded commandos were taken prisoner.

The sacrifices made by the Munich heroes were not entirely in vain. They didn't bring about the liberation of any of their comrades imprisoned in Israel as they had hoped, but they did attain the operation's other two objectives: World opinion was forced to take note of the Palestinian drama, and the Palestinian people imposed their presence on an international gathering that had sought to exclude them. As for the slaughter which ended the operation, the West German government must bear a heavy responsibility.

The German authorities, moved by a sense of guilt or perhaps out of cowardice, were clearly anxious to have the captured fedayeen off their hands. The occasion presented itself about two months later, on October 29, 1972, when a Lufthansa Boeing flying from Beirut to Frankfurt was hijacked to Zagreb, Yugoslavia, by Palestinian commandos. They demanded and obtained the immediate release of the three survivors of the Munich operation, who once again became anonymous soldiers in the ranks of the Resistance.

Meanwhile, the Israeli authorities had tried to cover up one crime with another, even more abominable. Forty-eight hours after the Munich massacre, Jewish aviation savagely pounded about ten refugee camps in Syria and Lebanon, killing or wounding more than 200 civilians. That same day, Abba Eban dropped his mask by declaring that Israel would henceforth give the struggle against terrorism priority over the search for peace.

The "shadow war" was declared, and could only intensify. The Zionist intelligence services dispatched booby-trapped objects to many of our militants in Beirut, Algiers (where the PLO representative Abu Khalil was gravely wounded), Tripoli (Mustafa Awad Zeid, PLO representative, was blinded and paralyzed), Cairo (a letter bomb meant for Fatah leaders Faruq Qaddumi and Hayel Abdel Hamid left them unharmed), Stockholm (Omar Sufan, director of the Red Crescent, lost the fingers of both hands), Bonn (Adnan Hammad of the Palestinian Student Union was seriously wounded), and Copenhagen (Ahmed Awadallah, a student, had to have his arm amputated). After the PLO representatives in Rome and Paris (Zuaiter and Hamshari) were killed, the PLO representative in Nicosia, Cyprus, Hussein Abul Kheir, was assassinated on January 25, 1973.

Black September fought back as best it could by mounting its own operations. Three days after Abul Kheir was murdered, the organization killed an Israeli agent calling himself Baruch Cohen in the heart of Madrid. Cohen, whose real name was Moshe Hanan Yshai, had a number of passports and was often on the move among European capitals, particularly Paris, Brussels, and Rome, using different identities.

Everything pointed to the fact that he had important duties within the Jewish state's special services. In Spain, he had set up a network of Palestinian students mainly from the West Bank and Gaza whom he assigned duties as agents provocateurs as well as espionage tasks. One of these was to find out about Palestinians residing in Spain, particularly their political sympathies and affiliations. Another involved gathering certain information in the Arab countries, Egypt and Lebanon for example, where a number of his recruits went for their school vacations. In a later stage, Cohen started laying plans for terrorist attacks against Spanish enterprises owned by Jews or having close business relations with Israel, with the aim of discrediting Palestinians in the eyes of the Spanish and provoking their expulsion from Spain.

What he didn't know was that several of the students he had recruited belonged to Black September and pretended to cooperate with him at the request of the organization. When he began to have serious doubts about the loyalty of those who failed to carry out the tasks assigned to them on various pretexts, it was decided to execute him. His elimination became urgent when in early January, shortly after Mahmud Hamshari's assassination in Paris, Cohen announced that he was leaving Spain to take up other duties.

Cohen set the date for his own execution by informing his Palestinian contact in Madrid that he would meet him for the last time on January 28. That day, the student went to the agreed-upon bar on one of the main arteries of the Spanish capital. Also at the rendezvous were two armed men, one inside the bar and one outside, waiting for the right moment.

Shortly after Cohen arrived, he informed the student that he was going to introduce him to his successor and invited him to follow. This was an unhoped-for windfall, but the student had no way of warning his two accomplices to put off the execution until he could meet the new Israeli agent. So when he and Cohen suddenly and unexpectedly left the bar, the other two were afraid their target would get away for good by following his habit of slipping into the crowd of pedestrians. One of them opened fire at short range, killing Cohen, while the other fired into the air to create a panic. The three fedayeen lost themselves in the confusion, and were soon on a plane leaving Spanish territory.

With this operation, Black September killed two birds with one stone. In addition to eliminating Cohen, who according to information reaching Black September was one of the architects of Hamshari's liquidation in Paris, it also necessitated the dismantling of the entire Israeli network in

Spain. The Israeli special services, not knowing which of the Palestinian recruits had suppressed their agent, were obliged as a precaution to break their relations with all the members of the organization which Cohen had so patiently constituted.

Black September killed another Israeli agent, Simha Gilzer, in Nicosia, on March 12, 1973. About a month later, on April 9, two operations took place in the Cypriot capital, one against the Israeli ambassador's residence, the other against an El Al plane parked at the airport. The day after this double attack, which coincided with the twenty-fifth anniversary of the Deir Yassin massacre, an Israeli commando unit landed in Beirut and assassinated three of the main leaders of the Resistance: Yusuf al-Najjar (Abu Yusuf), Kamal Adwan, and Kamal Nasir.

Kamal Nasir was one of my best friends. Not including our political meetings, we saw each other at least once a day, preferably in the evening when we had time to talk for long hours. Kamal was an accomplished poet, who knew how to sing both the despair of a prostrate people and the hopes of the Resistance. He radiated intelligence, sensitivity, and good humor, and was also witty and amusing. I also loved in him his uncompromising honesty and loyalty. A Baathist by conviction, he left the party when he realized that its actions were not always in keeping with the principles in which he believed. Despite his sympathy for Fatah he never joined the movement, with which he wasn't always in agreement. So he remained an independent, and it was as such that he occupied the delicate position of official spokesman for the PLO.

Both of us were deeply concerned about the unity of the Palestinian movement, often discussing the strong points and failings of the Resistance long into the night, trying to find ways to correct deviations or errors that had been committed. How many times did we play the part of conciliators or mediators!

The three Resistance members all lived in the same building: Kamal Adwan on the second floor, Kamal Nasir on the third, and Yusuf al-Najjar on the sixth. I remember an evening Yasir Arafat and I spent with all three of them in Kamal Nasir's apartment about ten days before the Israeli raid which was to cost them their lives. I'm not sure if you could say I had a premonition, but while entering the building I was suddenly struck by the absence of bodyguards or any other security measures, and told them half-jokingly: "You three certainly are careless! An Israeli helicopter will be landing soon in that vacant lot across from your building and kidnap all three of you!" The remark was taken lightly, but Arafat advised them in all seriousness to pay more attention to their security. They replied that they didn't want to upset their neighbors by instituting protective measures in the building which would be too obvious.

As fate would have it, the PLO Central Council, to which all five of us belonged, decided to meet in Beirut (instead of Damascus as was usually the case) on April 9 and 10. The April 9 meeting lasted until very late, and afterward I slept at Kamal Nasir's as I often did. At the end of the morning session the next day, Najjar, Adwan, and Nasir asked me to join them for lunch at a seaside restaurant where the fish is particularly good. As a rule I avoid public places for security reasons. I don't know what prompted me to accept the invitation that day; all I know is that I vaguely felt the need not to be separated from my three comrades even for a few hours. After a particularly agreeable meal, during which everyone was in high spirits, we returned to the PLO Central Council meeting which ended at about nine o'clock that night.

Yusuf al-Najjar and Kamal Adwan went home. I suggested to Kamal Nasir that we end the evening at his apartment. To my surprise he refused, saying he had to write an elegy to the poet Issa Nakhlah, who had just died, and that he was sure my presence would keep him from working. I left him with regret. Remembering I had to meet with the three survivors of the Munich operation, I decided to go listen to the account of their odyssey. As I was approaching their building, which was about ten meters from the one occupied by Nayif Hawatmah's Democratic Front for the Liberation of Palestine (DFLP), I noted that the DFLP militants in the street were preparing for some kind of action. I asked them what was going on, and they replied that their commandos were in a state of alert because they feared an attack from Dr. George Habash's PFLP. I became very angry and told them what I thought about this senseless quarrel between two Resistance organizations which should be devoting their energies to fighting the common enemy.

I didn't know how right I was. It was nine-thirty in the evening and no one imagined that three hours later the DFLP building would be stormed not by the PFLP but by Israeli commandos. Violating the most elementary rules of security, Nayif Hawatmah's followers had installed virtually all their departments—administrative, financial, information, and a large part of their archives—in this same nine-story building.

My conversation with the three Munich survivors carried me away from my immediate preoccupations. I was fascinated by their detailed recounting of the operation itself, and shocked by the tortures they underwent in the German prisons. The brutality inflicted on one of them had left permanent genital damage. The conversation veered to the current political situation. Suddenly we heard bursts of machine-gun fire. I looked at my watch: It was 12:30 A.M. I became angry once again and told them that the fighting was probably between the followers of Habash and those of Hawatmah.

The shooting intensified, followed by deafening explosions, at which point I began to have doubts. A hail of mortar shells began to pelt down on the Democratic Front's building, and I said to myself that it was highly unlikely, indeed impossible, for the Habash group to be attacking with mortars. It was then that the janitor of the building burst into the apartment shrieking in a choked voice: "The Jews! The Jews are here!" Trembling like a leaf, he was incapable of saying more.

The prediction I had made a week earlier, without really believing it myself, had come true. The Israelis were literally at our doorstep. If they had been able to locate the DFLP headquarters, I thought, wouldn't they also know that the three surviving members of the Munich commando were living next door? Or that Yasir Arafat lived in a house a few meters away?

All we had were ordinary revolvers, so there wasn't much for us to do but take refuge in the stairwell on the fourth floor. We got the elevator to the fifth floor and immobilized it by keeping the door open, so the attackers would be obliged to come up on foot and expose themselves to our resistance. We intended to defend ourselves to the last cartridge.

An incredible explosion, followed by a series of crashes and rumbling noises, gave us to suppose that the DFLP building had been blown up. The shooting died down. My companions ran down to the street and watched the Israeli commandos withdrawing, covering their retreat with sporadic shooting. Our enemies were wearing fedayeen battle dress, but spoke to each other in Hebrew. I then came down and recognized the three young DFLP militants whom I had reprimanded three hours earlier lying dead on the pavement. Most of their comrades who had been inside at the time of the assault were safe and sound, having left the building before it exploded to return the attackers' fire.

I crossed the street and went to Arafat's place. He hadn't been hurt either. The Israelis had pounded his building but, obviously unaware that he was inside, didn't persist since his bodyguards had put up a fierce resistance. The fedayeen locked up in the basement of the building for having committed misdemeanors had been released and armed as soon as the attack began and helped drive back the Israeli soldiers.

Arafat had followed the battle from the roof of his building while issuing orders to the fighters.

Arafat, who had heard that I was in a neighboring building during the battle, was convinced that I had been killed. So when I appeared he clasped me in his arms, visibly moved. He brought me up to date on the information he had received: The Israeli commandos, who had landed in the south, near Sidon and in Beirut, had simultaneously attacked a number of Palestinian targets. The most serious, he told me, was that they had gotten into the apartments of Yusuf al-Najjar, Kamal Adwan, and Kamal Nasir, but he didn't yet know whether they had been kidnapped or killed. A few minutes later, the terrible news reached us that our three comrades had been assassinated.

I decided to go straight to their building on Verdun Street despite Arafat's efforts to dissuade me due to the possible risks involved. I went to Kamal Nasir's apartment first. The sight that greeted me filled me with horror. Through a mist of smoke from a rocket the Israelis fired a few seconds before their assault, I saw my friend's body laid out in the form of a cross, the area around his mouth riddled with at least fifteen bullets. His killers hadn't neglected symbols in their sinister task: Kamal was in fact a Christian, and was the PLO spokesman. The assailants had sprayed the place with bullets, especially his bed and the couch in the living room where I usually slept, doubtless to drive out anyone who might be hiding underneath.

Kamal was in his pajamas. The window of his room was open and the venetian blinds ripped off as if he had initially tried to escape. He had shot back with his own revolver, which was found at his side, but his resistance had been short since only two bullets were missing. I then remembered how I had often teased him: "You're nothing but a poet and you'll never use a weapon in your life!" I hadn't been far off. And hadn't he been killed at the moment he was composing an elegy?

We know more about the circumstances under which our other comrades were assassinated thanks to the testimonies of their family members. The Israeli commandos, using a gun with a silencer, had killed the single fedayeen guarding the building as soon as they arrived. They then took the elevator to the sixth floor and blew the door off Najjar's apartment. Najjar, who generally went to bed early, was already sleeping. But his children—a boy, Yusuf, who was sixteen years old, and four girls—were doing their homework in their rooms. Yusuf ran toward the front hall and was stopped by the Israeli commandos who shouted to him in Arabic: "Tell us where your father is!" Seized with panic, the boy rushed to his room and, climbing out his window, slid down the drainpipe to the apartment on the fifth floor.

Awakened in the meantime by the clamor, Najjar locked himself in the living room which separated his bedroom from the entry hall. While the commandos were trying to break down the door, he asked his wife to bring him his revolver. The Israelis shot through the door, and the lock finally gave way. Najjar, seriously wounded, teetered while cursing his aggressors: "Cowards! Traitors!" His wife tried to protect him by throwing herself between him and the Israelis. But they continued to fire coldly, killing the couple.

While this was going on, another commando group was storming Kamal Adwan's apartment on the second floor. Adwan, who was still working, was alerted by suspicious sounds coming from the stairs. He scarcely had time to grab his submachine gun when the assailants began to force the main door. Before he could even fire back, he was shot in the back of the neck by a second group of Israeli commandos who had entered through the kitchen window by scaling the drainpipes. Adwan's wife and child, who had helplessly witnessed the atrocious scene, were spared by the Israelis, who continued to the third floor to take care of their third victim.

It goes without saying that Defense Minister Moshe Dayan's commandos would never have been able to operate with such impunity for three hours in the very heart of Beirut if they hadn't benefited from important local complicity. The Lebanese army, gendarmerie, and security forces made no effort to intervene. The attackers moved about with amazing ease, both in Beirut and in the south, displaying a perfect knowledge of the area. We didn't have any proof at the time to support our suspicions, but the close cooperation between the Lebanese rightist parties and Israel, which came out into the open two years later during the civil war, swept away our last doubts concerning the collusion that facilitated the April 10, 1973, operation.

Israel had enormous means at its disposal in the struggle it undertook against the Palestinian people. In the shadow war, it could count on large numbers of well-organized and well-equipped operatives, on an advanced technology, on numerous embassies abroad which provided logistical support, not to mention the unconditional assistance furnished by members of the Jewish community throughout the world. The Palestinians, on the other hand, lacking any state structures or even a sure sanctuary, were fighting not only the Israelis but also the hostility of various foreign powers, including certain Arab countries. Nonetheless, they managed in the face of terrible odds to score a few striking successes in this unequal struggle.

The Israelis have doubtless not renounced their plan to liquidate the fedayeen leaders, believing that in so doing they will be able to destroy the Palestinian national movement. I doubtless remain one of their primary targets. For years now, Israeli intelligence—along with its American and Jordanian accomplices—has fueled a press campaign presenting me not only as the chief of Black September, but also as the one who masterminded a number of other terrorist operations, even ones claimed by various other organizations. Several plots on my life have been uncovered these past years in Beirut or Damascus. One attempt, cleverer and thus more serious than the others, almost cost me my life along with members of my family in August 1973.

I was in Cairo at the time, where my wife and six children live. One of my bodyguards informed me that a young man insisted on seeing me, claiming that he had important information that could be communicated only to me in person. I had no other choice but to receive him. Right off the bat he said he had been assigned to kill me. As if to back up his claim, he opened his briefcase and gave me a pistol with a silencer. He said he didn't want to be killed or arrested, so he had decided to confess in exchange for which he asked me to assure his safety. He wanted to get a fresh start in life in a North African country or, failing that, somewhere in the socialist bloc.

He was a West Bank Palestinian, and had been assigned to kill me by an Israeli intelligence officer whom he cited by name. But while crossing over into Jordan where he was to catch a plane from Amman, he was arrested by the Jordanian police and subjected to a harsh interrogation. When he revealed the nature of his mission, the Jordanian intelligence officer, Falah al-Rifai (at the time head of the department in charge of combatting Fatah), promised him additional payment if he succeeded in killing me. This piece of information was particularly interesting to me, since I knew Falah al-Rifai well.

The Israelis and Jordanians, the young man told me, both had detailed plans of my Cairo residence, where I also maintained a private office. They had supplied him with exact information about the people working for me, the security measures set up by the Egyptian security police, and my usual movements. He added that he should have killed me two days earlier on the steps of the Radio Building, where indeed I had been for a Palestinian broadcast at the very time he specified.

I thanked him profusely and asked his name and address so I could contact him later. He told me he was staying in a modest hotel, the Lotus. He left after having given me his briefcase and, obviously, his revolver.

To be on the safe side I asked the Mokhabarat (Egyptian intelligence) to do a check on him. They reported back that he had not registered under the name he gave, which wasn't on his passport either, but that he was at the hotel. They had searched his room discreetly and found a small locked suitcase, which they had not been able to open without arousing suspicion.

Three days later, at seven o'clock in the morning, I was awakened by one of my bodyguards who told me that the same young man wanted to see me at once. Intrigued, I agreed to receive him. As soon as he entered the living room, I noticed he was carrying the little suitcase the Egyptian police had described. I asked him to open it. He blushed, started stammering, and finally broke down. The suitcase, he confessed, contained enough explosives to destroy my house and everything in it, including my wife and six children. According to the instructions he had received, he was to hide it under a chair before leaving. His previous visit and first "confession" were designed merely to gain my confidence and familiarize himself with the house before going on to the second and final phase of the operation as it had been conceived by the Israeli and Jordanian secret police. I declined his offer to open the suitcase and turned it over to the Egyptian police. The young man has since been locked up in a Cairo prison.

Other attempts have been made on the lives of my family. Twice my children have received boxes of chocolate which in fact were booby-trapped. Happily, my wife and I had taught them to be on guard at all times. They have become so cautious that they don't even open the packages of sweets I send them from abroad until they've been checked.

Although the life I have chosen subjects me to constant threat, I am not afraid of death. I am a believer without being a mystic. The divine protection which has spared me thus far does not keep me from taking a minimum of precautions to assure my safety and that of my loved ones.

I personally abhor bloodshed and have always taken pains to prevent young enthusiasts of the Resistance from undertaking operations I consider futile or damaging to our cause. One of the welcome results of the October 1973 war was that it pushed the policy of violence to the background, at least for the time being.

7

The October Interlude

IT WAS IN MARCH 1973—about a month before the Israeli commando raid on Beirut—that we heard for the first time that the war Sadat had been trumpeting for months on end was really imminent. Yasir Arafat, Yusuf al-Najjar, Abu Jihad, and I were in Cairo to meet with the Egyptian president, and before the interview top-ranking army officers told us confidentially that the date for the hostilities had been set for May. But Sadat himself talked a completely different line. Not only did he make no reference to an eventual conflict, he also complained at length about the USSR's reluctance to deliver him vital arms. In fact, he devoted a good part of the interview to reviewing Egyptian-Soviet relations and to railing against what he saw as the Kremlin's unfriendly attitude toward him.

In mid-August, Faruq Qaddumi and I asked for an audience with Sadat, with whom we wanted to discuss certain current issues. He replied that he was prepared to meet with one of us alone. Somewhat surprised, we said that since we didn't have secrets from each other we preferred to see him together. So he invited us to the Borj al-Arab Palace, a few miles from the Mediterranean between Alexandria and the Libyan border.

The Egyptian president, looking very relaxed in casual summer attire, received us on the veranda of his residence. He began with light pleasantries before asking a few questions on the general situation of the

Palestinian Resistance. But he seemed distracted, listening only half-heartedly to our replies. It wasn't long before we discovered the reason. Changing the subject abruptly, he announced without further ado that he was launching a war against Israel "before the end of the year." He implied the approximate date by adding that he would give us the details after the Nonaligned Summit Conference scheduled for early September, "or shortly before the hostilities begin." He had already named the operation "the Spark," and told us it would be waged jointly with Syria. The war, he hastened to add, would not be total since its aim was to break the deadlock in the Israeli-Arab crisis. He said calmly, almost in passing as if it were a foregone conclusion, "So we'll all go to the peace conference together!"

Qaddumi and I were so enthusiastic about the idea of a war against Israel that I confess we didn't take this last statement very seriously. Egypt and Syria, the two main confrontation states, had finally understood the necessity for armed struggle! Naturally, we assured Sadat of our support and asked what he wanted us to do. He replied that he needed as many fedayeen and Palestinian Liberation Army (PIA) units as possible for the battle. He asked us to use the utmost discretion, and expressly requested us not to mention the conversation to Syrian President Asad. He then called Abdel Salam Tewfik, who had just been appointed head of the Deuxième Bureau, and instructed him to meet with us to work out the practical aspects relating to our participation in the fighting.

As agreed, Sadat received Qaddumi, Arafat, and myself on September 9, immediately after the Nonaligned Conference and just before his meeting with Asad and Hussein. The Egyptian president had no intention of breathing a word to Hussein about the war plans. The main objective of the "summit" was for Egypt and Syria to reestablish the diplomatic relations with Jordan that had been severed in the wake of the Jerash and Ajlun massacres. This normalization was intended to create more favorable conditions on the "Eastern front" during the coming hostilities.

During the September 9 meeting, Sadat outlined his plan in detail, this time emphasizing the postwar phase. He himself would call for the convening of a peace conference. He didn't specify that it would be in Geneva, but did list the countries that would be represented, about the same as those which actually participated in December of the same year: the United States, the USSR, Israel, Egypt, Syria, Jordan, and the PLO. When asked on what basis Jordan would be invited, Sadat mumbled a few unconvincing arguments. As for our own participation, we didn't express any opinion either way since we would have to refer the matter to the decision-making bodies of the Resistance. Our main concern for the immediate future was to determine the conditions of our participation in the conflict.

To this end, Sadat met with Yasir Arafat on September 12. Just as Arafat was leaving, Sadat told him that he would be informed of the exact date of the hostilities at the proper time.

When we got back to Beirut, we convened first the Council of the Revolution and then the PLO Central Committee to inform them of Egypt's intentions—using, of course, the vaguest possible terms. Most of our comrades were not very impressed: Sadat had publicly threatened war so often that no one took him seriously any more.

On September 30, or six days before the war broke out, I received a message from the Egyptian Embassy in Beirut asking me to leave for Cairo immediately. I told the representatives of various fedayeen organizations with whom I was in a meeting at the time about the summons, adding that I thought it must be related to the imminence of the war. This remark provoked gales of laughter. Abu Ahmad al-Yamani of the PFLP (George Habash's group) exclaimed: "I'll bet you an entire sheep that Sadat won't make war!" I accepted the bet. However, not really believing that the conflict was so close at hand, I left Beirut only Thursday, October 4, landing in Cairo in the evening.

A high-ranking officer was waiting for me at the airport. He immediately took me to the defense minister, Marshal Ahmad Ismail, who told me: "We are launching the offensive after tomorrow. You have taken your time getting here, and Yasir Arafat must be advised immediately." I thought it would be less risky to send a message by hand with an emissary rather than trust a coded telegram. I wrote a note and put it in a sealed envelope, but since there were no more planes for Beirut that night I gave it to a Resistance member the next morning and told him to destroy it in case his plane was hijacked to Israel or elsewhere. When he expressed surprise at so much secrecy, I told him that the envelope he would personally hand to Yasir Arafat contained my resignation from the movement, and that I didn't want the news to get around before it was accepted.

Arafat is very difficult to reach on short notice, and unfortunately my messenger was unable to get my note to him until late Friday night. A few hours later, all the forces of the Resistance were put on alert. The following day, Egyptian troops set out to reconquer the Suez Canal while the Syrian army stormed the Golan plains and then heights.

The day of the attack, Faruk Qaddumi (who like me has a residence in Cairo) and I were asked not to leave our homes. We were supposed to remain available for President Sadat, who wanted to see us at some point during the day. At 2:00 P.M. we learned over the radio with great satisfaction that the hostilities had begun. At 5:00 P.M. we were informed that President Sadat would receive us at seven o'clock sharp at the Al Tahira Palace at Manchiet al-Bakri on the outskirts of Cairo.

The presidential residence, which is relatively small and tastefully decorated, had taken on the air of a fortress, surrounded by armored vehicles, heavy machine guns, and innumerable armed soldiers. The ground floor had been transformed into a sort of military headquarters. Sadat received us in a sitting room, fully decked out in a field marshal's uniform. (Under the constitution, the president is the supreme commander of the armed forces.) His eyes shining with pleasure, he greeted us at the doorway with a triumphant "Didn't I tell you I'd make war? Do you believe me now?"

I had never seen Sadat in such a high state of euphoria. He radiated self-satisfaction, overflowing with joy and enthusiasm. "We have virtually neutralized the Bar Lev line! We're throwing pontoon bridges across the canal! One of them is a bit worrisome—it isn't solid enough." Sadat kept us posted on the details of the military situation as he received them from the operations room or following brief telephone conversations. "Our first tanks just crossed the Suez Canal! The infantry will be following soon!" he gloated, more and more excited.

I described to him the joy that had exploded through the streets of Cairo when the offensive was announced. "The Egyptian people, all the Arab people," I added, "are hoping to wipe out the shame that Israel inflicted on us during the Six Day War in June 1967." Sadat listened, beside himself with delight, and cried: "How beautiful power is! We are strong! We will win!" For hours that night, Sadat spoke of nothing but violence, reconquest. It was the first and last time I ever heard him speak without constant references to "peace" or "negotiation." He absolutely astonished us by declaring: "My armies will push on to the Mitla and Giddi passes [which control the Sinai]. Then I'll leave it to the fedayeen to carry on the guerrilla war!"

The early successes fueled his optimism. At about 9:30 P.M., shortly after the Third Army crossed the canal, he cried: "This is fantastic! We had anticipated thousands of dead in our ranks during this phase of the operation. I have just learned that there have been fewer than two hundred! Isn't it marvelous?"

About 10:30, he was handed a telegram. His face suddenly darkened. He read the message over and over. Finally he said, with an impatient gesture, "I can't believe it! The Soviets are telling me that Hafiz al-Asad has asked their embassy in Damascus to try to get a cease-fire!" The news plunged us into the greatest perplexity. On the one hand, it seemed inconceivable that Moscow would have quite simply invented such a story. On the other, why in God's name would Asad ask for an end to the fighting when his army was scoring success after success in the Golan?

It was while we were pondering this question that Sadat, totally distraught, let slip a few sentences which have haunted us ever since: "But it was all agreed! Asad and I had agreed with Faisal [king of Saudi Arabia] to carry on the war for at least ten days! He needs at least that much time to lay the groundwork for the oil embargo!" Qaddumi and I were speechless at the enormity of the revelation. The war's objective was thus not to liberate the Sinai, but merely to favor economic pressures on the West?

Sadat was soon reassured. Shortly after the Soviet message arrived, he received a telephone call from Asad, which he answered in our presence. Asad said he was determined to pursue the combat. He adamantly denied ever having asked for a cease-fire from the Soviet ambassador in Damascus.

I have never had occasion to question our Soviet friends on this matter, but I did get President Asad's version during a meeting I had with him in January 1978. Asad was indignant when I told him what Sadat had said about a secret agreement with King Faisal (and in my opinion, with Washington as well, since the United States benefited greatly, both politically and economically, from the October 1973 war). The Syrian president told me that the only thing agreed upon was that Sadat and he would solicit a cease-fire together after the reconquest of the Golan and the Sinai up to the Mitla and Giddi passes. "If I had known that the Egyptian army would stop a few kilometers beyond the canal I certainly would have set a more modest target for my own army to spare it the setbacks it suffered thanks to Sadat!" Indeed, the halt in the Egyptian offensive enabled Israel to divert important forces to the Syrian front.

I understood then why Sadat had asked us in August not to tell Asad what he had said about the limited objectives of the attack he was plan-

ning. To encourage our discretion, he had told us that the Syrian president detested us, especially Yasir Arafat, and thus would not appreciate
our being closely associated with their joint undertaking. The October
War in Sadat's eyes must indeed have been a "spark"—as he told us in
August—and not the raging fire that the entire Arab world was hoping
for.

Our meeting with Sadat the night of October 6 lasted four consecutive
hours. Qaddumi and I were embarrassed to take so much of his precious
time, especially since he was so absorbed by his crucial task. But every
time we tried to leave, he insisted that we stay with him. We didn't understand why he was so accommodating toward us. In retrospect, I think
he was trying to make sure of Palestinian support either if he lost the
war—which would have been a catastrophe for his political future—or if
he won, in which case he hoped to win our confidence so as to integrate
us into the peace process he planned to initiate. He finally let us leave
about eleven o'clock, when two of his intimates, former vice-president
Hussein al-Shafei and current National Assembly president Sayed
Marei, were announced.

The October War unfolded without much talk of the Palestinians. The
military communiqués broadcast from Cairo and Damascus trumpeted
the Egyptian and Syrian victories, but more often than not omitted any
reference to our feats of arms or even our presence. In fact we were active on all fronts. A number of PLA units had been helicoptered behind
Israeli lines on the first day of the fighting and seized four hills of Kunei-
tra in the Golan. From South Lebanon, fedayeen commandos crossed
over into Israel to attack the rear lines of the Jewish army in Upper
Galilee. Others shelled a number of kibbutzim beyond the Lebanese
border. As of October 6, some 70,000 Palestinian workers employed by
Israeli enterprises went on strike in the West Bank and Gaza. In all, we
launched more than 100 operations during the first week of the war, according to no less a source than Golda Meir herself.

We didn't have access to the line of demarcation separating Jordan
from the West Bank and asked Sadat to intercede with King Hussein on
our behalf. When Hussein replied negatively to a written request from
the Egyptian president, an emissary from Cairo made a second attempt
but again was rebuffed. Faruq Qaddumi and I approached the Jordanian
ambassador in Cairo, assuring him that we were prepared to turn the
black page in the history of our relations if only his government would
authorize the fedayeen merely to cross through Jordanian territory. Finally, a PLO delegation under Abu Daud went to Amman to urge Hus-

sein to enter the war, but to no avail.

Pressed by numerous Arab countries to open a third front against Israel, the king dispatched a tank brigade to Syria on October 13 but refused to grant the Iraqi army the right to cross Jordanian territory or even to use Jordanian airfields. To justify its negative attitude, the government said its forces were ill prepared and its antiaircraft defense system weak, a situation it blamed largely on Egypt and Syria for not informing it of their war plans ahead of time. This was only an excuse, however, since several Arab and even non-Arab countries proposed to provide Jordan with the military support it needed.

Although some fine works have been devoted to the October War, its definitive history is yet to be written. Indeed, certain aspects remain in the shadow, others constitute unsolved enigmas. Not the least of these is without doubt the crossing of the Suez Canal by General Sharon's men, a breakthrough which was to reverse the course of events and seal the defeat of the Egyptian army.

To me, the behavior of the Egyptian high command and of Sadat himself regarding General Sharon's enterprise was, and still is, incredible. The facts are as follows: On October 10, or four days before the Israeli commando units crossed the canal at a point known as the Deversoir near the Great Bitter Lakes (Timsah), Egyptian intelligence agents disguised as bedouins alerted Cairo through radio transmitters that pontoon bridges and amphibian tanks were being transported through Al Arish. The nature of the matériel was in itself a proof that the Jewish army would try to cross the canal and encircle the Third Army, stationed on the east bank of the canal. In Cairo, the general staff had files containing several plans drawn up both during Nasser's time and recently to prevent breakthroughs at at least four vulnerable points, including the Deversoir. The Israeli plan thus had nothing unexpected about it. And what did the Egyptian high command do? Nothing. Was the information received from Al Arish on October 10 even transmitted to Sadat?

Two days later, when General Sharon's first men reached the Deversoir region, the alert was sounded once again, this time by our representatives. The PLA command officers and Fatah units responsible for defending the Deversoir region along with Kuwaiti troops informed Cairo that an Israeli attack was imminent. The Egyptian officials still didn't react, and sent no reinforcements to defend this crucial position. General Sharon launched his offensive on October 14, managed to infiltrate a few tanks, and concentrated on widening the breach. Our men fought heroically; many died.

The situation was critical, but still something could have been done. There was still time for the Egyptian high command to take measures designed to drive back the enemy. But the high command let it happen. Sadat spoke at length of the army's successes in his radio and television speech of October 16, but didn't breathe a word about the fighting in progress on the two banks of the canal. Yet it was impossible for him not to know about the catastrophe since I myself was fully informed about the situation.

How can his silence and the passivity of the army high command be explained? The mystery remains total.

The basic flaw of the October War was that Sadat had given it limited objectives, without realizing that he couldn't reach even those without carrying his offensive to the end. This doesn't change the fact that, despite our reservations, we fully supported the venture whose patriotic nature was demonstrated by the enthusiasm and self-sacrifice of the Egyptian and Syrian soldiers. They fought valiantly, erasing forever the image—which Israel helped spread after the June 1967 conflict—that Arabs are incapable of mastering modern techniques. The lightning advance of the Syrian tanks in the Golan and the Egyptian army's conquest of the Bar Lev line will remain to the credit of the Arab nation regardless of the reversals suffered later.

On the negative side of the balance sheet, meanwhile, is the failure of the Arab states to use, to the hilt, the oil weapon they had in their hands. Despite the enormous financial gains they reaped from the embargo, they ended it prematurely, before achieving the target they had set of forcing a full Israeli withdrawal from the occupied territories. Were they threatened by an American military intervention? It's possible. Did they strike a bargain with Washington under which the United States would save the Egyptian Third Army, trapped by the Israeli forces on the eastern bank of the canal, in exchange for the lifting of the embargo? It's plausible. Whatever the case, it is certain that powerful Western pressures—American and European—were brought to bear and that Egypt and Syria were unable to withstand them. Sadat, who in his October 16 speech proclaimed his determination not to go to the bargaining table before the departure of the last Israeli soldier from the occupied territories, let himself be dragged into the negotiations trap laid by U.S. Secretary of State Henry Kissinger.

The war was scarcely over and the Third Army was still under siege when Sadat already wanted to open negotiations with Israel. On October 26, forty-eight hours after the second cease-fire, Mohamed Has-

sanein Heikal, editor in chief of *Al Ahram* and at the time still one of
Sadat's influential advisors, arranged for Faruq Qaddumi and me to
meet with Sadat. He received us at the Al Tahira Palace, and before we
even had a chance to sit down he asked us point-blank: "Well now, will
you agree to participate in the Geneva Peace Conference?" Sadat struck
us as being both impatient and worried. In his October 16 speech, he
said that the "Palestinians" must necessarily be involved in the peace
process. Today, he wanted to know if the PLO would agree to represent
the Palestinians at the round table.

I told him that we couldn't answer his question on the basis of the
limited information we possessed. We wanted to know who exactly
would be present at the Geneva Conference and on what conditions we
would be invited to attend. He replied that he had just written to the
U.S. and Soviet governments proposing that they participate in the
meeting. He said he had suggested that France and Britain also be invited to take part alongside Egypt, Syria, Jordan, the Palestinians, and
naturally Israel. The note went on to say that the conference should be
held under the auspices of the United Nations either in New York or
Geneva, where appropriate facilities were available. "What harm is
there in that," he said to reassure us, "since in any case Arab diplomats
are always meeting Israeli representatives in various UN bodies?"

We raised the objection that the United Nations was charged with
implementing Security Council Resolution 242 of November 22, 1967,
which we rejected since it makes no mention of the legitimate rights of
the Palestinian people. If we went to Geneva in these conditions it
would mean that we agreed to negotiate merely on the problem of "refugees," the term used in the resolution. Sadat tried to dismiss our objection by declaring: "All you have to do is ignore the stipulation of this resolution. Come expose your viewpoints, submit your claims, no matter
which ones. Defend your thesis on the need to dismantle the Israeli
state in favor of a democratic and multiconfessional Palestine. The main
thing is for you to be present at the peace conference!"

We promised to submit his proposal to the governing bodies of the
Resistance without delay. In the meantime, we asked him a number of
questions on the military situation. Why had he accepted a cease-fire so
easily? How serious was General Sharon's breakthrough? Sadat tried to
minimize the importance of the Israeli penetration, insisting that the
Third Army was not threatened with extinction. On the other hand, he
did mention the American airlift of sophisticated weapons to Israel during
the last phase of the conflict and complained that the Soviet Union had

"dropped" him by refusing to furnish the military hardware needed to pursue the war.

His arguments, obviously designed to convince us of his powerlessness, didn't ring true. First of all, the Egyptian forces had launched the hostilities with Soviet arms in more than sufficient quantity and quality. Secondly, since I was staying near the Almaza military airport just outside Cairo, I was able to observe, personally, the extent and intensity of the Soviet arms deliveries all through the October War. According to the International Institute of Strategic Studies in London— which can hardly be accused of pro-Sovietism—the Russian airlift to Egypt and Syria involved 934 round-trip flights, not counting the deliveries made by sea to Egyptian ports or the electronic resources that Moscow utilized for them to gather information on Israeli troop movements. On October 26, the same day we met with Sadat, Henry Kissinger revealed that the USSR had considerably reinforced its war fleet in the Mediterranean and had placed several airborne units (about 50,000 men) in a state of alert. In so doing, the Russians wanted to dissuade Israel from pursuing its offensive against the Egyptian Third Army.

Sadat also complained bitterly about Colonel Qaddafi, who had publicly criticized the conduct of the war and its limited objectives. Despite his disagreement, the Libyan president had not stinted on his financial, economic, and military aid. He supplied Egypt not only with oil and ready cash in foreign currency, but also with Mirage planes purchased from France and seventy MIG-21s, twenty-six of which were purchased during the hostilities and flown directly from the Soviet Union to the Egyptian front. During the first hours of the war, Qaddafi dispatched two members of the Revolutionary Command Council, Majors Abdel Monein al-Huni and Omar al-Meheishi, to Cairo, where they were to remain at Sadat's disposal if he should need them. It was they who alerted Tripoli to the fact that Sharon had penetrated the west bank of the canal, adding that this military reversal had deeply affected President Sadat. Major Abdal Salam Jallud, Libyan prime minister, immediately flew to Cairo and at the end of a meeting with Sadat reported to Qaddafi that the Egyptian president's morale had "collapsed."

The Libyan president himself then rushed to Cairo where he found Sadat in bed, suffering from stomach pains and incapable, it seems, of carrying on a coherent conversation. Burning with impatience, Qaddafi proposed going to the armed forces headquarters himself to follow the evolving military situation. Sadat flatly refused, saying that his generals were perfectly capable of assuming their responsibilities. In reality, he didn't want the Libyan president to have any part in the venture he had so vigorously denounced.

Sadat and Qaddafi had never gotten along well. Qaddafi had virtually idolized Nasser, who had much affection for the young man who sought to emulate him even though he thought he lacked political experience. Qaddafi's devotion to Nasser was such that when the Egyptian president had rallied to the Rogers plan for a peaceful solution with Israel in 1970, he told me: "Even if Nasser betrays the cause, I will always be at his side." His attitude toward Sadat was exactly the opposite, and he generally ran counter to any position espoused by the man he considered unworthy to succeed Nasser.

As for myself, I've maintained close relations with Qaddafi ever since he seized power and know him well. I was in Cairo for the Palestinian National Council when we learned, on September 1, 1969, that the Sanusi monarchy had been overthrown by a group of young officers. Four or five days later, a few comrades and I went to Tripoli where I met Qaddafi for the first time. He made a good impression on me despite the fact that he didn't understand Arab problems very well. He did show a heartening enthusiasm for the Palestinian cause, to the point of choosing as password for the coup "Al Quds," the Arabic name for Jerusalem.

Contrary to widespread belief, Qaddafi is not against the Geneva Conference in principle. In fact, he was one of the first to advise us to demand our place at the bargaining table. But unlike Sadat, he wanted to exclude all the Arab countries! Failing this, he advised us to participate with them in the search for a solution to the Middle East conflict, pointing out that if they negotiated in our absence they would surely betray us. He also encouraged us to form a government in exile and set it up in Tripoli.

Other Arab governments also pushed us to take part in the peace process. The Algerian foreign minister Abdel Aziz Bouteflika, for example, while visiting me at my home in Cairo at the end of October 1973, said that the war which had just ended clearly heralded a long diplomatic phase. Although he added that it would doubtless not be the last Arab-Israeli conflict, he believed it indispensable for us to formulate clear positions concerning a possible negotiated settlement in the meantime. He didn't say anything explicit, but it was clear he wanted us to adopt a responsible attitude regarding the peace conference. Bouteflika, along with President Houari Boumedienne, whom I met later, added that Algeria would be at the side of the Palestinian Resistance as long as it pursued the armed struggle. The Algerian leaders in fact have always maintained a consistent policy concerning us. Faithful to their principle of noninterference, they support us whatever our choice: war or peace.

When we returned to Beirut on October 27, the day after our meeting with Sadat, we knew that the Arab states, whatever their ideological, tactical, or strategic differences, generally favored our participation in the diplomatic maneuvering that was opening on the international scene. We had to define a clear position as President Sadat had requested us to do. To this end, we called an enlarged meeting of the Fatah leadership as soon as we arrived.

A long discussion ensued. Sadat had placed us in a difficult, not to say impossible, situation. Everyone was agreed not to reject the principle of a peace conference out of hand, but it would have been just as imprudent to reply affirmatively. First of all, neither of the two superpowers had as yet approved Sadat's plan. Secondly, and especially, we hadn't received an invitation to the conference. Nor did we know in what form and under what conditions we would be asked to participate. We couldn't simply overlook the fact that the cease-fire had been established on the basis of Resolution 242, which as I said before denies the Palestinians their most elementary rights. So we decided not to reply either way until we received a formal invitation. It was only then that we would be in a position to define our position in a clear and precise manner.

On November 12, exactly two weeks after the Fatah leadership's meeting, Sadat received Yasir Arafat who had been charged to transmit our reply to the question he had asked us on October 26. Arafat found Sadat's attitude surprising: He seemed distant, practically indifferent as to what decision we had reached. Arafat got the distinct impression that Sadat was no longer concerned by our participation in the Geneva meeting. He didn't even mention the possibility of an invitation for the second phase of the peace conference. At the time, our comrade was at a loss to understand what could have led the Egyptian president to reverse his position within the space of fifteen days.

But something had taken place during this period which, in the light of what came later, would explain Sadat's strange behavior: Henry Kissinger had entered the picture. Kissinger had met with Sadat on November 6 for the first time since the war's end, and five days later, on the very eve of Arafat's November 12 meeting with the Egyptian president, a first Israeli-Egyptian agreement was concluded at Kilometer 101 under his sponsorship.

The so-called step-by-step policy of partial and interim agreements so dear to the U.S. secretary of state was now under way. It gradually became clear that Kissinger had convinced the Egyptian chief of state to exclude the PLO from a negotiating process aimed not at favoring a comprehensive Middle East settlement, but merely at fooling the concerned Arab states by getting Israel to return only part of the territories occupied in 1967. We were only at the beginning of Kissinger's "shuttle diplomacy," which was to weaken the Arab world by dividing it, lay the groundwork for the bloody clashes in Lebanon aimed at paralyzing the Palestinian Resistance, and, finally, serve the expansionist aims of Israel if not always the real interests of American imperialism.

For us, the Palestinians—as indeed for the entire Arab nation—the October War in the last analysis was merely a bright interlude. Far from opening the way to the liberation of the occupied territories, it consolidated American influence in the Middle East and set the stage for the plots to liquidate the Palestinian Resistance. On the other hand, the war and its consequences did give rise to healthy soul searching in our ranks, to a new awareness which was to help us adapt our objectives to the realities of the situation and make bold decisions bringing to an end the "all-or-nothing" policy.

8

The Challenge of Peace

THE ROOM WAS PACKED WITH PEOPLE, all tense with enthusiasm. One after another the speakers delivered impassioned oratories. The words *armed struggle, revolution, reconquest, liberation,* recurred incessantly. Seated on the rostrum—I was supposed to be the main speaker that night at the meeting organized by the Arab University of Beirut—I let my eyes wander over the posters and banners that decorated the walls of the amphitheater. I smiled to myself. There wasn't one that didn't sport in giant letters the word *NO!* No to negotiations. No to compromise. No to capitulation. No to the Palestinian state.

The colloquium had been organized to debate the pros and cons of a possible Resistance participation in the peace process inaugurated in the wake of the October War. Sadat's call for an Arab-Israeli conference aimed at a comprehensive and final settlement based on the recognition of Israel within its 1948 borders had profoundly shocked, disoriented, and divided Palestinian opinion. Heated arguments had been raging for weeks in refugee camps and in the press. The various fedayeen organizations split into two camps, hurling accusations and invective at each other. The groups which in the summer of 1974 were to constitute the Rejection Front bitterly denounced the "capitulationist" attitude—and indeed even the "betrayal"—of Fatah and Nayif Hawatmah's Democratic Front (DFLP), suspected of favoring the Geneva conference and a compromise that would give the Palestinians a ministate in the West Bank and Gaza.

The leaders of the various organizations belonging to the PLO had been invited by the Arab University of Beirut to present their respective positions in a series of meetings. Dr. George Habash of the Popular Front, Nayif Hawatmah, and Ahmad Jibril (leader of the Popular Front-General Command) had spoken at the earlier meetings. On that night of February 10, 1974, it fell to me to explain and justify Fatah's stance.

The chairman of the meeting was obviously either unaware of the line of conduct unanimously adopted by the Fatah leadership or mistaken as to my personal views. Whatever the case, he introduced me to the thousands of militants packed into the meeting hall as the "champion of rejection"! To listen to him, I was going to develop the various reasons that would incite the Palestinians to oppose a categorical "no" to all the vile compromises that leaped from the posters and banners around the room.

When I stood up to take the microphone, the audience greeted me with chanted slogans: "Down with peaceful solution!" "Down with the peace of capitulation!" "Long live the armed revolution until the liberation of Palestine!" Grinning, I started straight off with "I'm afraid I'm going to disappoint you. I'm perhaps not going to get much applause, but contrary to the banners that surround us, I would say 'yes' to certain questions the Resistance is being asked." All the commotion subsided, and I began my presentation in a tomblike silence.

"The October War, whatever our reservations and criticisms concerning it," I declared, "was essentially a patriotic war. It created a new situation in the Middle East, which calls for new and original decisions. We would be making a tragic mistake if we were to turn our eyes away from the realities we're now faced with. These realities are of various kinds. The successes of the Egyptian and Syrian armies, the newfound Arab solidarity, the psychological upheaval which has shaken Israel to its very roots, all these have contributed to making the evacuation of the territories occupied in June 1967 a possibility. Among these territories are the West Bank and Gaza, which belong by right to the Palestinian people. The question we must ask ourselves today is whether, by our refusal to accept anything less than the full liberation of all Palestine, we are prepared to abandon a portion of our patrimony to a third party. Is it possible to let King Hussein, the butcher of our people, negotiate in the name of the Palestinians? Do we have the right to turn our backs on the fate of the West Bank and Gaza populations, who are suffering from the oppression of occupation?

"It is impossible to answer these questions," I went on, "without taking into consideration the regional and international balance of power. The Palestinian movement does not evolve in a vacuum. It has enemies and friends throughout the world. So we must carefully measure our capacity to influence events, without deluding ourselves. Now the vast majority of our friends—a number of Arab states, the socialist camp and especially the USSR, the Third World countries—are encouraging us to compromise, or at least not to burn our bridges. Ben Gurion and the other Zionist leaders accepted the 1947 partition plan, agreeing to set up the state of Israel on part of Palestine which like us they claimed in its entirety. During the Geneva Conference of 1954, the leaders of the Vietnamese revolution agreed to the division of their country into two states while awaiting a balance of power more favorable to them. This still holds true for North and South Korea. Lenin himself, in the Brest-Litovsk treaty, sacrificed a large part of Soviet territory in order to save the essential, which was the Bolshevik government."

I asked my audience if we could pretend to be greater revolutionaries than the Soviets, Vietnamese, North Koreans, or East Germans, or if we should agree to deprive ourselves of the margin of flexibility and maneuver the Zionist movement had reserved for itself throughout its history. It was clear that we should make the distinction between compromise and surrender, that we should know how to take what was offered us without renouncing our strategic objective of a democratic state in all Palestine in which Arabs and Jews would live as equal citizens.

"We have to go beyond the negativism and outbidding of the past! The traditional 'no' which has characterized the Palestinian movement is not necessarily revolutionary, any more than 'yes' is necessarily a form of treason. Rejection, on the contrary, could be just another form of escapism, of draping ourselves in a cloak of doctrinal mock purity."

I ended my speech by outlining the resolutions adopted by the Fatah leadership: not to renounce the inalienable rights of the Palestinian people to self-determination and the liberation of their country; to prevent, in the meantime, King Hussein from seizing the West Bank and Gaza; and to set up a national government on any part of Palestine to be liberated.

These positions were actually the result of a long evolution, the culmination of a reflection which began in the early days of our political activism. When during the fifties and sixties we analyzed the actions of our predecessors at the head of the Palestinian national movement, we noted a certain negativism which we ourselves wanted to avoid. From 1917 to 1947, the Palestinian leaders were confronted with a series of proposals aimed at resolving the conflict. They rejected all of them. There is absolutely no doubt that none of these solutions corresponded to any criteria of justice or to the legitimate aspirations of our people. But the mistake the leaders made was to accept nothing if they couldn't get everything. In this they contributed to favoring the Zionist venture and the colonization which over the years was to deprive the Palestinian people of their lands and an ever-increasing part of their country. The partition plan of 1947 was certainly unjust in principle. But why didn't the Palestinian leaders accept a temporary solution just as the Zionists did, which would consist of founding a state on the portion of the national territory assigned by the United Nations?

When I discussed these issues with Hajj Amin al-Husayni, he gave several reasons to justify his inability to save at least part of our national patrimony. The Arab governments concerned, either on their own or under pressure from the British (who in his view bore him a particular grudge), stood in the way of the foundation of a state in the West Bank and Gaza, territories which the Jewish army had been unable to conquer. It goes without saying that King Abdallah of Transjordan, Hussein's grandfather, did not favor the constitution of a Palestinian entity since he intended to grab the West Bank for himself—which in fact he did shortly after the 1948 war.

King Farouk, on the other hand, didn't try to annex Gaza to Egypt. He authorized a Palestinian congress to be held in that city in September of 1948, which designated a government under Ahmad Hilmi Pasha whose principal objective, again according to Hajj Amin, was to extend its effective authority over Gaza and the West Bank. However, the Egyptian regime prevented the Palestinian government from even establishing itself in Gaza on the grounds that the Israelis might use the "provocation" as an excuse to occupy the enclave. So the Palestinian government had to set itself up in Cairo, where Ahmad Hilmi Pasha, a banker by profession, paid more attention to his business dealings than to the shadow cabinet he headed. Betrayed by the Arab states, Hajj Amin was abandoned by most of the Palestinian leaders who split into pro-Jordanian and pro-Egyptian factions.

Although plausible, Hajj Amin's justifications didn't strike me as entirely convincing. At the time, Egypt and Saudi Arabia were hostile to the Hashemite dynasty and thus disapproved of Abdallah's annexation of the West Bank. Couldn't Hajj Amin have used these two states to help him oppose Jordanian expansionism? And if that weren't possible, why didn't he appeal to the Arab world at large, or even to the United Nations which had decreed partition, to claim the West Bank and Gaza? In any case, no document in the Palestinian archives—which we have examined carefully—corroborates the thesis of Hajj Amin.

In short, although Hajj Amin and his companions did have a strategic vision of Palestine's future, they were sadly lacking in the qualities necessary to make tactical concessions. It was precisely that gap which Fatah tried to fill.

Contrary to appearances and general conviction, it wasn't in the wake of the October War that we decided to establish our state on any part of Palestine to be liberated. As of July 1967, or barely a month after the Arab debacle, Faruq Qaddumi submitted a policy paper to Fatah's Central Committee outlining what should be the strategy and tactics of our movement. In that document, he proposed that we take a stand in favor of a ministate in the West Bank and Gaza in the event that Israel would withdraw from these two territories it had just conquered. Qaddumi argued that in the short term such an objective was not only in keeping with the Palestinian people's right to the ownership of all Palestine, but also corresponded to an objective analysis of the present situation. Indeed, it was clear that whatever the growth and vigor of the guerrilla war, the Jewish state would remain invincible in the foreseeable future. In the light of this, it would be unrealistic not to provide for stages leading to the strategic objective of setting up a democratic state in all Palestine.

Although the Qaddumi report, and particularly the part concerning the ministate, was realistic and lucid, it gave rise to strong opposition within Fatah's leadership bodies. At the time we didn't have a wide enough popular base to be able to submit the document to the intermediate cadres of the movement, much less open a public debate on the issue. So we decided to table the Qaddumi report while awaiting a more opportune moment.

The strategic objective of a democratic state in all Palestine didn't have everyone's support either. But after more than a year of deliberations and discussions, we were unable to put off making it public any longer. On the one hand, journalists were hounding us with questions concerning the goals of our struggle and it was ridiculous—especially after the extraordinary growth of our movement after the 1967 war—to reply evasively. At the same time, the Israelis were exploiting our silence to claim that our intention of "liberating Palestine from the Zionist grip" was merely a cover-up for our true aim, which was to "drive the Jews into the sea." (In fact, none of us had ever explicitly or implicitly referred to such an absurd possibility.)

The Fatah leadership asked me to outline our viewpoint. At a press conference held October 10, 1968, I announced that our strategic objective was to work toward the creation of a democratic state in which Arabs and Jews would live together harmoniously as fully equal citizens in the whole of historic Palestine. I explained that we had no objection to coexisting with the Jews, a people who had suffered atrocious persecutions. However, I added, not being responsible for these sufferings, we had no intention of paying the bill. It was therefore out of the question for us to agree to giving up part of Palestine or to accept a Zionist regime which in essence excluded the Arabs and deprived them of their natural rights.

The journalists present at the press conference asked with which Israelis we envisaged coexistence: With those born in the country? With the immigrants? New? Old? I replied evasively, as I did to all questions on what exactly the democratic state would involve. First of all, we thought it would be wiser to wait for Israel's reaction before going into detail and working out a compromise (whereas to this day neither Israel nor any other country has expressed the slightest interest in our project or asked for the least clarification concerning it). Secondly, as expected, the proposal I announced even in such prudently vague terms triggered a storm of protest both within the ranks of the Resistance (including Fatah) and among Arab countries. The idea that after a half century of bloody struggles we could coexist with a people who had usurped and colonized our country was still too new not to be intolerable to many. A great deal of courage and boldness would be needed to go beyond the accumulated traumas and frustrations, not to mention a political mindset which had been decades in the making. Still, we succeeded, and four months after my press conference the Fifth Palestinian National Congress (February 1–4, 1969) passed a resolution confirming our strategic objective.

Yet for all that, the Fatah leadership was still bent on getting the policy of intermediate stages accepted by the Resistance as a whole. It was the tragic events in Jordan in 1970 and 1971 which succeeded in opening the militants' eyes to the realities. After the massacres of Amman and then those of Jerash and Ajlun, and especially after the expulsion of the last fedayeen from Hashemite territory, it was only too evident that the Palestinian revolution could not count on any Arab state to provide a sure sanctuary or an operational base against Israel. In order to forge ahead toward the democratic, intersectarian society that was our ideal, we had to have our own state, even on a square inch of Palestine. This idea began to gain favor among the movement's rank and file after King Hussein unveiled his United Arab Kingdom plan on March 15, 1972. The plan, postulated on an Israeli evacuation of the West Bank, provided for a kingdom on both sides of the Jordan to comprise two federated provinces, Transjordan and Palestine. We had to claim what was rightfully ours in order to thwart Hussein's plan to usurp what was left of our country. So toward the end of 1973, or shortly after the October War, the Fatah leadership decided to make public its policy of intermediary stages and its tactical objective.

The fedayeen organizations that subsequently formed the Rejection Front, and especially Dr. Habash's PFLP, immediately unleashed a defamatory campaign against us. We were accused of defeatism, denounced as advocates of capitulation. They took a position both against the ministate in the West Bank and Gaza and against an independent democratic state. For them, the armed struggle must be pursued until the total liberation of Palestine. They tried to exercise a sort of intellectual terrorism, with those advocating compromise being presented as traitors. I then recalled reading as a youth about the conflict between Lenin and Trotsky, which strengthened my conviction that we were right.

In keeping with the rule we had adopted at the time of Fatah's creation, we refrained from fighting abuse with abuse. There had been too many examples of revolutions ending by devouring their own children. Using the pretext of ideological or political differences, the settling of scores had too often led to bloodbaths, always in the name of revolutionary purity. We had thus sworn never to use weapons against our opponents within the Palestinian movement and never to substitute invective for clear argument. We have in fact largely succeeded in making what we call democratic dialogue the accepted practice within the Resistance.

We had intended to convene the Palestinian National Congress (the parliament of the Resistance) a little after the October War to discuss the role the Resistance should assume in the new diplomatic phase which was opening. But we decided to put off the meeting until we had reached a consensus on a program common to all fedayeen organizations. Since Nayif Hawatmah, president of the Democratic Front, largely agreed with Fatah (he was one of the first to advocate the creation of a ministate in the West Bank and Gaza), we opened negotiations with George Habash, leader of the Popular Front. We were confident of the outcome, especially since we were on good terms with him despite our profound differences. During the critical period of regrouping which followed the fedayeen massacres in Jordan, a tight cooperation in various fields had developed between his organization and ours, especially in the occupied territories and Lebanon.

In public, Habash is dogmatic, intransigent, and incredibly violent, mesmerizing the crowds with his fiery oratory. In private, he's an entirely different person. Soft-spoken, calm, even phlegmatic, he listens with utmost attention and not without modesty, and expresses reasonable opinions. Scrupulously honest, he defends his political beliefs with conviction, but with none of the fanaticism shown by some of his comrades on the Popular Front's politbureau. I know Habash well, although I've never been to his home about which he observes a great discretion. Moreover, he isn't seen very often since he suffered from a heart attack right after the October War.

The meeting Yasir Arafat, Abu Salah, and I had with Habash at the beginning of 1974 was extremely encouraging. Habash seemed sympathetic to our proposals. He even suggested that prominent Palestinians living in the occupied territories be asked to endorse the negotiations for a political solution to the Israeli-Arab conflict, and that our role should be to guide them and lend behind-the-scenes support.

We had no reason to doubt his sincerity or freedom of action. The Popular Front, like Hawatmah's Democratic Front and Fatah, and unlike all other Resistance organizations, has consistently refused the tutelage of any Arab country. Entering into and breaking tactical alliances, it has maintained its autonomy despite the financial and political aid it has received from its protectors of the moment. There was a time when Habash and Hawatmah criticized us for our cooperation with the "petty bourgeois" regimes, but experience led them to adopt a pragmatic attitude, identical to ours, which consisted of dealing with any state prepared to support them. In practice, however, they enjoy the active sympathy only of the "progressive" states, such as Iraq, Libya, the Democratic Republic of Yemen, and to a lesser extent Algeria.

During that same period early in 1974, we also met with the leaders of the other fedayeen organizations, particularly al-Saiqah (pro-Syrian) and the Arab Liberation Front (controlled by Iraq). These talks similarly met with success. The negotiations resulted in the formulation of a ten-point program, approved by all factions of the Resistance, which was adopted by the Palestinian National Congress meeting in Cairo in June that same year. This success exceeded our hopes. The representatives of

all the fedayeen unanimously proclaimed their determination to establish an independent state on "any part of Palestinian territory to be
liberated," adding however that "the strategic objective of the PLO continues to be the establishment of a democratic state on the whole of
Palestinian territory."

This unanimity was unfortunately short-lived. No sooner had the
Palestinian Congress session ended than arguments and outbidding
erupted within the various organizations, with the more radical elements in each accusing their comrades of having approved a "liquida-
tionist" text. Needless to say, it was the extremists who prevailed over
the moderates, as is usually the case in such debates. All the organizations except Fatah, the Democratic Front, and Saiqah (all of which have
unified leaderships) reversed their position and unleashed a campaign
against the ministate. Posters denouncing our policy began cropping up
on walls all over Beirut. I remember one depicting a map of Palestine
shot through with ten bullets symbolizing the ten articles of the joint
program which had just been adopted. Shortly thereafter, the all-or-
nothing organizations formally joined forces within the Rejection Front,
which was to dangerously divide the Resistance for years to come.

The only way to offset their adverse propaganda was to wage a coun-
tercampaign among the masses. The task turned out to be a difficult
one. I remember one day going to the Tal Zaatar refugee camp—whose
population was to be massacred by right-wing Christian militias two
years later during the Lebanese civil war—and finding to my amazement the walls of this desperately poor shanty town plastered with
slogans denouncing the Palestinian ministate! At a popular meeting
organized for me, the audience—or at least the majority of it—was
clearly won over to the intransigent policy of our opponents.

I began my speech by congratulating them on their fighting spirit,
adding that this combativeness was nonetheless strange. "For the past
twenty-five years you've been living in exile," I said in effect, "twenty-
five years of frustration, humiliation, deprivation, and yet you persist in
your rejection of any compromise solution, even provisional. Isn't it extraordinary that you would prefer to live in a ghetto in a strange land instead of settling in a liberated region of your native country?"

In fact, the people of Tal Zaatar were prey to a narrow regionalism.
Coming from the part of Palestine that became Israel in 1948, they considered themselves foreigners in the West Bank! They didn't feel they
were even concerned with the ministate proposal. The Rejection Front
had thus found fertile ground for its maximalist theses, its all-or-nothing

policy. Its natural following extended, however, to other strata of the population, and curiously enough to the rich or comfortable Palestinians of the diaspora, especially those established in countries far from the battlefield. Taking no physical risk, living in ideal social conditions, lacking for nothing, they could afford the luxury of intransigence without having to fear an eternal exile. The same holds true for certain intellectuals who love to hold forth at fashionable get-togethers with learned analyses divorced from reality and all leading to a sterile negativism.

Meanwhile, I kept on explaining that the rejection of the extremist Palestinians was not unlike that of the Israelis, who were trying to exclude us from any settlement process before annihilating us. Over and over again, I repeated that our enemies were determined not to give up so much as a square inch of occupied Palestine, and that those who believed that the mini-Palestine which was being so fiercely debated could be obtained without struggle were sadly mistaken. Unlike many of our comrades, I was convinced in 1974—and said so repeatedly at the time—that a negotiated settlement was out of the question as long as there wasn't a significant change in the balance of power.

About two years later, in the spring of 1976, while the Lebanese civil war was raging and the Syrian Army was preparing to launch its offensive against the Palestinians, George Habash came to visit me in Beirut to pay his condolences on my father's death. We avoided any reference to our differences, but just as he was leaving he asked a single question, which went a long way toward showing his state of mind. "Is there any hope left?" he asked. His face was filled with a profound sadness.

The organizations of the Rejection Front were not the only ones to fight us in 1974. Besides Israel, we had to contend with U.S. Secretary of State Kissinger, who was busy maneuvering in the shadow of his secret diplomacy to exclude us from the political scene. He manipulated King Hussein as much as he did Sadat, dangling before Hussein's eyes the restoration of the West Bank to the Hashemite crown. As a result, Hussein was the only Arab head of state at the Algiers Arab Summit (November 26–28, 1973) who refused to endorse the resolution recognizing for the first time the PLO as the sole legitimate representative of the Palestinian people. Due to his abstention, the decision was kept secret. Three days later, on December 1, the king publicly declared that it was Jordan's responsibility to secure Israel's withdrawal from all the occupied territories before a referendum could be held enabling the Palestinian people to decide their own future. In other words, he was claiming the right to represent us at the Geneva Conference.

None of the other Arab heads of state reacted to his statement. In fact, some of them clearly regretted their vote in our favor at the Algiers summit. Sadat showed his true colors some months later. At the end of King Hussein's visit to Alexandria on July 18, 1974, Sadat subscribed to the joint communiqué recognizing the king's right to speak in the name of all the Palestinians living in the Hashemite kingdom (more than 1,000,000). Simultaneously, the Egyptian press unburdened itself against the Resistance and its leaders, going so far as to call them dishonest. Alone among the Arab chiefs of state, President Boumedienne— with whom I had just had a long meeting—gave a vigorous speech at a student congress in Algiers denouncing the plot being hatched against the PLO.

The danger was taking shape when a new Arab summit was convened for October 26 in Rabat. The agenda naturally included the problem of Palestinian representation. Unknown to Fatah's leadership, a group of young militants decided to kill Hussein if he succeeded in convincing his fellow rulers to reverse the position they had adopted toward the PLO during the Algiers Summit of November 1973. Whatever the cost, the PLO was to remain the "sole legitimate representative of the Palestinian people." This time, they were determined that the Hashemite ruler would not escape from the punishment so long deserved. A number of assassination plans were drawn up and given to the various commando groups which would be posted at the airport, along the road Hussein would take to Rabat, in front of the conference hall, and elsewhere. The young guerrillas, armed with false passports which didn't require Moroccan visas, arrived in the country one at a time and fanned out among a number of cities while awaiting the signal to regroup in Rabat. Just as was the case for the Munich operation, the weapons were not to be delivered until a few hours before the attack.

Everything was ready to go when, about a month before the summit's opening, two members of the commando team unexpectedly ran into a Libyan businessman one of them knew in a Casablanca hotel. The Libyan, who passed himself off as an enthusiastic supporter of the Palestinian Resistance and an advocate of violent action to boot, actually worked for Moroccan intelligence, among others. Several hours later, the two militants noticed indications which led them to believe that they were under police surveillance. They decided on the spot to leave the country, but were immediately arrested, interrogated, and tortured. Meanwhile, security agents moved into the hotel room they had occupied to nab any visitors and answer the telephone. A third militant, the one in charge of delivering the weapons, soon called from Tangiers announcing his arrival that same night and giving his flight number. Since he was careless enough to telephone from his hotel, the police had no difficulty getting the name he was using and arrested him as soon as he stepped off the plane at the Casablanca airport.

It wasn't long before a fourth commando fell into the net, calling from a public phone in Agadir to announce his arrival and flight number. Since the police had no way of identifying him, they sequestered all the passengers of the plane and interrogated them for forty-eight hours. The fedayi, who was using a Pakistani passport, was finally caught when the investigators discovered he didn't know a single word in his "native" tongue. To make a long story short, with the help of various ruses the Moroccan security police were able to round up fourteen of the fedayeen on the team.

The report King Hassan II received from his special services was particularly alarming. It incorrectly stated that the plot provided not only for Hussein's assassination but also for Hassan's, King Faisal's, President Sadat's, and President Numeiry's. The report noted that the greatest cause for concern was that no weapons had been seized, so there was a danger that the accomplices still on the loose could proceed with the raid.

Hassan II placed all his security forces on alert, warned the concerned Arab leaders about the plot, and urgently summoned Yasir Arafat for explanations. During their meeting, which took place in mid-October, the Moroccan king accused me of being behind the plot just uncovered on the basis of his intelligence report. Arafat protested and defended me, assuring the king that the Fatah leadership—himself included—knew absolutely nothing about the matter. The king showed him photographs of the fourteen captured fedayeen, but the PLO president was only able to identify two of them.

Meanwhile, those in charge of the abortive operation tried to minimize the damage caused. The weapons for the operation, well hidden in a truck crossing Europe on its way to Gibraltar, were to be delivered any day in Tangiers. It was necessary at all costs to prevent the shipment from reaching its destination, for if it fell into the hands of the Moroccan police it would provide enough evidence to convict our comrades. One of the commando members who hadn't been arrested flew to Madrid and made an anonymous phone call to Spanish intelligence giving a detailed description of the truck, its cargo, and the road it was supposed to take. The police intercepted it and arrested the driver and another militant accompanying him. However, the Spanish authorities, not wishing to get involved in an affair between the fedayeen and Morocco, dropped the matter by discreetly expelling the two militants after confiscating the truck and the weapons.

The meeting of the Arab Foreign Ministers Council, held in Rabat a few days before the summit, unfolded in a climate of terror. The Moroccan capital was alive with the most alarmist rumors: To listen to them, a veritable army of terrorists was preparing a whole series of attacks, indeed a massacre; reports supposedly emanating from this or that intelligence service—American, French, West German, Jordanian—were cited to predict the apocalypse. The members of the PLO delegation participating in the working sessions of the council noted the extent to which the mounting anxiety influenced the attitude of the Arab ministers: even those known for their pro-Hussein bias were becoming ardent defenders of the PLO!

The Rabat Summit was an outstanding victory for us. All the Arab heads of state, including King Hussein, adopted a series of resolutions in our favor. The signers of the communiqué affirmed, among other things, "the right of the Palestinian people to return to their homeland" and the right "to establish an independent national government under the leadership of the PLO, in its capacity as the sole legitimate representative of the Palestinian people, on any part of Palestinian territory to be liberated. This government, once it is established, shall enjoy the support of the Arab states in all domains and at every level."

When the summit's final communiqué was published, an explosion of joy went up among the fourteen fedayeen in Moroccan jails. They believed, and rightly so, that they had achieved their goal. They had not been after bloodshed, all they wanted was for the Arab countries to come out clearly in favor of the legitimate rights of the Palestinian people and to recognize the PLO as the Palestinians' sole legitimate representative.

My own joy at the summit's outcome was marred by my concern over what lay in store for the commandos. Not only were they subjected to cruel prison conditions and in some cases inhuman tortures, they also had to suffer public disavowal by the official voices of the Resistance. They could well spend the rest of their lives in prison. Press campaigns, inspired by Morocco's special services, presented them as gangsters. Yet in reality they had rendered an inestimable service to the Palestinian cause without spilling a drop of blood. I was burning with impatience to defend them publicly, but had to hold my tongue in the higher interests of the Resistance. Obviously, to justify their action before or during the Rabat Summit would have provoked a major crisis between the PLO and the Arab countries and sabotaged all our efforts to win the recognition we so desired. Even after the summit ended, I was asked to remain silent longer so as not to compromise the activity of our friends at the United Nations aimed at securing the PLO's recognition by the international organization. This goal was crucial for our future.

My silence paid off. On November 13, 1974, two weeks after the Rabat Summit, Yasir Arafat was given a triumphal welcome at the UN General Assembly. The standing ovation he received from representatives of some 140 nations was one of the most moving moments in the history of the Palestinian people. The nations of the world thus paid homage to the struggles and sacrifices covering more than a half century. That day, we felt that in the eyes of world opinion we were no longer merely a people of refugees and destitute beggars, but also a national community, deprived and humiliated to be sure, but still proud and ready to carry on the struggle.

After Yasir Arafat's speech, the UN General Assembly adopted two resolutions without precedent in the history of the organization. Not only did it recognize the PLO as the sole legitimate representative of the Palestinian people, but especially, it granted our organization the status of observer at the United Nations and invited our representatives to participate in this capacity in its sessions and work. We thus held the signal privilege of being the first national liberation movement to be officially associated with the world organization, within which we enjoyed the same status as, for example, Switzerland, the two Koreas, and the Vatican. In addition, the UN General Assembly recognized the Palestinian people's "right to sovereignty and national independence."

All our objectives on the international scene had thus been reached. We were no longer outlaws, "bands of terrorists," "murderers." It was then that I decided to raise my voice on behalf of the fourteen fedayeen unjustly incarcerated in Morocco.

At a popular meeting held at the Arab University of Beirut on November 19, I surprised my audience not only by defending the fourteen commandos but also by fully supporting their venture. After mentioning the recent victories of our people, particularly at the Rabat Summit and the United Nations, I declared that these successes could not be dissociated from the struggle and sacrifices of our militants. "The fourteen fedayeen being held in Rabat," I added, "have done their duty. Contrary to the allegations of a malicious propaganda, they never had any intention of attacking all the Arab chiefs of state, but only one of them, King Hussein, the butcher of our people. And if it's true that they sought to execute him," I exclaimed, "I assume the full responsibility for it and the honor of supporting their action!"

Coming to the plight of the fourteen captive fedayeen, I proclaimed my determination to secure their release. I denounced the tortures inflicted on them by the Moroccan police and let it be understood that if Hassan II remained deaf to my appeals—I had already sent him a verbal message through a prominent Tunisian—we had ways of forcing him to give in.

I was just launching into a furious diatribe against Hassan II when one of my colleagues interrupted me to hand me a message. My eyes shot open as I read that our fourteen comrades had been released and handed over to Egypt, which in turn had locked them in the Citadel prison of Cairo. I continued my speech, extremely embarrassed, saying that perhaps I had been a bit hasty in criticizing Hassan II, who in reality was sensitive to the interests of the movement. I announced the news I had just received and from there moved on to the unspeakable attitude of Egypt which dared to imprison men who had just benefited from the indulgence of Morocco.

I had scarcely begun the transition from Hassan II to Sadat when I was interrupted a second time by a member of the audience who handed me a note which went something like this: "Sadat invites you to come see him immediately. I beg you not to criticize him before hearing him out." It was signed by a member of the Egyptian Embassy in Beirut whom I consider one of my dearest friends. A former intelligence officer, he had rendered us great services during the confrontation with Hussein in 1970. I had no other choice but to comply with his urgent request.

Still more embarrassed, I went back to my speech, searching for words that would enable me to make a gentle shift, to spare Sadat without contradicting myself. Finally I managed to tell my audience—by this time totally disconcerted—that our Egyptian friends had just given me the reassuring news that the fourteen fedayeen had been locked up as a "routine measure" and were being well treated. Cutting short my talk, I concluded on a vaguely optimistic note.

The next day I flew to Cairo. As on the eve of the October War, one of Sadat's representatives met me at the airport and drove me straight to the presidential palace. Embracing me, Sadat said with a smile: "So, it seems you were trying to assassinate me?" The accusation was so absurd that I didn't even bother defending myself. Sadat went on to mention the reports he had received before the Rabat Summit and the Moroccan ambassador's visit informing him of the investigation's alarmist conclusions. However, the president added in a friendly way that he had been skeptical about all this information. After all, didn't my family live near his own residence? Weren't we old and good friends? Moreover, he went on, the Egyptian intelligence officers dispatched to Morocco had come back convinced that Hussein had been the only target of the operation. They had questioned the arrested fedayeen at length, and even knew four of them who generally resided in Cairo.

In short, Sadat spared me the necessity of futile explanations about the past. I thanked him for the confidence he showed me before saying that it was unworthy of him to act as jailer for the Palestinian patriots. I would be profoundly disappointed if our militants remained another hour in the Citadel, I added. Sadat went to the telephone and dialed Mahmud Salem, then interior minister, and asked him to release the fourteen detainees immediately. I left the president with a light heart to join my wife and children.

Forty-eight hours later, on November 22, I received a call from Ismail Fahmy, the foreign minister, who asked me in an agitated voice to come see him at once. It was urgent and serious, he added mysteriously.

I found him in his office surrounded by the prime minister, the interior minister, and a few aides. Their faces were grim and the atmosphere tense. I felt as if I were appearing before a war council. Ismail Fahmy briefed me on the situation. A British European Airlines DC-10 had been hijacked that day to Tunis (after a forced stopover the night before in Dubai) by a group of Palestinians demanding the release of thirteen fedayeen imprisoned in Egypt: five who had carried out an attack at the Rome airport on April 5, 1973, and the eight responsible for the March 1973 operation at the Saudi Embassy in Khartoum. The hijackers were also demanding the release of two fedayeen who had been jailed in Holland following an abortive attack.

President Habib Bourguiba, anxious to avoid a drama at the Tunis airport, was insisting that the hijackers' demands be satisfied. "But we don't want to give in to blackmail," Ismail Fahmy said. "Can you help us? Can you secure the release of the hostages without giving anything in return?" I had to admit it was a pretty tall order. As to the hijacking, I must say I found it intolerable that the commando members were demanding the release, among others, of fedayeen imprisoned at the request of the PLO, as were those of the Khartoum operation. It was a form of one-upmanship and a sort of challenge to us, which we had to meet.

While I was hesitating as to whether or not to commit myself personally, I was called to the telephone. It was Sadat, who asked me to leave for Tunis immediately and offered to put a plane at my disposal. I agreed, saying that I would be ready to take off within an hour along with a few aides. Arriving in Tunis, I went directly to the control tower where I was to spend three days and two nights negotiating the hostages' release. It was one of the most curious missions I ever had to accomplish.

Taher Belkhodja, the Tunisian information minister, welcomed me to the control tower by having me listen to the tapes of his first exchanges with the hijackers. Holed up in the British aircraft, they were threatening to kill all the hostages. When they learned that I was coming from Cairo to talk with them, they pelted me with abuse, along with Yasir Arafat, the other PLO leaders, and the Arab heads of state, whom they denounced as traitors.

The commando members belong to the "Martyr Ahmad Abdel Ghaffur" group. Ghaffur, killed under mysterious circumstances in Beirut in 1974, had been a Fatah militant until 1972 when he joined the camp that was to become the Rejection Front. A political extremist, he was a fierce advocate of violence. Having gathered around him a number of admirers, he received support from Abu Nidal, another Fatah defector who had sought refuge in Iraq. It was thus that Ghaffur organized various bloody operations, notably in Rome and Athens, before being killed himself. So I was dealing with resolute adversaries who obstinately refused even to open any dialogue with me.

Using the transmitter in the control tower, I nonetheless talked to them, urging them to listen to me. I recalled the good relations I had had with Ahmad Abdel Ghaffur before he left Fatah, and assured them that the Tunisian authorities and I were determined not to resort to force. I said that our only concern was to save the hostages while safeguarding the good reputation of the Resistance and partially satisfying their demands. It was out of the question, I said, to hand over the eight fedayeen of the Khartoum operation since they were under Fatah's jurisdiction. On the other hand, I promised to do everything in my power to obtain the release of the seven other fedayeen on their list. I then had the hijackers listen to a tape of a press conference held the same day in Cairo by a member of the Khartoum commando team who declared on behalf of his comrades that they did not want to be exchanged against the hostages in Tunis.

"Think about it. Be reasonable, and give me a positive answer!" I concluded. Belkhodja took over and proposed that the negotations begin. A voice replied: "We don't trust Abu Iyad. We know he's a crafty one." The Tunisian interior minister insisted, assuring them that they could have confidence in us. They asked for a half hour to think it over. We waited all night, in a deathlike stillness. The next morning, just as we were beginning to lose hope, the voice of the chief commando—a certain Marwan—reverberated. He asked to speak to "Brother Abu Iyad." I sighed with relief. The battle was half won, I said to myself, since for the first time he was calling me brother.

Without losing any time, I contacted the Egyptian and Dutch governments and asked them to send the fedayeen I was proposing to exchange against the hostages. The plane from The Hague arrived first, but the Dutch consul informed me that the two Palestinians could not leave the aircraft until all the BEA passengers had been released. The hijackers, who demanded that the reverse process be applied, thought we were laying a trap for them. They became angry and threatened to begin executing the hostages one by one. I urged them to be patient and opened tedious negotiations to gain time until the five other fedayeen arrived from Cairo.

I would then be in a position to propose a compromise formula which had some chance of being accepted: The commandos from Egypt would join the Abdel Ghaffur group, which in turn would release the passengers. The two Palestinians being guarded by the Dutch police could then leave their plane and board the BEA aircraft. Finally, the hijackers and their companions would be flown to the country of their choice by the seven crew members, all British, who could then regain their freedom.

Before the five fedayeen from Cairo boarded the hijacked plane, I made sure of their cooperation. They knew me by reputation, and were grateful to me since I had interceded on their behalf at the time of their arrest. I asked them to do everything possible to convince the hijackers to accept my proposal, especially by showing them that they had no chance of imposing their point of view. First of all, they were isolated on the international scene: If they had been listening to the radio they would know that all the Arab states—including Libya, Iraq, and South Yemen, which generally sympathize with the Rejection Front— categorically condemned their action. Secondly, their blackmail had very little, if any, chance of succeeding since the vast majority of the hostages were neither European nor American. Who would care about Pakistanis, Indians, and other Asians? Unfortunately, Westerners only seem concerned with the lives of their own citizens, while those of the Third World are considered, and often treated, as subhumans.

It took the five fedayeen from Egypt several hours to persuade the hijackers to agree to my proposal. Finally, however, the twenty-seven passengers (including three Europeans) were released and the two fedayeen brought by the Dutch were delivered to the commando group. At that point there were thirteen Palestinians—including the six hijackers—and seven British crew members on board the BEA airliner, ready to take off for the country to be designated.

Suddenly, however, Marwan asked to speak to me alone. The meeting, painstakingly prepared, took place exactly halfway between the aircraft and the control tower. He said that he and his comrades wanted to obtain political asylum in Tunisia with the guarantee that they wouldn't be turned over to the PLO. I transmitted the request to President Bourguiba, who categorically refused. This time the hijackers threatened to blow up the airplane, killing the crew members along with themselves. We had to start from scratch. My pleas fell on deaf ears. I then proposed exchanging the seven crew members against seven of my aides. "At least spare us the shame of annihilating innocent Englishmen!" I shouted into the microphone. As I expected, President Bourguiba was moved by my proposal and, not wanting to take the responsibility for such a tragic epilogue, agreed to satisfy the demands of the Ahmad Abdel Ghaffur commando. We had made it—just barely!

During those sixty hours of feverish and anguishing negotiations, a man who was introduced as a British diplomat remained nearby, closely following the developments. The few words he spoke were always in English, so it never occurred to me that he understood our language and was amazed when, at the end of the ordeal, he warmly thanked me in a halting Arabic.

"We are profoundly grateful to you, Abu Iyad," he said, "for having saved the lives of our citizens. I was very impressed with your chivalrous spirit, and by your moving offer to sacrifice fedayeen in their place." He turned out to be a former ambassador to various Arab countries who had been sent on this mission by the Foreign Office. I told him that I was only doing my duty, but that if he insisted on thanking me, his government could give the PLO treasury half the value of the BEA plane that I had managed to save. The diplomat burst out laughing, and a few days later when I was back in Cairo, a sumptuous bouquet of flowers was delivered to my house by the British air company.

The day after the hostages were released, I held a press conference in Tunis. An American journalist asked tauntingly: "You must have been ill at ease in that control tower, Mister Abu Iyad. Wouldn't you have felt more at home in the airplane next to the terrorists?" I remained calm and replied: "I don't feel at home in the control tower or anywhere else. But you who have a country and a place to call your own, do you think it's too much to ask that you observe a minimum of courtesy toward those who have neither?"

Some time later I had a discussion with the hijackers on a subject we had managed to keep quiet during the hijacking. The demands of the Abdel Ghaffur group had actually not been limited to the liberation of imprisoned fedayeen. They had also demanded the recall of the PLO delegation from the United Nations. I asked the Tunisian authorities not to make anything about this public before getting the commando members to drop the demand, which they did at the end of arduous negotiations.

"Have you even read Arafat's speech at the UN General Assembly?" I asked them. Since they hadn't, I described the scenes of joy that took place in the refugee camps, explaining that the Palestinians were filled with pride that one of their own had been able to expose to the entire world a cause too long ignored, and that the man who spoke in their name had been applauded by representatives of peoples from all over the planet. "It's true," I added, "that the UN's attitude toward us in the past has been far from blameless. And of course there's no need to have any illusions regarding its effectiveness and power. But still, does this mean we should scorn a moral and political victory?"

At the end of the discussion, Marwan and his comrades admitted their error and even said they were sorry for having been so blind. All six of them have since joined the ranks of Fatah. The debate was also useful in that it gave me an idea of the extent to which the demagogic propaganda of the Rejection Front can influence young patriots if the realists within the movement don't take the trouble of countering with an objective analysis of the situation we're facing. Our task would be all the easier in that the theses of our adversaries are untenable from whatever perspective—nationalist, revolutionary, or Marxist. The leaders of the Popular Front, who claim to be Marxists, affirm that diplomacy is a form of defeatism and that only armed struggle is revolutionary. This was the argument they used to denounce our entry into the United Nations—

the organization that groups together all the socialist countries including the two giants of international communism! These pseudo-Marxists obviously don't know much about Lenin, who instructed the Bolsheviks to infiltrate all mass organizations and make their presence felt. And yet the Rejectionists pretend to shine by their absence in the biggest mass organization of them all, the one that gathers together all the peoples of the world.

George Habash, president of the Popular Front, apparently forgetting that he had opposed our entry into the United Nations as an observer in November 1974, proposed in September of 1977 that our delegation demand Israel's exclusion from the world body. But for Dr. Habash, one contradiction more or less wouldn't make much difference.

While we were fighting among ourselves as to how to take up the challenge of peace, Henry Kissinger was busily and discreetly at work to neutralize our successes on the international scene and more generally to divide the Arabs in the interests of Israel. On the surface, he was a tireless mediator with his successive Middle East tours, his shuttles back and forth between Tel Aviv, Cairo, Damascus, Amman, and Riyadh. But his objective, as soon became clear, was not to bring about a comprehensive settlement going to the roots of the conflict, but rather to conclude partial agreements designed to give the Israeli expansionists a long breathing space by setting the Arabs against one another.

The first agreement he engineered between Israel and Egypt, concluded November 11, 1973, seemed innocent enough. Didn't it save the Egyptian Third Army from suffocation and perhaps even destruction? The PLO didn't oppose it. But when he undertook a new shuttle to bring about a first military disengagement in the Sinai, our organization severely criticized the step-by-step diplomacy which clearly could only lead to serious dissension within the Arab world. Syria in particular took umbrage, understanding full well that a new Israeli-Egyptian agreement would inevitably weaken its own position with the Jewish state.

A few days before Egypt and Israel signed the first disengagement agreement on January 18, 1975, I flew to Cairo to beg Sadat not to get further involved in this dangerous spiral. The negotiations were at a standstill, and I was hoping that Israel's intransigence would once again prevail over the Egyptian president's weakness and defeatist attitude. I found Sadat extremely angry, not at the Zionist state or Kissinger, but at the PLO. He reproached me bitterly and violently criticized Yasir Arafat for a communiqué which had just been published by the PLO Executive

Committee concerning the new orientation of American diplomacy.

Using all my patience, I tried to calm Sadat and reason with him. I wanted to avoid a break at a time when I still hoped to win him over to our line of thinking. But he didn't budge. Once again he flew into anger, shouting: "If Kissinger offered me one square meter of the Sinai tomorrow, I'd grab it! I'll never give up the course I've set for myself!" I told him that in any case he should take into account the position of Syria, his ally during the October War. He ended by reluctantly agreeing to meet with President Hafiz al-Asad, whom I had seen just before coming to Cairo. The meeting between them took place a little later in Riyadh, but led to nothing since Sadat was hell-bent on pursuing the path Kissinger had charted for him.

The next milestone along that path was the second Sinai agreement of September 1, 1975, that fatal agreement which was to exclude Egypt from the confrontation states, widen the gulf between Cairo and Damascus, and fuel the raging fire of the Lebanese civil war.

The first clashes between Lebanese Christians and Muslims, between the Maronite parties and the Palestinians, had erupted in the early days of 1975. Entirely taken up with the problems facing the Resistance, I could no longer leave my post in Beirut. In July, however, I took advantage of the misleading truce then reigning and decided to take my first trip abroad in seven months.

I had received an invitation to Morocco in the meantime for a reconciliation with Hassan II. I didn't particularly want to make an official visit since the meeting might not lead to any positive results. So it was agreed that I would meet my wife and children for a vacation in Tunisia, and quietly travel to Morocco from there. I was delighted at the opportunity to escape for a few days from my grueling responsibilities in Lebanon, especially since I had always had a particular affection for the Tunisians and their president, Habib Bourguiba. Besides, I hadn't taken a rest in years and was ready for a vacation with my children, whom I saw all too rarely.

My family met me in Tunis on August 10, and about ten days later a special Moroccan plane flew us very discreetly to Casablanca. We were accompanied by some Moroccan Intelligence officers as well as by three of the fedayeen who had been implicated in the October 1974 operation against King Hussein and later released by Hassan II. I wanted to introduce them to the king to show him that they weren't the ruffians described by his police.

We were lodged in a magnificent residence in Casablanca, and five or six days later I was taken to Rabat to be received by the king. The audience unfolded with all the pomp and ceremony customary to the Sharifian court. Accompanied by innumerable bodyguards, I was swept to the palace in a luxurious car preceded by a motorcade. Greeted by the chief of protocol, I was shown into a vast office at the other end of which Hassan II was seated at his work table. He rose to his feet as soon as I entered and advanced regally to the middle of the room to greet me. I noticed that his cordiality did not go so far as the traditional Arab embrace, which was only natural since we hadn't yet settled the quarrel between us. His behavior moreover corresponded perfectly to mine: I can't bear artificial effusiveness and never embrace someone I'm meeting for the first time or for whom I don't have some affection.

The three fedayeen were with me; they had followed me into the room, and after greeting the monarch withdrew to leave us alone. Hassan II opened the conversation by saying: "Let's forget the past. I think the best thing would be to begin again in our relations." I agreed, but asked his permission to bring up at least one issue that concerned me, which was the unjust accusations against the fedayeen arrested before the Rabat Summit. "How is it possible, Sire," I asked, "that you were able to believe that a number of heads of state, including yourself, could be targeted along with King Hussein?" I mentioned the crimes Hussein had committed against the Palestinian people and reminded him that a few years earlier he himself had suggested that Hussein step down in favor of the Resistance. As for the future, I said straight off that we wouldn't stop pursuing Hussein until he gave up once and for all his dreams of recovering the occupied West Bank for himself or in our name. It wasn't only a question of principle for us, I explained, but a crucial problem involving the future of our people.

Hassan II listened attentively, and said that the Palestinian people deserved to exercise their right to self-determination. He nonetheless offered his good offices to reestablish the dialogue between the Resistance and King Hussein. We then discussed the conflict over the western Sahara which had just broken out between Morocco and Algeria. The sovereign outlined his point of view and suggested a compromise formula which he asked me to convey to President Boumedienne, whom I was to see on my way back to Beirut. The meeting, which had gone from cordial to warm, enabled me to gauge the competence and adroitness of Hassan II as well as his vast knowledge of international problems.

Before I took my leave, Hassan II questioned me about my immediate plans. When I told him I intended to leave Morocco the next day, he protested and insisted that I stay at least until September 1. Why September 1? When I asked one of the king's aides after the audience, he replied mysteriously: "Because your children insist upon it." I didn't know then that they were preparing a celebration for my birthday on August 31, which I had completely forgotten. I nonetheless stayed for the three or four days that remained in the beautiful seaside house put at our disposal, and used the time to meet various opposition figures.

The evening of August 31 was one of the most beautiful of my life. Because of my work and constant travel, I had never before had the chance to be with my family on such occasions. Surrounded by my six children, my wife, Palestinian militants, and a high official from the Sharifian palace, I was treated to a wonderful meal followed by a gigantic birthday cake covered with a multitude of candles corresponding to my age. We sang old Palestinian and Moroccan ballads long into the night to the accompaniment of the oud.

The next day in Algiers I heard over the radio that Egypt and Israel had concluded a new and important agreement for a military disengagement in the Sinai. I didn't yet know the details—especially the secret clauses of the protocol annex that were not to be revealed until some months later—but I had a strong feeling that this was the first step toward a separate peace treaty in keeping with Israel's strategy. Questioned by Algerian journalists, I was the first Palestinian leader to denounce Sadat's surrender in vigorous terms. I accused him of striking a harsh blow to Arab solidarity and the Palestinian cause, and launched an appeal to Arab public opinion everywhere for support.

When I was received by Boumedienne the next day, I outlined the Middle East situation as I saw it, especially the dangers implicit in the Sinai II agreement for the Arab cause and civil peace in Lebanon. The Algerian president declared his conviction that the Israeli-Egyptian accord would exacerbate the split between Cairo and Damascus, adding that he didn't exclude the possibility that the Americans would favor bloody confrontation in Lebanon so as to weaken the Palestinian movement. He also believed that the lives of the Resistance leaders were in danger and that we had to take additional precautions. I suggested that he publicly take a stand against the Sinai II agreement, but he replied that it was up to the PLO to take the lead; otherwise, a declaration from him would be premature and inopportune.

I landed in Beirut on September 5, just in time for the Fatah Central Committee meeting called to examine the Sinai agreement. At the end of our deliberations, we published a declaration vigorously criticizing the Israeli-Egyptian arrangement as well as its architect, Henry Kissinger. Most of the Arab countries remained silent, either because they approved the agreement or because they wanted to humor Egypt, the United States, or both.

The bloody madness could now wreak its havoc in Lebanon, with nothing to stop it.

9

The Lebanese Tragedy

IT IS FITTING THAT THE LEBANESE CIVIL WAR was triggered by a massacre. In the afternoon of April 13, 1975, a bus crowded with Palestinians and Lebanese on their way home to the Tal Zaatar refugee camp from a rally held at the camp of Sabra crossed through the predominately Christian sector of Ain al-Rummaneh. While the leader of the Falangist party, Pierre Gemayel, was inaugurating a church in Ain al-Rummaneh, the bus was caught under heavy machine-gun fire.

The passengers, many of them women and children, were all unarmed and had no means of defending themselves. Some of them were killed instantly, while the wounded had to be finished off by the attackers. By the time the forces of order arrived, some thirty bodies were strewn around the inside of the bus. Thus began the Lebanese war, one of the most atrocious in history, which aside from a deceptive truce in July and August was to rage with ever-increasing intensity for eighteen months.

In fact, the Ain al-Rummaneh killings merely punctured an abcess which had been festering for a decade. It further testified to the degradation of Palestinian-Lebanese relations despite periods of apparent harmony. As I noted in an earlier chapter, the Beirut authorities had opposed Resistance activities ever since Fatah launched its armed struggle in December 1965, arresting and sometimes torturing fedayeen who tried to cross the Lebanese border into the territories occupied by

Israel. After the June 1967 disaster, the Lebanese government, like the other Arab states, had felt obliged to adopt a tolerant attitude toward the Resistance, the only force in the Arab world which hadn't resigned itself to the defeat or laid down its arms against a reputedly invincible enemy. Meanwhile, the Palestinians residing in Lebanon regained a sense of self-confidence and enthusiastically set about breaking their chains in a country which treated them as second-class citizens. The refugee camps, subjected to regulations and restrictions that made them reminiscent of prisons, were transformed into fortresses. Men and women by the thousand flocked to join fedayeen organizations or self-defense militias. Our fighters established military bases in the south from which they launched operations against targets inside Israeli territory.

The Lebanese officials observed the autonomous development of our activities but were powerless to do anything about it. As was the case in Amman, the first signs of uneasiness in Beirut didn't appear until after the imposing funeral we organized for one of our militants, Izzedin Jamal, a Lebanese citizen who was killed during a raid on Israel. For the first time, thousands of armed fedayeen marched through the main streets of the capital.

Representatives of the government, public authorities, and all Lebanese political parties—both rightist and leftist—had insisted on participating in the ceremony in a show of solidarity. But it was obvious that the public display of our forces shocked many of them. It was very difficult, if not impossible, for us to contain our people's newfound freedom and their hope of reconquering Palestine, symbolized for them in the weapons they carried.

Six months after Izzedin Jamal's funeral, tensions were aggravated by a first skirmish between Palestinian commandos and a Lebanese army patrol in the south. Bloody clashes followed during the next months. In October 1969, violent fighting erupted in several regions of the country as a result of Lebanese efforts to impose restrictions and controls on fedayeen movements and activities. Lebanese President Charles Helou, under pressure from the Maronite parties, took a hostile stand against us while the prime minister, Rashid Karameh, did his best to preserve the interests of both camps.

Although the population on the whole was favorable to us, a split along sectarian lines reappeared dangerously, to the point where the chief of state confided to certain numbers of his entourage that the only solution was the partition of Lebanon into two states, one Christian and the other Muslim. It was under these circumstances that negotiations opened in Cairo under the sponsorship and through the mediation of President Nasser, resulting on November 3 in the agreements which to this day govern relations between the Resistance and the Lebanese state.

At the request of the Lebanese government, the Cairo agreements were not made public for fear of provoking reactions from the parliamentary opposition. Even so, they were vigorously fought by Raymond Eddé, president of the predominately Christian National Bloc party. I respect Eddé, a politician of high integrity, and have great affection for him despite our political differences. I cannot say the same for Pierre Gemayel and Camille Chamoun, the leaders of the Falange and the National Liberal party (NLP) respectively, who approved the Cairo agreements without reservations at the time and then later took up arms against us to abolish them.

Our relations with the Christian rightist leaders were not bad at the time. Our ambition then was to maintain friendly and cooperative relations with all parties, and especially with the two main religious components of the population. The Palestinian leaders, particularly Yasir Arafat, often met Pierre Gemayel and Camille Chamoun in an atmosphere marked by cordiality and even mutual respect. Chamoun always showed an exemplary moderation at these meetings, as indeed he did in his public statements.

Gemayel's behavior, on the other hand, intrigued us. In private he was always understanding, reasonable, inclined to compromise. But no sooner would the meeting be over than he would rush off to issue a decidedly anti-Palestinian communiqué or declaration. One day when we remarked upon this contradictory attitude, he explained that he had no other choice since his followers were quite hostile to any dialogue with the Resistance leaders. It was only later that we realized the Falangists were already mobilizing public opinion for the armed confrontation they were preparing against the Palestinians.

Nevertheless, the period from 1970 to 1972 was relatively calm. Of course, problems arose, but they were resolved in a friendly manner thanks to the lines of communication we succeeded in keeping open with the Christian leaders and the Lebanese government they dominated.

Things began to deteriorate in the spring of 1973. The Israeli raid on Beirut on April 10, which claimed the lives of the three PLO leaders, triggered a conflict over the army's failure to act. In the government crisis which followed, Prime Minister Saeb Salam resigned. Salam, along with the other Muslim leaders, called for an investigation of the army's passivity and demanded the punishment of those responsible, especially the dismissal of the army commander-in-chief, Iskandar Ghanem. President Suleiman Franjieh, meanwhile, supported by the main Christian parties, asked that the armed forces enter the refugee camps to "assure their defense." Needless to say, we rejected this request, which also was contrary to the Cairo agreements. More and more incidents took place and more and more Palestinian militants were arrested.

We couldn't help noticing that while we were taking measures aimed at appeasement, the army high command was carrying out provocations. It was as if it favored bloodshed and wanted to reach the point of no return. The violent clashes which shook Beirut at the beginning of May soon spread to the rest of the country. The Lebanese air force intervened for the first time on May 3 and bombed the Bourj Brajnhy refugee camp, while other Palestinian settlements were pounded with mortar.

I had occasion to meet the top army leaders during the negotiations which began in mid-May between the Palestinians and the Lebanese under Amin al-Hafiz, who had just been named prime minister. I would never have imagined then that these same officers would one day show a fanatical hatred for both Lebanese Muslims and Palestinians. General Iskandar Ghanem, who started sporting a large cross during the 1975–1976 civil war, spoke little during our meetings with the prime minister. Serious and courteous, he struck me as a professional soldier devoid of preconceived political opinions. Colonel Jules Bustani, chief of the Deuxième Bureau, and Colonel Musa Kanaan, assistant chief of staff, actually seemed likeable. Intelligent, perfectly informed about the political and military situation, their arguments were moderate. Kanaan also had a fine sense of humor, and seemed jovial and even friendly toward us.

The negotiations resulted in the Melkart protocol, concluded on May 17 thanks largely to the combined pressure of Egypt and Syria, anxious to restore order in Lebanon in anticipation of the war they were planning for October. The compromise involved setting up various mechanisms designed to facilitate a better application of the Cairo agreements. It reestablished a modus vivendi between the Palestinians and Lebanese which was to last until the beginning of 1975.

We tried to institute a cooperation on more solid bases. For instance, we took the initiative of opening a serious dialogue with the Falangist party. Throughout the entire month of June, a delegation under my leadership representing the main fedayeen organizations held a series of meetings with members of the Falangist politbureau, particularly Amin Gemayel (son of Pierre), Joseph Chader, and Karim Pakraduni. The talks were extremely frank. The Falangists accused us of acting as if we were on conquered territory, of having created a state within a state, of having secretly brought in thousands of fedayeen who had fled Jordan after the 1970–1971 massacres.

We countered each of these accusations calmly, trying to reassure them with rational arguments. It wasn't true that we had brought our militants into Lebanon from Jordan, since the vast majority of them had sought refuge in Syria. It was true that we had made Beirut our center of communications, but the leaders of the Palestinian movement remained scattered throughout the Arab world, particularly in Damascus, and our activities were not, as they believed, concentrated in Beirut. We had no intention of taking any power from the Lebanese authorities or even of interfering in their internal affairs. It was in the interests of the Palestinian movement to remain outside any government framework so as to be able to pursue its national liberation struggle.

We had the impression that these meetings brought mutual understanding. They also led to one concrete result: A joint declaration was drawn up mentioning our points of agreement, particularly in South Lebanon. In this regard, the declaration stated that the Israeli aggressions against the border villages were motivated not by the presence of fedayeen in the area but by the Zionist state's territorial ambitions. Initialed by Joseph Chader and myself at the end of June, the document was to be published in September during the celebrations marking the anniversary of the Falangist Party's founding. When the time came, however, the Falangist leaders found a number of excuses for not making the joint declaration public.

The October War and the diplomatic negotiations that followed absorbed everyone's energies for the closing months of 1973 and throughout 1974. Besides, we had no reason to worry over the situation in Lebanon since all the political leaders, Christian and Muslim alike, were supportive and accommodating. It's too often forgotten that it was President Franjieh, accompanied by Lebanese former prime ministers and presidents—including Camille Chamoun—who went to New York in November 1974 to sponsor our admission to the United Nations as observers.

The euphoria created by this event didn't last long. In January 1975, Pierre Gemayel gave a speech accusing the Palestinians of abusing

Lebanese hospitality and demanded "the reestablishment of state authority over the whole of Lebanese territory." By February he was calling for a "referendum on the Palestinian presence in Lebanon."

From then on, things began to move fast. In March, the army brutally crushed a fisherman's strike in Sidon. A Muslim former deputy, Maaruf Saad, was killed. Protest demonstrations organized against the army (which was headed by a Maronite general) further widened the breach between Christians and Muslims, rightists and leftists, anti-Palestinians and pro-Palestinians—all dangerous cleavages which were to facilitate the task of those who wanted civil war. It was against this background of rising tension and polarization that the Ain al-Rummaneh bus massacre was perpetrated on April 13.

On the surface, everything seemed to indicate that Pierre Gemayel's party had prepared and carried out the attack. We learned, among other things, that two of the killers were Falangist militants. But curiously enough, the party leaders turned them over to the police the very next day. I began to have some doubts when several members of the Falangist politbureau, particularly Joseph Chader and Karim Pakraduni, whose intellectual honesty is beyond question, proposed that we set up a neutral commission of inquiry to determine who was behind the massacre. At the same time, they assured me categorically that the Falangist party leadership had absolutely nothing to do with the crime, which moreover they condemned vigorously.

It was close to a year before I was to learn the shocking truth. After the disintegration of the Lebanese army in the spring of 1976, Muslim officers of the Deuxième Bureau gave me some damning documents revealing that the Ain al-Rummaneh massacre had been jointly organized and brought off by the Deuxième Bureau, led by Colonel Jules Bustani and the National Liberal party of Camille Chamoun! The two killers the Falangist party had handed over to the police were in fact NLP militants who had infiltrated the Falangists.

It would have been the perfect crime if it hadn't been for the leak, only possible under exceptional circumstances, which was later to unmask them. I happened to meet Colonel Bustani shortly after my discovery. He flatly denied all the proofs I held on his responsibility in the affair. However, some months later, when relations between the Resistance and Syria began to improve, Syrian intelligence gave me information confirming the documents I received from the dissident officers of the Lebanese Deuxième Bureau.

The bloody provocation behind the April 13, 1975, massacre shocked me all the more in that I was a thousand miles from imagining Camille Chamoun capable of such a revolting act. I had met with the former president of the republic at least four times during June 1975. At the first meeting, which was held in the presence of Yasir Arafat at the home of a Palestinian Christian, Chamoun was full of kind words for the Resistance and made statements worthy of an Arab nationalist. I observed him in silence. This venerable old white-haired gentleman, playing coquettishly with his horn-rimmed glasses while speaking with calm and poise, could disarm even the most incorrigible of skeptics.

Abruptly turning toward me, he said teasingly: "Well, Abu Iyad, did the cat get your tongue? I would very much like to hear what your voice sounds like." I smiled and said: "Allow me, Mr. President, to ask you a question which has been troubling me ever since this meeting began. Do you think the Ain al-Rummaneh massacre is merely an incident, or was it rather the first step in the implementation of a plot concocted by the Falangist party against the Resistance?"

Looking back on it, it is clear that Chamoun is a consummate actor. He assumed an inspired air, put on his glasses, furrowed his brow, and fell into deep thought. After a few minutes, he raised his eyes and said: "My son, it's difficult for me to give you an immediate reply, since I lack the necessary elements. It would take me a few weeks to gather the information enabling me to express an opinion. In the meantime, I must confess that, like yourself, I don't exclude the hypothesis of a plot." Some months later we learned that at the very moment he was speaking, the president of the NLP was importing massive quantities of weapons and arming his militias while reselling the surplus at high profits to various extreme-rightist Christian groups, including his Falangist allies.

It was only gradually that we understood Chamoun's game. His strategy—clearly mapped out in his autobiography which was published later—covered three successive objectives. The first (the one he had set his sights on when we met him in June 1975) was to get himself accepted as a national leader, sensitive to the demands of Lebanese Muslims and Palestinians. The second was to occupy a choice position within the government, which would enable him to maneuver toward reaching his ultimate ambition: to replace Suleiman Franjieh as head of state.

I hardly knew President Franjieh in the spring of 1975, having met him only once—and quite by chance—in Cairo shortly after his election in August 1970. At the time we were in the midst of our conflict with Hussein, and I explained to him the difficulties we were having in Jordan. After hearing me out, he said he was convinced that nothing of the sort could happen in Lebanon under his presidency since he would permit the Resistance to pursue its activities within the framework of the existing agreements.

I had heard that he was well disposed toward us from our comrade Yusuf al-Najjar and the socialist leader Kamal Junblatt, who had met him just before his election. His presidential opponent, Elias Sarkis, had been much more reserved when sounded out about his attitude toward the Resistance. The PLO had thus given Franjieh's candidacy its moral support and perhaps even contributed to his election. Indeed, although the influence of the Lebanese of Palestinian origin was not decisive, it was far from being negligible.

Franjieh, in an effort to end the violent clashes that were spreading throughout the country after the Ain al-Rummaneh massacre, received Yasir Arafat on May 17. Given the lack of confidence between the two men, nothing came of the meeting. The situation only got worse, and on June 23, Franjieh summoned Arafat and myself to the presidential palace.

We were immediately taken aback by the presence of the Egyptian and Saudi ambassadors at President Franjieh's side, totally unprecedented and contrary to the rules of protocol for such meetings. As if this weren't enough, no sooner were we seated than a number of high-ranking Lebanese army officers, all Muslims, joined us one after another at Franjieh's request.

Our host seemed extremely nervous, smoking cigarette after cigarette, his face set. He was the first to speak. "You have doubtless noticed," he said, "that I am the only Christian present at this meeting. I have invited the ambassadors of Egypt and Saudi Arabia, as well as officers of my army whom you can't suspect of systematic hostility to the Palestinian cause, so that they can witness our exchanges. Your behavior is intolerable for the Lebanese population. The other day, while driving with my wife in the mountains, I was shocked to see the walls of Christian villages plastered with posters exalting the fedayeen's armed struggle. No doubt your leftist friends are responsible for this indecent propaganda. Don't be astonished, then, that massacres like that of Ain al-Rummaneh can occur."

Arafat couldn't stand it any longer and interrupted him to declare that the reality was quite different. He said it was the Christian rightist parties which had long been preparing a war of extermination against the Palestinians and that to this end they had received massive quantities of arms. Suleiman Franjieh lost his temper and shouted: "Proofs! Proofs! Be honest for once and give me documents supporting your allegations!"

Arafat was deeply hurt by the insult, made worse by the presence of witnesses. He actually had tears in his eyes. Red with anger, he snapped shut the little booklet he generally uses for taking notes and exclaimed: "I won't tolerate being talked to like that! I am a fighter, and it was as such that I was elected to head the Palestinian movement and not thanks to a one-vote majority in an assembly of notables!"

His answer was cruel, to be sure, but I found it to the point and justified. If Arafat hadn't reacted that way, I probably would have come down on Franjieh even harder. It was inconceivable that we should allow anyone to insult the leaders of the Palestinian people. Moreover, Arafat's indignant reply had the salutary effect of calming Franjieh, who immediately excused himself by declaring that he had had no intention of offending us. He merely wanted the arguments that we advanced backed up by irrefutable proofs.

Arafat then told him that before coming to the presidential palace we had learned that Christian officers of the Lebanese army had just delivered 6,000 firearms to the Falangists which had been sold to Lebanon by Bulgaria and Poland. This illicit transfer had been made through false documents drawn up by the Deuxième Bureau.

Franjieh claimed he knew nothing about this transaction, but said he found it normal that the Lebanese Christians should arm themselves just as the Palestinians had done. "I have ordered the interior minister to grant an arms permit to any Christian who requests one," he said. "I authorized you, indeed encouraged you, to fortify your camps, to import any weapons you needed to defend yourselves against Israeli aggression. You are equipped with heavy artillery, antiaircraft guns, even ground-to-air missiles. I am asking you today—indeed, I am insisting—in the presence of two Arab ambassadors friendly to your cause, to confine yourselves to the limits of your camps and sectors. The rest of Lebanon doesn't concern you. And since we don't agree on this subject, I propose that we invite officers from Arab countries here to arbitrate in our dispute. They will judge which of the two parties, you or us, is violating the Cairo agreements."

Having kept silent since the beginning of the session, I asked to speak. My presentation lasted over an hour without interruption. I began by thanking President Franjieh for having sponsored the PLO's admission to the United Nations the previous November by personally pleading our case before the General Assembly. He had spoken in the

name of the entire Arab nation. That being the case, I said, it wasn't
necessary to "Arabize" the Lebanese conflict by calling in officers to arbitrate our differences. Such an initiative could be dangerous in that it
might encourage intrigues on the part of this or that Arab state. We
should, on the contrary, come to an understanding without any foreign
interference.

It was true, I added, that the fedayeen had committed errors, that at
times they had ruffled the Lebanese people's national sensibilities. We
didn't deny it. But President Franjieh was making a mistake in confusing the reprehensible acts of individuals with the policy of their leaders.
The leaders of the Palestinian movement were neither ruffians nor anar-
chists. They had just as much at stake as the Lebanese themselves in the
well-being of Lebanon and the harmonious coexistence of Palestinians
and Lebanese. They couldn't afford a breakdown in order, or having the
struggle for the liberation of Palestine hindered or deflected by marginal
conflicts. President Franjieh should understand that it was difficult for
us to control all the acts and gestures of our militants, who came from a
people that had been disarmed, persecuted, and humiliated for decades.

The Christian rightist parties in Lebanon, I continued, scorned us and
were pursuing dubious objectives. For years we had tried to maintain a
dialogue with them, to reach an understanding on mutually profitable
bases. But we never got anywhere. Their claim that we tried to ally ourselves with the Lebanese Muslims and the left against them simply
wasn't true. It wasn't even logical. By definition we couldn't be fanatical
Muslims and progressives at the same time. The truth was that we had
tried to maintain an equal balance between all Lebanese communities,
first because it was in our interests to have good relations with the entire
population and second because the Palestinian movement was resolutely
secular. It was well known that Palestinians had never been bitten by
the sectarian virus, that we had never made distinctions between Muslims and Christians. Discrimination was so foreign to our mentality that
some of the best-known leaders of the Resistance, such as George Habash and Nayif Hawatmah, were Christians.

Countless times we had shared our deepest motivations with the
Christian rightist leaders. We were Palestinian nationalists, hounded
and frightened. We were not ashamed to admit our fears and anxieties.
The Lebanese government, controlled by the Maronites, frightened us.
That's why we wanted to get along with the Christian parties, the in-
struments of power. And yet they had rejected us. If we were close to
the Muslims, to the Muslim right—represented by men such as Saeb

Salam and Rashid Karameh—it was because we had nothing to fear from them. For electoral and political, local and regional reasons, the Muslim right was condemned to support our movement. The same held true for the left, which for similar reasons wouldn't strike us. When the socialist leader Kamal Junblatt was minister of interior, he was tougher on us than the Christian leaders had ever been. But we knew he would never go so far as to stab us in the back.

President Franjieh, who was listening with great interest, interrupted to object: "You nonetheless supported the decision of the left, which has impertinently named itself the National Movement, to boycott the Falangist party by demanding its dissolution and exclusion from the government. That was a major mistake on your part. The Falangists represent a significant segment of the Christian population. Your decision, moreover, will have no other effect than to spread its influence."

I defended our position as best I could, but was somewhat embarrassed. I couldn't admit to President Franjieh that I didn't even know exactly what the decision to boycott the Falangists meant. We had rallied to it more by solidarity with Kamal Junblatt's National Movement than by conviction. And how could we have been less severe regarding the Falangist party, which had sworn to destroy us and organized—or so we thought at the time—the Ain al-Rummaneh massacre?

It was one o'clock and our meeting with Franjieh had lasted four hours. Arafat and I asked permission to withdraw. To our great surprise, Franjieh protested and swore by heaven that he wouldn't let us leave before we had lunch with him. Franjieh may be lacking in culture and may not always have been equal to his responsibilities, but I'll say one thing for him: He does have a certain generosity of spirit. At least he doesn't resort to the tricks or duplicity of a Camille Chamoun.

The lunch was a veritable feast. The president gave Arafat the place of honor across from himself, while the rest of us—including the two Arab ambassadors, the high-ranking Muslim officers who had been present at our meeting, as well as Christian officers who had remained in the antechamber at Franjieh's request—all took seats around the table. Franjieh's mood had changed entirely. Friendly, sometimes playful, freely drinking arak, he dispensed a typical Arab hospitality, reaching across the table to offer a tender piece of meat to one guest, a crisp pastry to another. His son Tony—who along with his wife and little daughter was assassinated by the Falangists in June 1978—joined us toward the end of the meal, which lasted more than three hours.

On the whole, the meeting was very positive. We agreed to exclude an Arab arbitration. Lebanese-Palestinian joint military committees were to be set up to take adequate measures to halt the fighting. We agreed to use our influence to tone down the National Movement and encourage it to reduce its pressure against the Falangist party. Finally, Yasir Arafat would address a message to the Lebanese people calling for national union. The text of the appeal, drawn up by a group of Palestinians who were specialists in Lebanese affairs, was designed to reassure the Lebanese, especially the Christians, on our intentions and to reiterate our determination not to jeopardize the confessional, political, or economic structures of Lebanon.

Still, we weren't sure this was enough to exorcise the demons of the Lebanese right, especially since about that time Arafat and I had had a long meeting with two leading members of the order of Maronite monks which had profoundly shocked us. At the beginning of the interview, which took place at the Beirut residence of a Palestinian Christian, the two monks showed us documents attesting to the Maronite Church's support of the Palestinian cause in the early years of the struggle against the Zionist colonial venture. But the monks' opening remarks were merely a prelude to their denunciation of our "ingratitude" and their claim that we were no longer "worthy" of their sympathy.

The two monks then launched into a lecture on history. The Maronites, they explained, had fought heroically to conquer and preserve the independence of Mount Lebanon, and they would defend it to the last man against what they called Palestinian colonization. "We are a people of stubborn peasants, warriors, and we are prepared to pay whatever price is necessary to drive you away," they said.

One of the two, a teacher of philosophy whom we thought to be a man of religion, a humanist despite his bull-like appearance, sent shivers up our spines with his bloodthirsty claims of what he himself had done to a Lebanese Muslim and a Palestinian as an example to be followed "in the name of God and our holy church" by the other monks heading militias under his command.

Arafat and I were struck speechless. It was as if we had suddenly been transported back to the religious wars of the dark ages. When I finally found my tongue, the only thing I could think of to say was that I didn't believe the good father's boasting, any more than I believed the violent declarations of Abu Arz, leader of the Guardians of the Cedar militia, who at the time was cordially inviting every Lebanese to kill at least one Palestinian. Nor did we take very seriously the calls to murder issued by certain bishops from their episcopal thrones. Unfortunately, we later discovered that our skepticism was ill-founded, and that the atrocities committed by the right-wing Christian militias far exceeded their threats.

"Why such hatred?" I asked the two monks. One of them replied: "You understand nothing of our history and our mentality. As I already told you, we are attached to Mount Lebanon with every fiber of our being. All our monasteries have been transformed into fortresses and arsenals. We have collected funds reaching fifty million pounds with which to buy more arms."

On this point, we weren't learning anything new. As of 1970—a little after "Black September" in Jordan—we noted that the Falangists were beginning to expand their military camps and develop their militias. Young members of the Falangist party and Chamoun's National Liberal party were sent to Jordan and West Germany for training. Thanks to fund-raising drives organized by Lebanese emigrés, ever-increasing quantities of arms began to pour into the country from 1973 onward. The weapons, purchased in Belgium, Switzerland, the United States, and France, were generally delivered via Moroccan ports to the port of Juniyah north of Beirut. The arms transactions were carried out through middlemen, such as a Saudi businessman well known in the West, and often were guaranteed by Western governments.

The Falangists, unlike the Chamounists, didn't try to hide their military preparations. At the invitation of Amin Gemayel, the Falangist leader's oldest son, I visited a Falangist training camp twice in 1973 where I was able to get an idea of the extent and quality of their militia. Gemayel assured me that these preparations were strictly defensive. "But whom are you going to defend yourselves against?" I asked. "Against you, the Palestinians," he replied.

At the time, we were naive enough to believe the Christian parties when they said they had no intention of starting an armed conflict. Otherwise, we never would have waited for the outbreak of the civil war before arming and training the militias of the leftist groups. Indeed, up to the Ain al-Rummaneh massacre in April 1975, we had limited ourselves to helping organize the inhabitants of South Lebanon's border regions so they could resist incursions of the Israeli army. By the same token, it wasn't until after the Israeli commandos descended on Beirut in April 1973 and killed the three PLO leaders that we began to seriously fortify the refugee camps and accelerate the training of Palestinian militias. All this was in anticipation of Israeli aggression: It never occurred to us that one day we would have to turn our weapons against Lebanese.

As of early 1975, there were a number of indications that we were threatened not only by local forces but also—and especially—by a veritable international conspiracy. Arms sold to Lebanon by Saudi Arabia, Kuwait, Libya, Syria, and Egypt were promptly resold to the Christian militias. Even worse, we learned that Arab—particularly Saudi and Kuwaiti—companies and businessmen were generously financing arms purchases by the Falangists and Chamounists. On top of all this, certain Gulf countries, including Kuwait, were interrupting or delaying payment of their subsidies to Fatah and other fedayeen organizations. The situation became such that in December 1975, in the middle of the civil war, I decided to tour the Arab oil-producing countries.

I began with Kuwait, where I spent about ten days. The PLO office organized a series of public meetings for me, and I used the opportunity to severely criticize certain Arab countries whose attitudes concerning us were ambiguous, if not downright hostile. It was during one of these speeches that I denounced Colonel Qaddafi, who had cut off his financial aid to us since the beginning of the year.

I also lit into the rich Palestinians who had slowed down their contributions to the PLO. "Whether they like it or not, they will pay!" I shouted. The threat wasn't very subtle, but I couldn't do otherwise at a time when the Resistance was in the midst of a severe crisis. As it turned out, the strong-arm approach paid off, since the very next day our millionaires organized a meeting and came up with a considerable sum for the movement.

I didn't call on any of the Kuwaiti officials as I usually do, and they were affected by my public utterances. They were convinced that my attacks against certain Arab countries and wealthy Palestinians were really aimed at their own government, with which in fact we did have a rather large disagreement. We had several reasons to be irritated with the Kuwaiti authorities: for instance, their refusal to cover a ridiculously modest deficit (about 150,000 dinars) in the budget of the Palestinian schools in Kuwait, which prevented the admission of new students. Such pettiness was unworthy of this fabulously rich country which had always been sympathetic and generous to us before.

At the time, the Kuwaiti population and government circles alike were gripped by a totally irrational fear. Everyone was convinced that the civil war in Lebanon would soon spread to Kuwait, where some

200,000 Palestinians were living. Now that the PLO was threatened in Beirut, they said, it was going to transfer its headquarters and the bulk of its activities to Kuwait. Even more alarmist rumors were circulating—to listen to them, Iraq was going to arm the Palestinians and incite them to seize power in the emirate.

All these allegations were utterly absurd. If the Palestinians in Kuwait weren't treated as equal citizens, at least they were treated as privileged guests. They were thus deeply grateful, and have always shown an unfailing loyalty toward the country they consider their second home. It would never occur to any of us to compromise the security, territorial integrity, or sovereignty of the emirate. It's not a coincidence that we supported Kuwait every time it was involved in a dispute with a third party, notably Iraq. All this to say how unfounded the Kuwaiti anxieties were.

When I heard that my public statements, which the Kuwaiti leaders interpreted as a kind of blackmail, were increasing their fears, I decided to reassure them on our intentions. Prominent Palestinians close to the rulers arranged meetings for me with certain officials, including Deputy Prime Minister Sheikh Jabar al-Ali. After convincing each of them of my good faith, I outlined our grievances, emphasizing the most serious one which was the financing by Kuwaiti businessmen of arms purchases for the Christian rightist parties.

I had never met Jabar al-Ali before, and he made a strong impression on me. Intelligent and lively, he had a pleasant manner and wonderful sense of humor. He wanted our meeting to be strictly private, so I went to his residence where he welcomed me with extreme warmth. There was already a certain bond between us as his two sons had been students of mine when I was teaching in Kuwait.

We had, nonetheless, a stormy political discussion. Known for his frankness, the deputy prime minister announced straight off: "If I were a Lebanese, I'd be a Falangist!" He explained his viewpoint, which I countered with arguments based on the realities of the situation, but we each remained solidly entrenched in our own positions. In fact, the thing that struck me most during my entire Gulf tour was that all the leaders I met, whether in Kuwait, Bahrain, or Qatar, expressed exactly the same opinion as Sheikh Jabar al-Ali. Naturally, they all began by assuring me of the sympathy they had for the Resistance and for our struggle against Israel. But they promptly added that we were wrong in Lebanon, where the conflict as they saw it pitted the right—which they supported—against the "International Left," the bogeyman trotted out by Pierre Gemayel, Camille Chamoun, and Henry Kissinger.

Three months after the Sinai II agreement was concluded, it was clearly in the interests of the Americans and their agents in the Middle East to strike at the Resistance, to reduce it to silence and paralysis. My Gulf tour gave me ample evidence that America's representatives, including the CIA, had been doing a good job. They had succeeded in setting against us the rulers who feared the spread of communism above all else. For certain of them, who to put it mildly lacked a highly developed sense of nuance, the socialist Kamal Junblatt was nothing but a tool—conscious or otherwise—of a vast Marxist conspiracy. Many of those I met begged me not to fall into the communist trap and urged us to break our solidarity with the National Movement. They didn't realize that what they were asking us to do in practice was to place ourselves at the mercy of the Americans and their Israeli and Arab allies.

While I was winding up my tour in Qatar in January 1976, I received an official invitation to return to Kuwait where Sheikh al-Jabar al-Ahmad, presently Kuwait's ruler but at the time prime minister, would receive me. I was given a very different welcome from the one I had received some days earlier. There was a red carpet and official reception at the airport and limousines waiting to take me to the Hilton hotel where a suite had been reserved. However, since I can't bear formalities and protocol, I politely declined the offer and insisted on staying with my brother in his modest apartment.

My meeting with the prime minister was extremely positive. It soon became clear that he knew all the ins and outs of the Palestinian case and the Lebanese situation. Our talk, which lasted three hours, was marked by total frankness and led to concrete results. When I left Kuwait for Beirut, I had the impression that we had succeeded in clearing up three-quarters of our differences.

I got back to Beirut in mid-January. The fighting had been escalating in an ever-increasing spiral, and a conversation I had had in July 1973 with Joseph Chader, one of the principal members of the Falangist politbureau, came to mind. Chader had showed me a certain sympathy ever since I told him that his Armenian origins made me feel close to him. "We both belong to traditionally persecuted minorities," I had said. During that July 1973 meeting, Chader confidentially told me something which turned out to be prophetic. He had learned from a "good source" at the U.S. Embassy that an Israeli-Arab war would be breaking out "in the near future" and that "a peace conference would be called soon afterward." Then he added, carefully emphasizing each word: "There is some talk of inviting the PLO to the conference table, *if you are not liquidated beforehand.*" When I asked him to elaborate, he answered evasively that we had to be careful if we really wanted to take part in the peace conference.

Reflecting on this conversation two and a half years later, I told myself that we had undoubtedly not been "careful" enough: We had expressed serious reservations on the way the October War was conducted, we had denounced Kissinger's step-by-step diplomacy, we had resisted the spread of U.S. influence in the region, and, finally, we had fought the shameful Sinai agreement. The nomination of George M. Godley as U.S. ambassador to Lebanon not long before the civil war erupted couldn't have been mere chance. He had planned and carried out a number of "dirty tricks" throughout the world, especially in Chile and Vietnam. I remember when he arrived in Beirut, the whole town was asking in anguish what catastrophe was in the making.

I hasten to add that I'm not so naive as to think that American agents simply dropped in on Pierre Gemayel and Camille Chamoun and asked them to exterminate us. Nor do I believe that the authors of the bloody attack at Ain al-Rummaneh acted on orders emanating directly from Washington. Not that the United States suffered from a lack of paid agents in Lebanon or elsewhere, or that they couldn't intervene through the intelligence networks of Israel or Jordan, among others. What's important is that the Americans had a whole panoply of means at their disposal to achieve their ends, especially given the situation, which was certainly ripe. If they didn't actually physically provoke the civil war in Lebanon, there is no doubt that they contributed to tending the fire of the conflict and to fanning its flames.

A number of Arab states, deliberately or otherwise, also contributed their share. Yet most analyses of the causes of the civil war attribute the major responsibility to the fedayeen, who by their excesses supposedly pushed the Christian rightist parties to take action against the Palestinians.

Advocates of this thesis overlook the fact that most of the provocations to which they refer were committed by fedayeen organizations manipulated by various Arab regimes, which traditionally settle their scores on Lebanese territory. For instance, when an article offensive to Iraq is published in the Lebanese weekly *Al Hawadess*, it is the Arab Liberation Front, a mere puppet of the Baghdad regime, which takes the matter in hand by dynamiting the publication's building and killing about a

dozen people in the process. But the press doesn't accuse Iraq or even
the ALF. It denounces the "terrorism of the Palestinians." And when
Saiqah, which dances to the tune of Damascus, kidnaps Lebanese belonging to the pro-Iraqi Baath party, the PLO is accused of interfering in
Lebanon's internal affairs. Or when Libya decides to seize an opponent,
as was the case with its former prime minister Mustafa Ben Halim, it
digs up some obscure Palestinian splinter group to do its dirty work. I
could go on and on.

This situation places the PLO leaders in an intolerable position. We
are told that if we disapprove of these acts and if we are convinced that
they compromise the Resistance, we should do something to stop them.
But here again our critics are either ill-informed or feigning naiveté.

First of all, it goes without saying that we don't necessarily know who
is responsible for every such act. And secondly, even if we do know, it
would be suicidal to incur the wrath of the various Arab regimes on the
pretext of maintaining order. Could we afford the luxury of breaking
with Syria or Saudi Arabia, for instance?

It is a well-known fact that Lebanon has always been a favorite stamp-
ing ground for intelligence services of foreign powers, large and small,
Eastern and Western, Arab and Israeli. The shadowy struggles played
out on Lebanese soil make our position all the more difficult. Numerous
bombings, kidnappings, assassinations, and other "uncontrolled" incidents throughout the civil war were attributed all too quickly to the
Resistance or the left, but in fact were nothing more than manifestations
of the secret wars being waged among the various intelligence services.
For those whose interests were served by the war's prolongation, the incidents were yet another way to revive it when it seemed to lag. Such
was and remains our dilemma and our drama.

Objectively speaking, the Lebanese—or those who didn't have ulterior motives politically—were right to find the situation unbearable. But
when we tried to explain that we, as much as they, were victims, they
didn't believe us. Even those we considered friends were skeptical. It's
difficult to understand us without being in our shoes.

As I said over and over again to the Christian rightist leaders before
the civil war, the fedayeen—after having been driven from Jordan—had
no other place to go but Lebanon. If we had to yield, the gains made in
decades of struggle would be lost. Of course, the Palestinian revolution
would ultimately survive, but a decisive defeat in Lebanon would compromise it for years to come. We are in about the same situation as the
Arab warrior Tarek Ben Ziad, the conqueror of Spain. After disembark-

ing on the Spanish shores, he burned the ships and told his troops: "The enemy is in front of you, the sea is behind." I had pleaded with the Maronite leaders not to resort to violence, not to push us in our last refuge, for we wouldn't have any choice but to fight to the finish.

The Christian rightist leaders acted with untold cynicism. Hypocritically posing as the defenders of national sovereignty, they marched off to war with ostentatious crosses on their chests, supposedly to free their compatriots from the Palestinians and more generally from the Arabs. Yet who played up to the Arab regimes and allowed them to interfere in Lebanese affairs? Who profited from the capital, the labor force, the weapons coming from Arab countries? Certainly not the Palestinians, the scapegoats singled out for the baseness and treachery of a handful of unscrupulous men.

We were all the more determined to fight since we knew from the very beginning of the civil war that we would also be fighting the Israeli enemy, who had slipped in behind the banner of the Lebanese crusades. Indeed, we had noticed among other things that the defense system installed around certain Maronite monasteries was identical to that of Israeli military settlements. The same held true for various war techniques, too lengthy to go into here, but which had obviously been introduced into Lebanon by Israeli officers.

In any case, there's no longer any need to demonstrate the close collaboration that existed between the Christian right and Israel throughout the entire war. Menachem Begin's government officially recognized it during the summer of 1977, even indicating the extent of the aid furnished to its Lebanese allies. The Lebanese rightists, meanwhile, repeatedly bragged about their alliance with the Zionists, justifying it by the need to assure their survival.

Major Saad Haddad, head of the Maronite militias in South Lebanon, is no longer anything more than a paid Israeli agent. Bashir Gemayel, commander-in-chief of the Falangist troops, admitted in the presence of witnesses that he consulted with Israeli officials in the Israeli village of Nahariya. We have proof that he and Dany Chamoun, son of the National Liberal party's president Camille Chamoun, met with Israeli officers on numerous occasions. The meetings, when not actually held on Lebanese territory, took place on a pleasure boat in the port of Juniyah, headquarters of the Christian right. Juniyah was also the scene of Israeli Defense Minister Shimon Peres's talks with Camille Chamoun and other Christian leaders at the end of January 1976. Only President Suleiman Franjieh and Falangist leader Pierre Gemayel declined to have any direct contact with the Israelis, leaving this task to their subordinates.

Personally, I don't believe that the Falangist party leadership had any contact whatsoever with Israel at the beginning of the civil war. On the other hand, I have reason to believe that Camille Chamoun and certain officers of the Lebanese Deuxième Bureau maintained close relations with the Israeli, American, and British intelligence services. The Ain al-Rummaneh massacre was conceived not only to trigger the hostilities but also to drag the Falangists into the conflict. It certainly wasn't an accident that the killings took place when Pierre Gemayel was known to be in Ain al-Rummaneh inaugurating a church or that two of the assailants were Chamoun followers masquerading as Falangists. It was only at a later stage that the Falangists were led to collaborate with Israel.

The many forms of aid provided by Israel must have been very tempting. The most sophisticated U.S.-made armaments poured into Juniyah, to the point that the Ford Administration was challenged on the Senate floor, the unauthorized transfer of military matériel to a third country being forbidden under U.S. legislation. Moreoever, a number of ships transporting arms for the Palestinian Resistance and the Lebanese left were intercepted by the Israeli navy and brought to Juniyah where the cargos were turned over to the Christian militias.

These arms were used to commit the most atrocious crimes in Lebanon's history, attesting to the fascist character of the Maronite militias. When I got back to Beirut from the Gulf on January 10, 1976, I noticed that the brutality had reached new heights. A week earlier, the Palestinian camp of Tal Zaatar had been encircled and subjected to a blockade which was so severe that the population couldn't even provision itself.

Four days after my arrival, Falangists and commandos of the Guardians of the Cedar militia stormed the refugee camp of Dbayeh. Despite the fact that it was inhabited by Christian Palestinians who had not been involved in the conflict, the place was largely destroyed and its population massacred. About a week later, on Jauary 19, the Muslim shanty town known as the Qarantina was burned and then totally razed to the ground by bulldozers. Hundreds of people were killed, many of them savagely mutilated. The soldiers of Pierre Gemayel and Camille Chamoun, their crosses prominently displayed, celebrated their victory by guzzling champagne over piles of cadavers to the accompaniment of songs on the guitar—grisly images which were broadcast across the world by various television networks. The survivors of the Qarantina, herded away with machine guns at their backs, crowded into other refugee camps which were later to be decimated by the Maronite forces.

These massacres faced us with a serious dilemma. On the one hand, we didn't want to massively intervene in the conflict in keeping with our initial decision not to let ourselves be drawn into the trap laid for us. On the other hand, it was difficult not to react to the challenges from the Christian rightist parties. The effect of their bloody offensive was to strike a moral blow at the fedayeen, the Palestinian population, and the Lebanese Muslims, who were becoming indignant at our passivity. The only thing to do was to take the initiative.

The joint military command of the Resistance and the National Movement decided to occupy Damur, a Christian village located about twenty kilometers south of Beirut. The choice was determined by two factors. First of all, Damur occupied a strategic position on the highway linking Beirut to Sidon, and thus the Muslim pro-Palestinian south. Secondly, the population, mainly supporters of Camille Chamoun, had erected barricades along the road where Maronite snipers had picked off dozens of innocent travelers, Palestinian and Lebanese alike.

Despite the anger in our ranks following the atrocities of Dbayeh and the Qarantina, we took various measures to spare the civilian population of Damur. The shelling of the village lasted about forty-eight hours, giving the population ample time to flee. In fact the siege against the town was only partial, as we left open an exit leading to Saadiyat, the village where Camille Chamoun's palace stood. We further refrained from firing on the small boats in which some of the inhabitants were escaping. When we finally stormed Damur on January 20, about half the population had already managed to leave the village safe and sound.

We gave our men very strict orders not to attack civilians, especially old people, women, and children. Unfortunately, war is war, particularly when it is waged in a climate charged with exasperation and frustration. Excesses were committed, innocent people were killed. Yet how could our soldiers distinguish between the Christian militiamen and the nonfighters? And if a sniper was entrenched in a house, was there a way of getting him without destroying the building and its occupants, including women and children? To insist that such things were avoidable, as the rightist parties did for their propaganda purposes, is nothing but hypocrisy.

I was invited to Damor after its capture, but I stubbornly refused to go for political and humanitarian reasons. First of all, I didn't want to appear to sanction the excesses, albeit unintentional, which had taken place. Secondly, I had no reason to rejoice over a military victory I didn't consider ours. After all, the rightful place for the Palestinians was not on Lebanese battlefields but on those of the territories occupied by Israel.

After Damur, we had to occupy two neighboring villages, Jieh and Saadiyat, where, according to the Maronite separatists' radio station, Camille Chamoun was holed up in his palace. We had a thousand reasons to kill the man responsible for so much bloodshed, one whom the Syrians were accusing at the time of being an agent of the CIA and Israeli intelligence. However, numerous political figures friendly to the Resistance, including Kamal Junblatt and Saeb Salam, intervened in his favor. So the decision was made to send a delegation representing all the fedayeen organizations and the Lebanese leftist parties to offer him safe-conduct.

The delegation was received at the Saadiyat palace by Dany Chamoun, who informed them that his father had left the place days ago aboard a helicopter. So much for the legendary heroism of Camille Chamoun, who was said to prefer to die shooting rather than flee the advancing Palestinian-Progressive forces.

The palace of Saadiyat was looted and reduced to rubble by destitute peasants from villages in the south. Chamoun claimed to be disconsolate over the disappearance of a portrait of his deceased wife. Yasir Arafat immediately opened an investigation and tracked it down, paying the villager who stole it 5,000 Lebanese pounds and then returning it to Chamoun.

It was about this time that Syria launched its first large-scale initiative aimed at ending the fighting. An important delegation from Damascus led by Foreign Minister Abdal Halim Khaddam arrived in Beirut on January 21. After making contact with the various parties concerned, the Syrians brought about a cease-fire on the basis of a compromise. Syria was to act as guarantor for the strict application of the Cairo agreements by the PLO, in exchange for which the Christian rightist parties would cooperate with the Syrian mediators. President Asad had been trying for some time to strike a balance between the two camps. While supplying many forms of aid to the Resistance and the National Movement, he had invited Pierre Gemayel to Damascus on December 6, 1975, giving him a welcome fit for a chief of state and thus provoking the anger of Kamal Junblatt.

The leader of the Lebanese left was even more displeased by President Franjieh's visit to Damascus on February 7, 1976, and especially by Franjieh's publication on February 14 of a seventeen-point program aimed at settling the crisis (which had received the green light from Asad). The PLO kept out of it, considering that a compromise between Lebanese was not its concern. The right and left rallied to the program only half-heartedly, since each felt exaggered concessions were being asked of it. Junblatt thought Syria had once again abandoned the National Movement, which in his view would have been able to impose at least part of its program of institutional, economic, and social reforms if Damascus had supported the left's military strategy a little longer. President Asad, on the other hand, claimed that continued fighting would have hardened the rightist parties and brought about a disastrous foreign intervention, particularly by Israel. In short, the Palestinian Resistance was torn between the need to maintain its good relations with its Syrian ally and the moral obligation to stand by the Lebanese left.

It was about this time that the Lebanese Army split, which further complicated our relations with Damascus. Ever since the beginning of the war, Prime Minister Rashid Karameh had taken pains to avoid the army's rupture along sectarian lines by opposing its utilization for restoring order. The army was led and officered mainly by Christians—most of them sympathizers of the right—so its intervention on the terrain ran a high risk of taking on partisan overtones which in turn would engender an opposite reaction from the Muslim soldiers. However, Suleiman Franjieh—incited by Camille Chamoun who had managed to get himself appointed interior minister in Karameh's cabinet—had succeeded in using the army on several occasions, especially on January 16, 1976, to defend the Christian militias.

The inevitable took place a few days after that. Units under the leadership of Ahmad al-Khatib broke away from the army, triggering a disintegration which spread from barracks to barracks. In no time the army was split into two distinct parts, one Christian and the other Muslim. Ahmad al-Khatib's part, which was favorable to us, managed to set itself up over most of the south, reinforcing our positions near the Israeli border.

The Christian right and the Syrians quite naturally accused us of being behind Khatib's initiative. It's true that under the circumstances we weren't unhappy about it. But all things being equal, we would have preferred a strong and united army so as to prevent the spread of anarchy and a consequent Arab intervention, which moreover took place and caused us grave damage. This is why we tried to help army Commander-in-Chief General Hanna Said by proposing that the rebel officers be granted amnesty as an appeasement measure. However, Suleiman Franjieh rejected our suggestion and stubbornly insisted that severe sanctions be inflicted on all those involved in Khatib's rebellion.

It was against this background that a stormy meeting took place in my presence on March 9 between an official delegation from Damascus headed by Abdal Halim Khaddam and representatives of the National Movement led by Kamal Junblatt. The Syrian mediators had been pushing for two specific objectives: the reunification of the army on the basis of a general amnesty, and the formation of a government of national union which would implement the seventeen-point reform program Franjieh had announced the month before.

The Syrian chief of staff, General Hikmet al-Shihabi, was visibly angry. Rigid in his military uniform, his face set, he subjected Kamal Junblatt to a veritable interrogation, asking him aggressive questions and jotting down the responses in a little notebook. "Is it true that you are supporting the traitor Ahmad al-Khatib?" he asked.

The socialist leader, a man of extreme refinement who generally expresses himself in subtle terms, replied in the same heated tone. "Khatib," he exclaimed, "is a great patriot! A national glory! It's the corrupt regime of Suleiman Franjieh you're supporting that is responsible for the disintegration of the army!"

The language became increasingly violent. Fearing the irreparable, I asked Khaddam and General Naji Jamil, the Syrian deputy defense minister, to join me in the next room and admonished them for the offensive way they were treating Junblatt, especially in front of third parties. I advised them to talk with the head of the National Movement alone so as to pursue the discussion in a more relaxed atmosphere.

They did, and with apparent success. They emerged smiling a half-hour later. Not only had Junblatt promised his assistance in reconstituting the army, he also gave them the names of four political figures who could represent his movement within a cabinet of national union. What the Syrian mediators didn't know at the time was that the socialist leader had purposely designated candidates he knew would be unacceptable to President Franjieh.

Two days later, on March 11, I saw the members of the Syrian delegation again. Khaddam was gloomy. "Franjieh is absolutely exasperating," he told me. "He refuses to form a government of national union before the entire army high command, which favors a general amnesty, is dismissed. The situation is serious. According to our information, a coup d'etat is in the making."

As it happened, it was later that same evening that General Aziz Ahdab was to carry out his coup de force, which I was accused of instigating. Although the accusation was totally false, I did have some precise information on the subject which I shared with Khaddam. I pulled a slip of paper from my pocket listing five high-ranking officers, each of whom, according to my sources, was separately preparing a coup. The third name on my list, Aziz Ahdab, commander of Beirut's garrison, struck us as the most plausible in view of his religion (Sunni Muslim) and the sympathy he enjoyed in Maronite circles. He represented a sort of national synthesis.

None of us had any illusions concerning the chances for a coup d'etat to succeed in a country having as many militias as it had sects, all virtually free of any government control. The Syrians feared the event for essentially political reasons. Worried, the delegation left Beirut for Damascus scarcely an hour and a half before General Ahdab declared his coup.

A little before eight-thirty that night, Abu Hassan Salameh, a Fatah intelligence officer, burst into my office to announce that in a few minutes General Ahdab was going to read a proclamation on television demanding Franjieh's resignation. There were about ten people in my office at the time, including Yasir Arafat, Zuheir Mohsen (chief of Saiqah), and Ali Madani, chief of Syrian general intelligence. Abu Hassan told us what he knew. He said that Aziz Ahdab was convinced that the Syrian government and the Lebanese army high command would support his action to oust the man (that is, the president of the republic) who had become an obstacle to national reconciliation. Salameh had supplied him with a Fatah escort to the television building. This assistance, which I considered out of place, naturally encouraged the rumors citing me as Ahdab's accomplice. But if that had been the case, Salameh certainly wouldn't have spoken so freely in front of Syrian officials close to President Asad. Nor would I myself ever have told Khaddam that Ahdab was one of the possible candidates for a coup.

This didn't change the fact that General Ahdab's hopeless enterprise caused the first crack in Syrian-Resistance relations. President Asad, convinced that we were trying to sabotage the compromise plan he had worked out jointly with Franjieh, invited a PLO delegation to Damascus.

The meeting, which took place on March 16, was a marathon, lasting twelve straight hours. Yasir Arafat and I had a great deal of difficulty convincing the Syrian president of our good faith. He remained un-

moved by our arguments, repeating that he couldn't continue a cooperation with men who betrayed his confidence while pretending to be his
friends. Above all, he insisted on standing by President Franjieh, who in
his eyes was a symbol of legality and stability in Lebanon. Nonetheless,
knowing that various factions of the Lebanese army and a majority of the
parliament, as well as public opinion, were demanding Franjieh's resignation, Asad ended up by agreeing to a compromise formula designed to
provide a graceful exit for his protégé. The Lebanese parliament would
amend Article 76 of the constitution so as to make possible the election
of a new president six months before the end of the actual president's
term of office. Franjieh could then resign with dignity without compromising the country's institutions.

Everything seemed settled when President Asad received a telephone
call informing him that Kamal Junblatt had made a declaration denouncing Syrian meddling in Lebanese affairs. Flying into a rage, Asad asked
General Shihabi to get President Franjieh on the phone at once to assure him of the Syrian army's support against those who pushed him to
resign. We were back to square one.

Nayif Hawatmah, head of the Democratic Front who was on excellent
terms with Asad, tried to explain that it would be a grave mistake to
alienate a political leader as prestigious as Junblatt, who moreover could
bring the entire Druze community into the conflict along with him. We
finally managed to convince Asad to meet with Junblatt in an effort to
end their misunderstandings and differences once and for all.

Asad received Junblatt on March 27 despite the offensive launched by
the joint Palestinian-Progressive forces against rightist-controlled villages in the Upper Metn region. Their nine-hour meeting had no other
effect than to seal the break between Syria and the Lebanese left. According to Asad, Junblatt remained totally uncompromising, flatly refusing to end the fighting. Quite the contrary, Asad reported, the socialist
leader had advocated the massacre of Maronites by the Druze sect in a
sinister replay of history. Asad, who swore he'd never receive the head
of the National Movement again as long as he remained president of
Syria, was in fact never to see Junblatt again. The socialist leader, from
that time forward denounced by the Syrians as an American agent and a
traitor, was to be assassinated a year later.

Still hoping to bring about a reconciliation between Syria and the
Lebanese left, a PLO delegation including Yasir Arafat, Nayif Hawatmah, Zuheir Mohsen, and myself set off for Damascus on April 16 for
another long meeting with Asad. It was immediately clear that he had

not yet forgiven us either for General Ahdab's ill-fated coup de force or for the ongoing fighting in the Christian mountain area, for which he held us responsible. Dismissing our vigorous protests, he also suspected us of maintaining dubious relations with President Sadat despite the Sinai II agreement.

Asad had reinforced his support for Pierre Gemayel's and Camille Chamoun's Lebanese Front. He justified this cooperation by the behavior of Junblatt (whom he referred to as "that dealer in revolutions and progressivism") and by his concern for the unity and territorial integrity of Lebanon.

Despite everything, we did manage to conclude a seven-point agreement with President Asad. In essence, it provided for a cease-fire in Lebanon, the rejection of any partition of the country, and the refusal to Arabize the conflict, which boiled down to excluding Egypt and its allies from a settlement of the Lebanese dispute. A protocol agreement, which we decided not to make public, stipulated that Syria would withdraw its army from the border villages it occupied if we would respect all our commitments. Junblatt, whom we consulted upon our return to Beirut, judged the compromise unsatisfactory and only agreed to the cease-fire reluctantly.

Shortly after the cease-fire—which like all the others was doomed to be short-lived—took effect, Ghassan Tuéni came to see me with a message from Dean Brown, Henry Kissinger's special envoy to Lebanon during the last few weeks. Tuéni, a minister in the Karameh government and the publisher-editor of the Lebanese newspaper *An Nahar*, told me that Brown wanted to know if the Resistance was in a position to guarantee the National Movement's application of the cease-fire. If not, Tuéni added, the United States would not oppose Syrian military intervention in Lebanon.

I considered the move unprecedented and the American meddling intolerable. My response was evasive but polite. On the one hand, I told Tuéni, it was not for me to become involved in the labyrinthine intrigues of Mr. Kissinger. On the other, the source of the problem was not in our camp but in that of the Christian separatists who had violated all the cease-fires concluded in the past.

During our April 16 meeting with Asad in Damascus, the Syrian president had broached another vital issue by asking: "Who is your candidate for the Lebanese presidency?" A week earlier, the parliament had amended Article 76 of the constitution, and under Syrian pressure Franjieh had agreed that his successor be elected May 1. He nonetheless kept his option to remain in office until the end of his term in August.

I told Asad that we respected Lebanese sovereignty too highly to have a presidential candidate. I did say, however, that I had a great deal of esteem for my friend Raymond Eddé and admired him for his honesty despite his profound differences with the Resistance. I added that the National Movement had mixed feelings about Eddé, but had finally decided to support him against Elias Sarkis who was being sponsored by the Christian Right and Syria. I concluded by advising President Asad against judging from appearances, saying that Raymond Eddé was highly respected and popular among the "silent majority"—Christian and Muslim, conservative and progressive.

"You are mistaken," Asad replied. "Syria does not have a candidate in the presidential elections, since we have no intention of interfering in Lebanese affairs." He then spoke in general terms about the two candidates, but it was all too clear that his sympathies lay with Sarkis and that he was not very fond of Eddé, who indeed never missed an opportunity to denounce what he continues to call the "expansionist designs" of Syria.

I knew from the beginning that Raymond Eddé didn't have much of a chance in the elections. Not only were the Lebanese Front and Syria against him, the United States was as well. Dean Brown had made his choice after meeting with the two candidates separately and questioning each of them on his intentions in the event of election. Raymond Eddé's answers, which he told me himself, quite obviously disqualified him in the eyes of the Americans.

The Resistance leaders were at a loss as to what attitude to adopt. Should we prevent the parliament from electing a new president, and thus come into open conflict with Syria? Or should we abandon the Lebanese left and allow Elias Sarkis to be elected? We were in a quandry. A good part of the National Movement was actually in favor of Sarkis, but had decided to vote against him solely to defy Syria. One wing of the Lebanese Front preferred Raymond Eddé but rallied to Sarkis since Eddé was being backed by the left. Camille Chamoun, meanwhile, avoided all soul-searching by opting to sell the votes of his parliamentary bloc to the highest bidder.

The Resistance finally decided that it wasn't worth it to incur the terrible wrath of Damascus, even if it were true that Eddé if elected could have ended the civil war, dismantled the partisan militias, reunited the army, and assured the unity of the country on new bases. On the other hand, as a gesture to the left the fedayeen subjected the building where the deputies met on May 8 (the session had been delayed a week) to a heavy shelling, just enough to show their displeasure but not enough to block the election of a new president. In any case, we considered Sarkis a man of goodwill and a patriot who could serve the higher interests of the country if given the chance. This was the impression I got from several meetings with him before and after the vote.

So Sarkis was elected, but the problems, far from being resolved, actually seemed to worsen. The right, reinvigorated, continued to harass us in an effort to recapture lost positions. On May 12 the left and the Resistance opened a new "mountain front." The reversals suffered by the Maronite militias greatly worried the Syrians, who claimed that a clear-cut victory for the Palestinian-Progressive forces could only lead to a foreign military intervention, Israeli or American.

New consultations with President Asad became urgent, so on May 15 Yasir Arafat and I set off for Damascus. Libya's Prime Minister Abdal Salam Jallud, who at the time was passing himself off as a mediator, was waiting for us. I refused straight off even to see Jallud. He had recently signed a joint communiqué with the Iraqi vice-president criticizing PLO policy, and I really didn't think they were in a position to give us lessons on Palestinian patriotism. His president, Colonel Qaddafi, had cut off subsidies to Fatah in an effort to pressure us and contrary to popular belief was far from generous toward the organizations of the Rejection Front.

Pressured by some mutual friends, I ended by consenting to meet with Jallud who immediately launched into an exasperating argument. I finally cut him short with the words: "Despite my differences with Qaddafi, I have not lost any of my friendship and respect for him. I only wish that you would show him as much loyalty." Jallud immediately caught the allusion (which I leave the reader to guess), and hastened to adopt a more amiable tone.

Referring to a meeting he had with President Asad, he reported statements which seemed so excessive that I suspected he had made them up. According to him, Asad said that Fatah had armed and trained 30,000 communist militiamen in Lebanon, that most of the mayors recently elected with PLO support in the occupied West Bank were also Communists, that we had systematically sabotaged all the cease-fire agreements concluded in Lebanon, and, finally, that the Resistance opposed Damascus's plan to reunite Syria and Lebanon in a single state. In the light of such gross statements, I asked that Jallud be invited to our meeting with Asad the next day, which he was.

Thanks to Jallud, our talks with the Syrian president were stormy. Asad rejected our arguments one after another and informed us of his intention to dispatch his army to Lebanon to restore order. Our pleading and admonishments were futile. Two weeks later, 6,000 men (later increased to 30,000) along with hundreds of tanks and heavy artillery pieces began to pour over the Lebanese border.

While President Asad's forces were advancing along two axes—one in the north toward the mountain village of Sofar and the other in the south toward the coastal town of Sidon—I learned a vital piece of information from a Saiqah leader close to Zuheir Mohsen. He told me that the Syrian-controlled organization was going to carry out a provocation on June 6 designed to paralyze all the fedayeen organizations in Beirut. Saiqah was planning to storm the offices of all the leftist parties and Rejection Front formations, at which point a Syrian army unit stationed at the sports stadium would move in, ostensibly to separate the fighters but actually to overcome Fatah's political and military apparatus. I received this information on June 3, and so had three days in which to make arrangements for defense.

Indeed, Saiqah launched its attack a little before noon on June 6. Our commandos immediately went into action to occupy the bases and offices of the pro-Syrian organizations, to disarm their militias and arrest their leaders. The operation was successful and ended six hours later. It's true that our adversaries didn't put up a very strong resistance, and many of them voluntarily handed over their weapons. No one in either camp was very happy about this new phase in the fratricidal war which was to cause much bloodshed, unfortunately in vain. We personally believe that our Syrian brothers fell into the American trap laid by Henry Kissinger, who infinitely preferred a Syrian-Palestinian confrontation to a calm which might enable the Arabs to get a closer look at his intrigues aimed at furthering Israeli and U.S. interests in the region.

Not long after the confrontation with Saiqah, a stupid and ignoble crime was committed. On June 16, Francis Melloy, the new U.S. ambassador to Lebanon who had arrived the month before, and Robert Warring, his economic advisor, were to be received by President-elect Elias Sarkis (who was still waiting for President Franjieh to step down in order to assume office). Since the embassy was located in western Beirut and Sarkis lived in the eastern sector under Maronite control, the two diplomats were obliged to take the Rue du Musée, the only street still open which linked the two warring sectors of the city.

The ambassador's car, followed by that of his bodyguards, drove toward the demarcation line between east and west Beirut. When they reached the Rue du Musée, the bodyguards' vehicle suddenly turned around, leaving the car carrying the ambassador and his economic advisor. Why? The mystery has not been cleared up to this day. Whatever the case, the ambassador's car disappeared before reaching the checkpoint at the intersection between the two sectors. A few hours later, we discovered the bullet-riddled bodies of Francis Melloy, Robert Warring, and their Lebanese chauffeur, Zuheir Moghrabi.

All the fedayeen organizations denounced this triple assassination. However, a group we had never heard of before, the "Socialist Arab Action" party, came out in favor of the deed without going so far as to actually claim it. These were the only facts made public before the case was closed.

I decided to open an inquiry. After eight days of investigations, I got a tip that the ambassador's car was in a warehouse. I had some fedayeen storm the building, and we found the vehicle being guarded by a sixteen-year-old boy. The adolescent had only an insignificant role in the affair but was able to supply a few indications on what had taken place. It was from him that I learned that Zuheir Moghrabi, Melloy's personal chauffeur and a loyal employee of the embassy for years, had been approached by the killers several days before the crime. They asked for his cooperation, assuring him that they wanted to kidnap the ambassador merely for a ransom and that they would free him unharmed along with the others in the car afterward. They offered the chauffeur a share of the ransom, a considerable sum which would have meant material security for his family for many years to come. Moghrabi's life was too miserable to resist the temptation, and he agreed to be the tool of the kidnappers. He stopped the car at a point agreed on in advance, where armed men seized their victims without firing a shot. After an interrogation, about which my young informer could tell me nothing, Melloy, Warring, and Moghrabi were shot down in cold blood. The murderers left Lebanon a few hours later, leaving no traces.

Since no ransom had been asked and no demand of any sort had been formulated, what exactly was their objective? The adolescent, who had overheard a conversation between the killers, told me that they had hoped to trigger an American landing in Lebanon! Deploring—as indeed we all do—the fratricidal Syrian-Palestinian war, they apparently thought they could end it by transforming Lebanon into a new Vietnam, and the civil war into a struggle for national liberation! Given such outrageously simplistic logic, one is tempted to assume that the authors of this senseless act were either fools or paid agents of Iraq, a country with which I was later to learn they maintained close relations.

Six days after the triple assassination, the battle of Tal Zaatar—the longest and most murderous of the civil war—began. The refugee camp had been subjected to a blockade by the Christian right ever since January. Then on June 22, several hundred Maronite militiamen— mainly Camille Chamoun's followers but joined, after some hesitation, by the Falangists five days later—launched a full-scale offensive against Tal Zaatar and the neighboring settlements of Jisr al-Basha and Nabaa. Continuously from dawn until dusk, mortars and rockets mercilessly pounded the area for fifty-two consecutive days. In all, it has been es- timated that some 55,000 shells fell on Tal Zaatar alone, where 20,000 Palestinian refugees and 15,000 Lebanese Muslims were entrenched.

It is not a coincidence that the siege began about ten days after the Syrian army entered Lebanon: The rightist forces had clearly waited for Damascus's initiative before embarking on the genocide. I need no proof other than the Christian right's reaction to a compromise offer presented jointly by Kamal Junblatt and the Resistance on May 25, or one week before the Syrian invasion. We had offered to withdraw from all the villages we had conquered in the mountains and to put them under the joint control of Junblatt's Progressive Socialist party and the Falangists. The letter outlining this proposal, which was designed precisely to pre- vent a Syrian intervention, was written in my own hand and given to Pierre Gemayel personally by my associate Abu Hassan Salameh. The Falangist chief never even bothered to reply to my missive.

The Tal Zaatar "victory" was actually an exercise in extermination in the purest fascist style. Pierre Gemayel and Camille Chamoun knew full well that we had no efficient way of liberating the Tal Zaatar and Jisr al- Basha refugee camps and the Nabaa Muslim quarter, which were en- tirely encircled by Christian separatists. Technically speaking, we had enough forces to launch a counteroffensive and break the siege. But despite the cease-fire concluded a few days before with the Syrian army, the Syrians paralyzed us as much in the north as in the south. It would have been disastrous for the Resistance to withdraw from the positions it occupied across from the Syrian forces.

Nevertheless, we did contribute to defending the camp by pounding the assailants and trying to destroy their field guns dispersed throughout the city and surrounding hills. We succeeded in locating them thanks to logistical information radioed us by the military leaders of Tal Zaatar. It was thanks to this "belt of fire" we kept up that the Maronite forces were unable to storm the camp.

On the whole, the camp was threatened more from within than without. The blockade, which had lasted more than five months, had brought the population to the brink of famine. Crueler still was the water shortage. The Christian militias had succeeded in blowing up the water pipes, and the Tal Zaatar inhabitants were left with nothing but a polluted well. Since it was exposed to the torrent of mortar shells pelting the camp, they had to mount expeditions to get water. Each attempt cost the lives of at least two or three of those who volunteered for the mission, which gave rise to the saying in Tal Zaatar that a glass of water was worth a glass of blood.

Young children suffered greatly from the shortage. Needless to say, there was no milk for the infants. The bread-and-water rations distributed to the families were too limited to satisfy even the youngest, not to mention the adults. And when we talked with the camp leaders by radio, the moans and cries in the background of "I'm thirsty, I'm thirsty Mama" wrenched our hearts. Not counting the adults, more than 300 children and babies died of starvation or thirst during the siege.

We didn't fully realize the gravity of the situation at the beginning of the battle. Then one day two doctors in the camp called to ask for help, insisting on speaking to the political rather than military leaders of the Resistance. I could sense the exasperation in their voices when they told me, almost harshly: "If you are unable to halt the carnage, at least find some way of getting us food and water!"

We immediately began to organize small teams, each with a handful of men, to try to infiltrate enemy lines to reach Tal Zaatar. Generally skirting the Christian forces, they had to crawl nights on end through the surrounding hills, fields, and forests. Under such conditions it was impossible to carry water, and their equipment, weapons, and ammunition didn't allow them to carry large quantities of food either. Many were killed before reaching the camp. The others brought only temporary relief: Remaining in the camp, they only increased the number of mouths to feed.

On the fifth day of the battle, Father Mubarak, a Maronite priest imbued with humanitarian sentiments and opposed to the Syrian military intervention, came to see me with a proposal for ending the fighting. The fedayeen of Tal Zaatar would surrender with their weapons to representatives of the International Red Cross who would await them at the gates of the camp, after which the civilian population would be evacuated under the best conditions. I rejected the offer on the spot, since it seemed unworthy of our fighters. My counterproposal—which in turn was rejected—was to evacuate the wounded, women, and children, or at the very least the children alone, while the men would carry on their resistance inside the camp. We received a number of other offers, each more humiliating than the last. They wanted to make us surrender in shame.

We would no doubt have been more flexible if the camp's military and political leaders, or more generally its inhabitants, had wanted us to. But on the contrary, they showed an intransigence even greater than ours. Tal Zaatar, after Palestine—they said—was their adopted country. They would leave only if they were carried out feet first. When the situation worsened beyond all hope, the father of the camp's political chief, whose name was Mohsen, came with all the members of his family to beg his son to raise the white flag. Mohsen became furious, scornfully sent his father away, and didn't speak to him for the duration of the battle.

The Palestinian refugee camp Jisr al-Basha fell to the Christian forces on June 29 and the Muslim enclave of Nabaa on August 6. Tal Zaatar's days were numbered. On August 11, an agreement was concluded through Arab League mediators concerning an evacuation which was to take place the following day. The terms were relatively honorable insofar as the fighters, who were to leave the camp at the same time as the civilians, were not compelled to surrender to the Maronite militias. Instead, they would be taken in hand by the Arab "Peace-keeping Force" and the Red Cross, which were to provide the transportation.

But our enemies could not resist a final and cruel treachery. While the inhabitants of Tal Zaatar were leaving their fortified camp, unarmed in keeping with the agreement concluded, militiamen of Camille Chamoun and Pierre Gemayel opened fire, indiscriminately cutting down hundreds of people. Others pushed into the camp and started shooting everyone they met on sight. Still others, manning the barricades along the road, stopped the buses in which the Tal Zaatar survivors were crammed and dragged out those they wanted—generally young people they suspected of being fedayeen—and either coldbloodedly killed them on the spot or took them off to unknown destinations.

The Christian rightist militias killed as many people on that one day as they had during the entire fifty-two-day siege. In all, their venture claimed more than 3,000 lives. However, of the 1,000 fedayeen in the camp, fewer than a dozen lost their lives on that fateful day of August

12, the others having taken advantage of the bloody free-for-all to flee through the surrounding forests and hills.

The Tal Zaatar tragedy was but another proof that we could rely on no one but ourselves. The so-called civilized world chastely averted its eyes from the carnage. It's true that there were men and women in Europe who were outraged, who organized protest meetings and demonstrations, but their action was on too small a scale to influence the course of events.

The real scandal, however, lies elsewhere: in the Arab world where no government, friendly to the Palestinians or otherwise, lifted a finger to save the 35,000 "brothers" of Tal Zaatar. I refuse to believe that 100,000,000 Arabs were incapable of breaking a siege imposed by a few hundred men, that they couldn't so much as raise their voices to exert pressure, if not on the Christian militias, then at least on Syria which was protecting them.

As I said earlier, the Arab states feared a victory of the Palestinian-Progressive forces more than anything. Forced by their public opinions to pay lip service to our cause and sometimes even to pay us generous subsidies, they simultaneously assured the predominance of the Christian right by financing and encouraging Syria's enterprise. And even when they didn't wish for the elimination of Fatah, they pushed for the destruction of the Resistance's left wing.

As for the Arab countries which, better informed, discounted the "red menace" thesis in Lebanon, they generally pursued a policy aimed at defending not the Palestinian Resistance but rather their own selfish interests. Egypt, for instance, supported us to the hilt, encouraging us to be even more intransigent since its chief desire was to widen the breach between the Resistance and its own rival, Syria. Iraq acted similarly, while Libya on the contrary tried to isolate Egypt to Syria's benefit. Algeria helped us but didn't take any bold initiative, explaining to us that it couldn't divert its energies at a time when the western Sahara problem threatened to degenerate into an open conflict with Morocco at any moment.

As curious as it may seem at first sight, even Israel's attitude was ambiguous. It sent war matériel to the Christian right, but we noticed that it sometimes closed its eyes when intercepting ships carrying arms for the Resistance and the Lebanese left. The Zionist state obviously didn't want such a profitable civil war to end prematurely for lack of weapons.

Among the foreign powers, the USSR had a relatively positive attitude concerning us. At the beginning, the Soviets didn't understand very clearly the nature of the civil war, taking it to be a sectarian conflict. Despite the tireless explanations given by us and the Lebanese Communists, the Soviet leaders advised us "not to get mixed up" in a "family affair." It was only after the massacres of Dbayeh and the Qarantina in January 1976 that they began to grasp the dimensions of the conflict. They openly rallied to our side after the Syrian military intervention in Lebanon. Of course, their communiqués and newspapers only criticized the Syrians by allusion. But President Asad later confided to me that Moscow interrupted the delivery of spare parts to the Syrian army as of June 1976. At the same time, he received a number of messages from the Soviet government encouraging him to rebuild his bridges with the Lebanese left and the Resistance.

However, to our deep regret, the USSR did nothing to break the sea and land blockade to which we were subjected by Israel, the Christian separatists, and Syria. The weapons we had been receiving via Syrian territory stopped reaching us. At a time when we lacked everything, including gasoline and milk, the Soviets didn't even try to send a supply ship. I strongly criticized them in this regard, along with the other socialist countries, at a press conference I gave during the Tal Zaatar siege, but there was no response. Looking back on it, I don't think Moscow wanted to become implicated in the conflict for fear of being dragged into a confrontation with the United States. The imperatives of security and détente must have taken precedence over the desire to help us.

If the Soviets were slow to seize all the implications of the Lebanese conflict, our Chinese friends never did understand anything about it. Right up to the very end they persisted in believing that it was nothing more than a religious war. Perhaps they were too absorbed in the internal crisis brewing in Peking. Whatever the case, they abstained from helping us in any area, political or military.

So we were virtually left to ourselves when the Syrians launched their vast offensive on September 28 to dislodge the Palestinian-Progressive forces from the positions they occupied in the Upper Metn. The pretext they used to justify their violation of the cease-fire in effect was the occupation two days earlier of Damascus' Semiramis Hotel and the seizure of hostages by four Palestinians. One of the Palestinians was killed during the operation and the other three were hanged on a public square the very next day.

But it was only a pretext, since the Syrians knew perfectly well that the commandos belonged to a Rejection Front organization under Iraqi control. Not only did they have no connection whatsoever with the Resistance leadership, they were adamantly opposed to our political line. Some days before that, on September 11, Syrian Defense Minister Naji Jamil had asked during a meeting at Sofar for the unconditional withdrawal of all our forces and our return to positions authorized by the Cairo agreements. We had rejected the demand because our ally Kamal Junblatt opposed it.

We had the greatest respect for the head of the Lebanese National Movement despite certain tactical differences which occasionally separated us. Kamal Junblatt was a sincere patriot and a political leader of genius. He had a profound knowledge and an instinctive understanding of Lebanon and the Lebanese, whom he loved with every fiber of his being. Unfortunately, he didn't always grasp the complexities of the Arab situation and the power play unfolding on the international scene.

A case in point was our respective analyses of the Syrian and U.S. intentions. The American special envoy Dean Brown, acting on instructions from Henry Kissinger, had assured him that Washington was against a Syrian military intervention and that in any case the Syrian army wouldn't dare push farther than the town of Sofar. Kamal Junblatt believed him. Hence his obstinate refusal to withdraw his forces from the Upper Metn.

We were of the opposite view. We were expecting a Syrian offensive supported by the United States and certain Arab countries. We also knew that the intervention by Damascus had tipped the balance of power against us. Our military leaders warned Junblatt that even if we could hold out against the Christian militias indefinitely, any resistance against the Syrian regular army with its heavy artillery, tanks, and ground-to-ground missiles would be suicidal and futile.

The entire leadership of the Resistance favored a withdrawal of the Palestinian-Progressive joint forces, especially since we wanted to avoid a confrontation with Syria which would be politically disastrous in the long run. Some of us wanted to go ahead with the retreat immediately, disregarding Junblatt's objections. Others, myself included, advocated pursuing the dialogue with the socialist leader in an effort to convince him of the wisdom of our analysis.

Under no circumstances, I argued, should we break our solidarity with the Lebanese National Movement. First of all, it would be an intolerable breach of loyalty to abandon political organizations that had faithfully supported us since the end of the sixties and a segment of the Lebanese people that had made heavy sacrifices fighting with us for eighteen months of civil war. Secondly, it would be a serious political blunder to break with Kamal Junblatt, who enjoyed immense popular support.

We finally settled on a compromise. We rejected Damascus' demands, but at the same time instructed our military leaders in the Upper Metn to retreat as soon as the Syrians launched their offensive. In so doing we were able to avoid futile losses. The vast majority of the fedayeen and their Lebanese comrades thus succeeded in withdrawing unscathed to new positions.

However, following unsuccessful negotiations between representatives of the Resistance and Damascus, Syria renewed its offensive on October 12, this time in South Lebanon. The next day it sent its tanks off to conquer the mountain towns of Bhamdun and Aley where the Palestinian-Progressive forces had dug in after the Upper Metn battle. While our troops resisted fiercely in Bhamdun, Yasir Arafat telephoned various Arab chiefs of state begging them to intervene.

He couldn't get hold of any of them: They were "too busy" to reply. Finally, on October 14, he was able to reach Saudi Arabia's Crown Prince Fahd, who said at the end of their conversation: "I will settle the problem. Give me a few hours." The next day, an official communiqué was issued by Riyadh announcing a "minisummit" for October 16 in the Saudi capital. The same day, President Asad interrupted his offensive and proclaimed a cease-fire on all fronts. Under the circumstances, the only way Arafat could get out of Lebanon was to accept President Asad's offer of a helicopter to take him to a Syrian airport, from where he flew to Riyadh on a Saudi plane.

Within forty-eight hours, six men—King Khaled (Saudi Arabia), Sheikh Sabah (Kuwait), Presidents Asad, Sadat, and Sarkis, and Yasir Arafat—succeeded in bringing the Lebanese civil war to an end. The first meeting was taken up entirely by the violent recriminations Sadat and Asad hurled at each other. The Saudi monarch then brought to bear the entire weight of his financial and political influence, and the Egyptian and Syrian presidents arrived at the second session relaxed and smiling in their renewed "friendship." One of the characteristics of the Arab world is that reconciliations are sealed as quickly as quarrels erupt, both being equally artificial—or superficial.

The decisions reached at the Riyadh summit suited us perfectly: cease-fire, respect and application of the Cairo agreements governing our relations with the Lebanese state, reaffirmation of Arab support for the PLO, and—the ultimate satisfaction—replacement of the Syrian army by an Arab Deterrent Force (ADF) which was to comprise units of various Arab countries.

Our rejoicing was premature. A week later at the enlarged summit in Cairo we discovered to our consternation that no Arab country was prepared to send a contingent to Lebanon—except Syria! Iraq justified its refusal by tensions with Syria; Algeria said it needed all its forces for the situation in the western Sahara; Morocco proclaimed that its army couldn't be used outside its borders except to "liberate Jerusalem" (which didn't prevent Hassan II from dispatching troops to Zaïre to defend Mobutu's regime); Libya invoked the danger of an Egyptian aggression; while Egypt refused to send troops because it feared an attack from Libya.

In short, the ADF was for all practical purposes a Syrian force, with 30,000 Syrian soldiers. Later, symbolic contingents were added from Saudi Arabia, Sudan, South Yemen, and Abu Dhabi. The Arab countries clearly didn't want to get caught in the Lebanese hornet's nest. More importantly, deep down inside most of them wanted Syria alone to shoulder the burden of cutting the Palestinian Resistance and the Lebanese left down to size.

Kamal Junblatt, who had been pulling every string to Arabize the Lebanese conflict so as to end the Syrian presence, was deeply affected. Disappointed by the results of the Arab summit and worried for the future of the National Movement, he called a press conference and invited me to participate. While I refused to make any declaration whatsoever—what could I have said without going back on my judgment?—the socialist leader announced that he would go along with the Riyadh decisions, but insisted on referring to the ADF as a "security" rather than a "deterrent" force. It was a final and vain little gesture of defiance from a broken man. Four months to the day after the Syrian ADF troops entered Beirut, he was to fall under assassins' bullets in an ambush laid along a deserted mountain road.

The shocking news of Junblatt's tragic assassination on March 16, 1977, reached us while we were attending a session of the Palestinian National Council in Cairo. We were deeply affected, but our grief could not take our attention away from the realities we were facing. The most important of these was the preponderant role Syria was playing in Lebanon. Syrian troops, this time under the banner of the ADF, had peaceably fanned out over the entire country. Yasir Arafat and President Asad had embraced at the minisummit of Riyadh and had theoretically put the past behind them. All my other comrades of the Fatah leadership had made their peace with Damascus, and went there frequently to confer with the Syrian political and military leaders.

I was virtually the only one who hadn't participated in these reunions dictated by the supreme interests of both parties. My quarrel with Damascus was particularly bitter for several reasons. I had been the one, in the absence of other Resistance leaders, who had made the difficult decision to resist the Syrian military intervention on June 6, 1976. Furthermore, I had made some extremely violent statements denouncing Damascus at various press conferences during the civil war. Meanwhile, I myself had been the object of virulent attacks in the Syrian mass media, which denounced me as a Saudi or American agent and made some personal accusations of doubtful taste. So neither side was anxious for a reconciliation.

My comrades began to worry over my refusal to make amends. Something could happen to me: My office in Beirut was a few meters from a Syrian unit; I had to cross ADF-manned barricades; I was always on the move around the city. In addition, as a Resistance leader I was reduced to virtual powerlessness since I had no contact with the Baathist regime. This sterile and dangerous situation could not continue. My comrades finally asked me to choose between two alternatives: either go to Damascus on my own and come to terms with Asad, or take an indefinite "leave" outside Lebanon.

For the first time in my life, I violated Fatah's rules of discipline, stubbornly rejecting both proposals. On the one hand, I thought it was unfair and an affront to my dignity to have to humble myself in Damascus. On the other, I didn't want to give my enemies the satisfaction of seeing me flee my responsibilities. I decided I wouldn't leave Beirut even for Cairo to visit my wife and children, whom I hadn't seen for over a year. It was only for the Palestinian National Council meeting mentioned above that I finally did go, reluctantly, to the Egyptian capital.

When I returned to Beirut, President Sarkis summoned me to say that it was absolutely imperative that I normalize my relations with the Syrian leaders. He had taken the initiative of broaching the subject to President Asad, telling him how much esteem he had for me. My friendship for the Lebanese president combined with the prodding of various other political figures finally induced me to go to Damascus, where President Asad had said he was ready to receive me.

So one fine day in April I set off for the Syrian capital with three other Fatah leaders—Abu Jihad, Abu Salah, and Abu Amer. We were greeted by our usual contacts during the civil war: Foreign Minster Khaddam, Deputy Defense Minister Naji Jamal, and Chief of Staff Hikmet Shihabi. The conversation, courteous without being warm, was in essence limited to small talk. But it did relax the tension before they led us to the presidential palace where Asad was waiting for us.

We had just been seated in an antechamber when to our great astonishment the chief of protocol asked us to give him our weapons before being ushered into the president's office. After the initial shock, Abu Jihad replied calmly that he wasn't armed. The other two, with a gesture of indignation, tossed their revolvers on the table. I refused point-blank to hand over mine, saying in a cold rage that it was up to the president to decide whether or not he had confidence in me. I was in no way seeking to set myself apart from the others, but given the prospect of a clash between Asad and me, I felt it would be a tactical error to give in at the first challenge. The chief of protocol disappeared for a few seconds and returned, saying: "The president will receive you now."

Asad, faithful to Arab tradition, embraced us one after the other. He then launched into a rambling conversation with my three comrades, questioning each of them about the health of their children and similar topics. He didn't say a word to me and acted as if I didn't exist. Asad, like me, can't even look someone he doesn't like in the face. He did try to lighten the atmosphere by asking Abu Salah: "How is it that a young man like you already has gray hair?" When Abu Salah said it was hereditary, Assad commented half-jokingly: "No, I'm sure it's by spending time with Abu Iyad that you've aged prematurely!"

Making light of the remark, I quoted a few lines of the Abbasid poet Bouhtouri to the effect that blood ties among the Arabian tribes always prevail over the rancors of war. The ice was broken. I took advantage of it and went on to say that we had all acted according to our consciences, he by sending his army into Lebanon, we by resisting it. History would be the judge of our respective actions.

I also mentioned the pettiness of his propaganda organs. "They thought to insult me," I said, "by saying that my mother was Jewish. Unfortunately, she is not. I say unfortunately because that would have helped me to better defend our strategic goal of founding a Judeo-Arab state in Palestine." In any case, I added, I hoped we could turn over a new leaf and henceforth discuss only the future of Syrian-Palestinian relations.

President Asad then started in on a long review of the situation. His army, he said, had intervened in Lebanon because the other attempts to end the civil war had failed, and because something had to be done to prevent the internationalization of the conflict. In passing, he mentioned that he had been suspicious of Junblatt's delaying tactics ever since I had warned him that the socialist leader was really an American agent! "What? But that isn't true!" I exclaimed indignantly. "I never said such a thing!" I reminded him that I had merely said that Junblatt trusted the American envoy Dean Brown, who had completely pulled the wool over his eyes. But Asad didn't budge from his conviction, and the long discussion that followed on this point did not result in any agreement.

I lost my temper a second time when he claimed that, appearances to the contrary, the Palestinians had been in favor of Sadat's Sinai II agreement and that the secret contacts between certain Palestinians and prominent Israelis were actually directed against him and Syrian policy.

I leapt to my feet, shouting: "There are limits to what I can stand! It is the entire Palestinian movement which is insulted by such unjust accusations! We were the first in the Arab world to denounce the Sinai agreement, to fight it, to have suffered from it since this shameful compromise led to the civil war in Lebanon. But allow me, Mr. President, to ask you a question. How is it that the Americans gave you free rein in Lebanon, when a single warning from Washington in September 1970 was sufficient to have you withdraw your troops from Jordan, three days after they entered?"

Cut to the quick, Asad retorted that he had decided to intervene in Lebanon entirely on his own, against warnings and pressures not only from the United States but also from the Soviet Union. And if I had any doubts in this regard, he added, he could show me documents corroborating his statements. It was at that moment that he revealed that the Soviets had interrupted their delivery of spare parts to the Syrian armed forces.

When the president moved on to the more general subject of cooperation between Syria and the Resistance, the dispute almost reached the breaking point. "We have decided," he told me, "not to take the PLO leaders into account any more. For some time now I have had doubts as to your seriousness and your capacity to lead the Palestinian movement. You have led your people to disaster and carnage in Jordan in September 1970. You have done the same thing in Lebanon. You have quarreled with all the Arab regimes. I am worried about the future of the Palestinian cause, for it is quite clear that you are not equal to the task."

That was the last straw. Once again I was on my feet, and replied angrily: "You are correct, Mr. President, to judge us like that. But you should have added that the Arab governments, including your own, are equally powerless to deal with the Palestinian problem. And it is because they are not, never have been, and never will be capable of resolving this problem that the Resistance exists and will continue to exist and grow!"

Hours had passed since the beginning of our meeting. Five hours of reproaches, recriminations, and violent clashes. But far from being negative, the meeting enabled us to clear the air, to go beyond our differences, and open a new page in the Syrian-Palestinian cooperation so indispensable for defending the Arab cause. The American-Israeli intrigues aimed at stifling the rights of the Palestinian people were soon to present us with one of the greatest challenges of our history.

10

The Sadat Initiative: From Illusion to Betrayal

THE PRESIDENTIAL BOEING gently glided onto a runway of the Tel Aviv airport. Seated tensely in front of a television set in Beirut, I watched the mass of Israeli dignitaries, some of whom I recognized, waiting for Sadat's arrival on that fateful day of November 19, 1977.

The aircraft taxied to a complete stop. Unfamiliar figures—doubtless newsmen, photographers, plainclothes security agents, officials—emerged hurriedly. A cluster of Zionist leaders, headed by Menachem Begin, stood stiffly at the foot of the boarding ramp, their eyes riveted on the door of the plane, a gaping hole. I held my breath. A mad hope suddenly seized me: Sadat won't come out! He has decided at the last minute not to go to Israel after all!

Then it was as though I received a kick in the stomach. My throat tightened. The Egyptian president appeared, a light against the darkness under the projectors' beams. He started shaking hands. The butchers of my people filed before our eyes: Begin, Dayan, Sharon, generals in full-dress uniform. Sadat, "the victor of the October War," stood at attention in front of the occupiers' flag while the Zionist anthem blared. Tears were streaming down the cheeks of some of my comrades. For forty hours straight, I hardly took my eyes off the television set. I was to follow, minute by minute, the visit of dishonor and shame.

The next day, Sadat listened complacently to Begin's speech at the Knesset, and then warmly congratulated him. I blushed doubly. Was it possible that the Egyptian president didn't feel, as I did, the slaps in the face the Israeli prime minister was giving us? From beginning to end, it was an aggressively nationalistic speech, a shockingly chauvinistic speech. The reference to the Balfour Declaration filled me with rage. The man who supposedly fought the British actually trotted out the guarantee of British imperialism to bolster his denial of the rights of a people rooted in the land for more than a millennium!

He called himself a "Palestinian Jew" with as much justification as I would have to call myself a Polish Muslim! He paid homage to the Zionist fighters who "liberated their land"—my land! The same land that was irrigated with the blood of Palestinians massacred by him and those like him! The image of Deir Yassin raced to mind, the butchery organized and carried out by Begin's followers in April 1948, the pregnant women disemboweled, the children and old men with gaping throats. The exodus, the long columns of my compatriots fleeing along the roadways before the advance of the colonizers' soldiers, the departure of my own family on the makeshift boat, the suffering of exile, all these thoughts rushed through my mind in a mad jumble while listening to Begin speak of what he dared to call the "Zionist epic."

And as for Sadat, he sat there nodding his head. In approval? Or simply impervious?

Up to the very end of Begin's speech, I tried to convince myself that the Egyptian president wouldn't stand for this insult to the entire Arab nation. I fantasized him walking to the podium to declare: "Thank you for your invitation, gentlemen, but I really must return to Cairo immediately. Please excuse me, but I made a mistake, a terrible mistake. I didn't understand the Israelis."

Before the Knesset session that afternoon of November 20, Sadat had spent the entire day making conciliatory gestures toward his hosts, political gestures with far-reaching consequences which I still naively believed would be compensated by equivalent concessions. I could understand his visit to Yad Vashem, commemorating the victims of the Nazi Holocaust. But how could he allow himself to pray at the al-Aqsa mosque, under the protection of the occupiers' bayonets, in territory conquered in 1967? And how could he have placed a wreath at the unknown soldier's monument, erected for those who died in a war which still hadn't ended?

His Knesset speech left a profoundly bitter taste in my mouth. He had erased all reference to the PLO—on Begin's request, as I later discovered. This concession was not, nor could it be, a mere formality. It amounted to forsaking the fundamental rights of the Palestinian people as embodied in our organization. In exchange, he obtained nothing, absolutely nothing, from Begin! Not even in the form of vague polite formulas. He arrived in Israel on his knees; he left groveling.

He didn't even have the satisfaction of hearing heartening words from the opposition. During the public debate he had with the Knesset members a few hours before leaving Israeli territory, the Labor party deputies expressed opinions similar to those of their colleagues from the Likud, but with fewer biblical references and in a language more suited to our times.

For the first time, I felt something in me snap. The friendship I'd had for Sadat, despite everything, for over fifteen years was irrevocably broken. Despite our differences, I had never lost my respect for him. The things he'd done which I considered mistakes still were not enough to tarnish his image as a patriot. But his behavior in Israel and later at the Camp David Summit exceeded all limits.

He claimed to speak in the name of the entire Arab nation, in the name of the Palestinian people, but he abandoned our rights without even consulting us. He sold a territory that didn't belong to him dirt cheap, at the expense of a people without a country! The friendship— I'm ashamed to admit I even had it—changed to hatred. It became clear that he had mounted a vast public relations operation to pass himself off to world opinion as a great statesman selflessly working for peace.

As I was to learn later, he first got the idea during a meeting in Washington with President Jimmy Carter at the beginning of April 1977. Carter was suggesting Israeli-Egyptian talks at the highest level, assuring Sadat that direct negotiations would go a long way toward eliminating Israeli intransigence. Sadat accepted the principle of such a meeting—the Labor party was still in power in Israel—which was to be organized by the foreign ministers of Egypt and the United States.

It wasn't until the end of August, when the Likud party was already in power, that Secretary of State Cyrus Vance proposed a formula which seemed likely to be accepted by both parties: Sadat and Begin would attend the fall session of the UN General Assembly, after which Carter would invite them to Washington where he would bring them together.

But the Egyptian president didn't consider this scenario sufficiently spectacular. "Why should I go to Washington to meet Begin?" he asked Ismail Fahmy, his foreign minister and the only member of his government whom he had informed of the plan he and Carter had discussed. "I might just as well go to Israel," he went on, "accompanied by the presidents of the five superpowers on the Security Council (the United States, the Soviet Union, China, Great Britain, and France). The event would create infinitely greater stir and would force Israel to conclude peace." On Fahmy's suggestion, Sadat agreed to consult the American government beforehand. Washington advised against the proposal, considering that even if it were to materialize it had little likelihood of success.

From September to early November, Sadat wasn't very clear on what to do next. The Geneva Conference, which Carter was doing his best to convene, was deadlocked. Israel was piling up obstacles, and Syria didn't share Egypt's ideas on procedural matters. The American president sent a personal letter to Sadat admitting his helplessness. His margin of maneuver, he confessed, was virtually nil due to the pressure of the Jewish lobby in the United States. "I need your help," he wrote.

It was about that time that an emissary of Sadat secretly met General Dayan in Morocco. The Israeli foreign minister was full of tempting promises. "If President Sadat were to visit us," he declared, "we would go far, very far, toward making concessions." Meanwhile, Hassan II was encouraging Sadat to make the journey. "It would be a historic event, a decisive initiative, and I would be the first to support you," the Moroccan king assured him. Hassan shared the conviction, which is very widespread among the North African leaders—Tunisian, Algerian, and Libyan alike—that only direct contacts with the adversary are productive. Hadn't Hassan proposed several times that Arafat meet secretly with Nahum Goldmann, then president of the World Jewish Congress?

So President Sadat decided to go to Israel. He didn't tell a soul, not even Ismail Fahmy who he knew was against the idea. From then on, he concentrated on throwing everyone off the scent.

Yasir Arafat, summoned urgently to Cairo, was received on November 8 by Vice-President Husni Mubarak, who conveyed to him two messages from Sadat. First of all, the Egyptian president invited him to attend a speech he was giving in parliament the next day. Secondly, he asked him to fly to Tripoli beforehand to get Colonel Qaddafi's final answer on the request he had made as the price for a reconciliation between the two countries. In fact, the Egyptian president was asking Qaddafi to supply him with the means to resume the war against Israel! To this end, he wanted Tripoli to replace, at its own expense, all the armaments destroyed in the course of the October 1973 war.

Colonel Qaddafi gave Arafat a warm welcome. He said he was prepared to send Egypt arms, but pointed out that even if he put his country's entire financial resources on the line, he still couldn't supply all the military matériel Sadat requested. He also said he was prepared to meet Sadat "on neutral territory," such as the Egyptian-Libyan border, but not in Cairo as Sadat had proposed.

Back in Cairo, Arafat went directly to the parliament where the session had already begun. He was somewhat surprised by the repeated praises Sadat showered on him during his speech for no apparent reason. Aside from this unusual detail, the speech contained nothing which seemed to justify the solemn character conferred upon the session. As usual, the president enumerated the fruitless efforts he had made to reach a just solution to the Middle East conflict. Then, straying from the text he was reading, Sadat suddenly dropped a bombshell. He was prepared, he exclaimed, to go anywhere, "even to Israel," if it would favor the conclusion of peace.

Frantic applause exploded throughout the assembly. The television cameras immediately zeroed in on Yasir Arafat, who ostentatiously crossed his arms. Needless to say, he didn't appreciate the little sentence Sadat had dropped and, like Husni Mubarak seated next to him, didn't know whether it had any significance or not. After the session, however, Sadat took pains to reassure him. While Arafat was standing by, Sadat—surrounded by his ministers and various dignitaries of the regime—pushed his strategem to the point of calling to his foreign minister: "Ismail, you'll have to find a way to cover my unfortunate slip."

So Arafat returned to Beirut convinced that the president had been carried away by his own oratory. I personally believed the remark was a skillful bit of propaganda designed for Western consumption. It was only a week later, when Sadat announced his intention of flying to Damascus to consult with President Asad, that I advised Arafat to write Sadat asking for clarifications.

By November 16, there was no longer any doubt. Fatah's leadership decided to publish a relatively mild communiqué inviting Sadat to renounce his project. But once the visit to Israel had taken place, the Central Committee of our organization split into two factions. One believed that we couldn't afford to break with Egypt due to its decisive role in the Arab world, and that we should confine ourselves to criticizing the president's move without going any farther.

I took the opposite viewpoint. Naturally, I said, Egypt is a major factor in the equation, but it is only as powerful as the legitimacy and popularity of its regime. In any event, I added, the price of humoring it in this case was too high. I advocated a frontal and sustained attack against

Sadat and any states that supported him. Certain that 99 percent of the Resistance rank and file would be with me, I denounced Hassan II, Oman's Sultan Qabus, and especially the Sudanese president General Numeiry, who had been so enthusiastic about Sadat's November 9 speech that the next day he informed his cabinet that he wanted to precede Sadat to Israel! With some difficulty, his ministers succeeded in restraining him.

I knew that my campaign would go against the current, at least initially. World opinion by and large was extremely impressed by Sadat's spectacularly bold move. Despite the fact that numerous governments, including that of the United States, were convinced that the Egyptian initiative was doomed to failure, Nasser's successor was seen as the champion of peace by Americans, Europeans, and even the citizens of the socialist countries. Even part of the Arab world was taken in by the move, which promised to satisfy their aspirations by a means other than war.

Many Arab countries observed an embarrassed silence. During a tour I made of the Gulf emirates, the leaders assured me that they didn't approve Sadat's move, especially since he had embarked upon the venture without consulting them. But, they hastily added, they didn't want to risk provoking his anger. He could retaliate by recalling thousands of Egyptian expatriates—teachers, engineers, doctors, skilled workers— who were contributing to the smooth functioning and prosperity of their principalities. To be on the safe side, they had decided to follow Saudi Arabia's example and take an apparently neutral stance. Despite these considerations, the governments of Kuwait, Qatar, and Abu Dhabi agreed to publish communiqués at the end of my visit reaffirming their support of the PLO as the sole legitimate representative of the Palestinian people.

Sadat's gamble initially appeared to be paying off. He had won over world opinion, neutralized part of Arab opinion, and consolidated his position in Egypt. Indeed, he had managed to persuade his countrymen that all the economic and social ills plaguing them would magically vanish with the advent of peace to the Middle East. In a way he had taken advantage of the Egyptian people's poverty and war weariness in order to rally them to the adventure he had launched. Similarly, he had deflected the discontent within the armed forces by blaming their defective equipment on Soviet bad will and by convincing them that Egypt had no other choice but to come to terms with Israel.

Time has shown that Sadat's strategy was built on sand. The sympathy

he aroused in world opinion, particularly in America, in no way affected
the racist and expansionist policy of the Zionist state. Nor did he succeed in weaning the Israeli people away from the intransigence of their
leaders. Quite the contrary, by going to Jerusalem he proved that Ben
Gurion was right when he used to say that time would work in Israel's
favor and that it was the Arabs who would end up by giving in. Did he
succeed, as he intended, in destroying the "psychological barrier" between the two peoples? If such had been the case, he would have played
us a very bad turn. The Israelis, made to feel even more secure, would
have less reason than ever to work for a settlement, while the resulting
climate of détente would demobilize the Arabs.

I don't think Sadat understood the psychological motivations driving
the Israelis and the Palestinians, two peoples made similar by the suffering each has endured—the Israelis by Nazism, the Palestinians by colonialism—similar also in their determination to attain their objectives
whatever the price, similar in their intransigence which far exceeds that
of their respective leaderships. Sadat was wrong to believe that the
Israelis would be more conciliatory than Menachem Begin and his ministers, or that the Palestinians would accept less than what was demanded by the PLO leaders. In the absolute, our two peoples were
made to get along. But each of us must first come to grips with the realities, mutually recongize each other, and accept the fact that we must
coexist on the same territory.

Sadat was wrong, too, in imagining that by signing the Camp David
agreements he could impose a settlement while excluding the PLO and
Syria. Without his natural partners, he weakened his position even further. It was all very well and good to proclaim that he was speaking for
all the Arabs. Begin had no reason to believe him. What guarantee
would Begin have that a peace settlement would be accepted and applied by the other belligerents? Even King Hussein, who all the same is
ready for any surrender, didn't dare get involved in the enterprise. So
Begin confined himself to presenting bogus plans that would take years
to implement, thereby buying time for himself or his successors to test
Sadat's ability to impose his will on the Arab world. Israel proposed a
progressive evacuation of the Sinai. The Golan was simply put on ice
until Syria would agree to negotiate. As for the West Bank, the so-called
autonomy offered by Begin for a five-year period provides neither for
the retreat of the Israeli forces, nor independence of the territory, nor
even its reintegration into Jordan.

And when Sadat insisted, during his December 1977 talks with Begin in Ismalia, that the Palestinians' right to self-determination be recognized, the Israeli prime minister asked him: "And if I agreed, what would you give me in exchange?" "The juridical recognition of the Israeli state," the Egyptian president replied. According to witnesses present, the Likud leader laughed in his face, saying: "I don't need your recognition. The Jews are on their ancestral land by right." As a supreme humiliation, Begin made Sadat include the biblical names Judea and Samaria to designate the Arab West Bank in the final declaration of the conference.

In short, Sadat didn't get anything and couldn't get anything from Begin—not only because of Begin's expansionist ideology, but also because the balance of power—overwhelmingly in Israel's favor, thanks to Sadat's "good friends" the Americans—wouldn't allow it. It is on this fundamental and decisive point that we differ with Sadat, much more than on the principle of his visit to Israel.

Contrary to widespread belief, we are not systematically opposed to direct negotiations. Our ultimate goal is to live in harmony and understanding with the Jews in a democratic Palestine. It goes without saying that we can't reach this objective by negotiating with stones. The resolution adopted by the Palestinian National Council in March 1977 is clear in this regard: we are prepared to cooperate with all progressive and democratic Jews, Israeli or otherwise, who recognize our right to self-determination. This is the most we can accept today, taking into account local, regional, and international balance of forces. To go beyond that limit could only lead to capitulation. The results of Camp David have amply demonstrated this.

The Egyptian president should have discontinued the negotiations the minute he realized Israel's intentions. He could have recovered his honor and dignity by submitting his resignation after admitting his failure and denouncing the Israelis' intransigence and bad faith as well as Carter's inability to induce them to greater flexibility. I would have been the first to rush to Cairo to congratulate him and ask him to remain in power. Mistakes are only human, but to persist so stubbornly in a like case is criminal. Sadat, by defending narrowly selfish interests, preferred to sacrifice peace—real peace—on the altar of his pride.

The Palestinian leadership was consistent with its principles and analyses. We refused to attend the "Meeting of Experts" held in Cairo just before the Ismailia Summit in December 1977. The Egyptian leaders hypocritically criticized our refusal by claiming it contributed to the failure of the meeting. Lebanon's former prime minister Rashid Karameh's comment to Sadat is worth mentioning: "If you can't even manage to raise the Palestinian flag over Mena House [the hotel where the experts were meeting], how can you expect to get the PLO representatives together with Israel's?"

On the other hand, we enthusiastically agreed to participate in the Tripoli Conference, called on Colonel Qaddafi's initiative with a view toward forming a front of Arab countries hostile to the Sadat initiative. The participants in the conference, which opened December 2, were Libya, Algeria, Syria, Iraq, and the Democratic Republic of Yemen.

This was the first time I had set foot in Libya for over three years, and a quarrel broke out between Qaddafi and me the minute I landed at the Tripoli airport. In front of President Boumedienne, whose plane had landed at the same time as ours, the Libyan president called to me: "I refuse to greet you, since you attacked me publicly by defending Sadat's position not so long ago!" "I criticized you because you were trying to pressure us," I replied. Boumedienne intervened, asking Qaddafi to apologize. I refused to accept it, saying I wouldn't remain another minute in Libya. But I was nonetheless packed into the car that drove Yasir Arafat and me to the place we were to stay.

When we got there, Prime Minister Abdal Salam Jallud and two other highly placed Libyan officials were waiting for us to talk me out of leaving the country. To my astonishment, Arafat announced that he'd leave with me. He also considered himself insulted by Qaddafi, who had said to him at the airport: "Sadat was able to take off to Israel thanks to an airplane one of whose wings bore the seal of Asad, the other that of Arafat." In other words, he was accusing the Syrian chief of state and the PLO president of having been Sadat's accomplices, intentional or otherwise.

Having heard Arafat's story, Jallud committed the supreme blunder of declaring: "If Qaddafi was wrong concerning Abu Iyad, he had good reason to talk to you that way. There is no denying that we disapprove of your policy." I don't think I've ever seen Arafat in such a rage. Shouting insults, he left the house slamming the door. Our hosts ran out after him, but weren't able to catch him as he sped off in a car. It later turned out that he had started for Tunisia, and it was only three hours later that the Libyan authorities succeeded in intercepting him and bringing him back to Tripoli. Qaddafi put an end to the incident by coming to explain himself and to clear up what he called a regrettable misunderstanding. It was only in July 1978, however, that our reconciliation was sealed following long talks in Algiers and then in Tripoli.

But this was only the beginning. At the conference round table where the five Arab representatives (one from each of the participating states) were seated, we noted that seven chairs had been reserved for the PLO. This was meant to indicate that Arafat, whom they had surrounded with the leaders of six other fedayeen organizations, was not recognized as the sole spokesman of the Resistance. Undaunted, Arafat gave the opening address which had been written jointly. But he vehemently protested when immediately afterward Qaddafi gave the floor to George Habash. "Have you invited us here to divide the Palestinians?" Arafat asked, turning to the Libyan president. After a long discussion, we agreed to a compromise formula whereby Habash could express his viewpoint after getting Arafat's authorization.

George Habash rattled off his usual accusations. To listen to him, the PLO leadership, and above all Arafat, was responsible for Sadat's betrayal through its policy of appeasement and indecisiveness toward the Egyptian president. I couldn't stand any more. I interrupted him and said: "You're confusing the issue. In the Middle East there are advocates of three distinct paths. One leads to capitulation, which is that chosen by Sadat. The second, which leads to adventurism, is yours. The third, which is ours, is the one which avoids these two pitfalls by taking into account the concrete realities of the situation."

When Abdal Salam Jallud intervened in the debate to support Habash's point of view, I turned, exasperated, to the Arab presidents and said: "Since this is the way it's going to be, I request that the meeting be adjourned to enable each of you to summon the representatives of the oppositional groups in your respective countries so that they too may participate in the conference. You're not going to make me believe that you enjoy the unanimous support of your populations. It isn't fair that the Palestinian movement—the only one that applies the principles of democratic dialogue—is obliged to flaunt its divisions at this conference!"

An embarrassed silence fell over the group. Qaddafi adjourned the meeting without comment. I used the recess to try to convince Habash and the other fedayeen leaders to present a united front. We finally agreed to stay in the background while waiting for the Arab chiefs of state to settle their own differences. The spectacle went on, but with different actors. The disputes now pitted Asad against Qaddafi, Boumedienne against Yassin Ramadan, the Iraqi representative, who also lit into the Syrian president. Arafat, who was the only one of us to attend the closed-door session, contented himself with the role of spectator.

Asad, the prime target of the Libyans and Iraqis, answered their criticisms with an exposé of flawless logic. He explained to those who were pressing him to denounce Resolution 242 that the UN resolution could not be held responsible for Sadat's visit to Israel. In passing, he reminded Qaddafi that his idol, Nasser, had subscribed to this same text without prostrating himself before the Israelis. Asad carried the day, thanks notably to President Boumedienne who tried to set the tone of reason throughout the entire conference.

The conference almost ended in failure, with the participants unable to agree on the formation of a front opposing the Egyptian betrayal. I then got all the fedayeen leaders together. I said that if we could work out a common platform we could present it to the Arab chiefs of state and implore them not to separate without creating a front based on our consensus. Habash conceded that the document could advocate the creation of a Palestinian state "on any part of Palestine to be liberated"; in exchange, I agreed to put down that the PLO should not negotiate with Israel or give it juridical recognition. So the "Tripoli platform" was born, on the basis of which the "Steadfastness Front" was proclaimed in the Libyan capital despite the withdrawal of the Iraqi delegation in protest.

Because of Sadat and his American friends, we had no other choice but to harden our positions. What else could we have done—follow the example of the Egyptian president? Even if all the Resistance leaders, starting with Yasir Arafat and George Habash, were to grovel at Begin's feet begging him to give us a ministate, the Likud leader would toss them into prison if indeed he didn't have them executed. Whatever we do or say, the Zionists perceive us as dangerous enemies. Do they really want peace? They didn't even satisfy Sadat's minimum demands, yet they have confidence in him. It's obvious that they won't try to conclude a just settlement as long as they have the unconditional support of the United States, which supplies Israel with everything it needs, "from bread to cannon," in Sadat's own words.

How, then, could we trust the Americans? It's true that Jimmy Carter was more explicit than his predecessors concerning the Palestinian people's right to a country. But his term *homeland* was nebulous, and he didn't spell out the location or contours of the territory that would be attributed to us. All this is academic anyway, since in no time he backtracked, no longer speaking of our rights, or a national homeland, or our participation in future negotiations. We soon realized that we could expect nothing from him. He was tied by the commitments Gerald Ford and Henry Kissinger had made toward Israel in the three secret texts included in the annexes of the Sinai II agreement concluded September 1, 1975. In essence, these texts stipulate that the Geneva Conference could not be enlarged to include new participants without Israel's consent, and that the United States had no right to establish contacts with the PLO unless it subscribed to Resolution 242.

When Secretary of State Cyrus Vance toured the Middle East in April 1977, he asked us through the intermediary of various Arab countries to accept the resolution as it stood, even if we published a declaration expressing our reservations on its content. We rejected the offer, since a unilateral step of this sort would have no legal value. Some of my comrades made counterproposals providing for the amendment of the UN Resolution, but Washington in turn rejected these. I personally was against this kind of bargaining. If the price for mere dialogue with the United States was the PLO's acceptance of Resolution 242, what additional concessions would be asked of us in exchange for our admission to the Geneva Conference and the recognition of our national rights?

In my opinion, we should stick to our line of conduct and our allies, notably the Soviet Union and friendly Arab countries led by Syria. We had very few cards in our hand—one of them being our "positive rejection" of Resolution 242—and rather than turn them over to the enemy we should shuffle them with those of our associates. It was only thus that we could ever succeed in progressively changing the balance of power to our favor. There would always be time to make concessions later in a situation where we would be more likely to make them pay off.

The working documents drawn up by the United States and Israel to pave the way for the Geneva Conference confirmed my convictions. The Americans and Israelis were trying to reduce the Palestinian problem to a question of refugees and indemnities in keeping with the spirit and the letter of Resolution 242. The "geographic" procedure they envisaged for the conference had no other purpose than to initiate parallel negotiations between the Zionist state on the one hand and Egypt, Syria, and Jordan on the other which would ultimately lead to separate peace treaties. The Camp David agreements were the first step. British imperialism's motto "Divide and rule" was adopted by the Israeli colonialists and their American associates. And to make certain that their plan would be realized without interference, they excluded the Soviet Union, our principal ally on the international scene, from the peace process.

I am not one of those who believes that Israel is an American satellite or, conversely, that Washington carries out Zionist policy to the letter.

Nor do I believe that the interests of these two countries always coincide. But despite their differences, Carter is compelled to conform to the Zionists' will. There is nothing to offset the pressures brought to bear by the Jewish lobby, since the Arab oil-producing states remain accommodating. In 1977, Saudi Arabia guaranteed the U.S. energy supply for five years, while at the same time pledging to work for a price stabilization within OPEC. Everything seems to point to the fact that the Arab countries, willingly or unwillingly, will never again resort to the oil weapon that they so feebly used in 1973–74.

But Washington's strategy is geared to longer-term goals, seeking to establish its dominance over a vast sweep of territory from the Gulf to Morocco. Many governments in this belt are not to its liking. The United States would like to replace the oil sheikhs with more modern and thus more solid regimes that would assure a better distribution of the national wealth. I wouldn't be the least surprised if the United States were to foment coups d'etat to this end. In so doing, it would guarantee for years to come its own interests in the region as well as those of Israel, which in the last analysis remains the privileged instrument of American imperialism.

The most powerful nation in the world is not omnipotent, however. There is no doubt that it can impose its will on this or that state. Obviously, it can influence the policy of a Sadat, a King Hussein, or an Asad, whose primary concern is to assure the survival or stability of their respective regimes. But what can it do against us, who have neither regime nor state nor country to defend?

It has no grip on us, for we have nothing to lose—and in fact everything to gain—by pursuing the struggle by any means at our disposal. In a way we are comparable to a breeze, being everywhere and nowhere even while influencing the surrounding climate. We are feared precisely because we have the ability to blow hot or cold over the entire Middle East.

We weren't going to let Carter, Begin, and Sadat get away with a so-called peace which would deprive the Palestinian people of their future. We had to show Israel that it was futile to exclude us from a settlement and remind the Arabs that it was dangerous to sacrifice us to their selfish interests. This was the dual political objective of the "Tel Aviv bus operation," which on March 11, 1978, was to end—against our will—with the frightful killing of civilians and our own militants.

The attack as originally planned was to be a strictly military one. About fifteen fedayeen in two small craft were to land secretly on a Tel

Aviv beach, where they were to be met by members of the Resistance inside Israel. The commando would then move toward an army training camp in a nearby suburb and try to seize soldiers as hostages for exchange against an equivalent number of Palestinian prisoners. But a huge storm came up, preventing the two small craft from reaching the rendezvous spot. One of them managed to turn back. The other was swept by the storm about forty kilometers north of Tel Aviv, not far from Haifa, reaching the shores of the Zionist state three or four days behind schedule.

The commando team, now composed of eleven militants, was led by Dalal al-Maghrabi, a young woman who had survived the Tal Zaatar inferno. Barely twenty years old, she was full of fun, radiating optimism and joy of life. She never talked about the ordeal she had gone through except to express her horror for war. But she was no less convinced of the need to carry the struggle to occupied territory.

Faced with an unforeseen situation, she assumed the responsibility of improvising an alternate plan of action for her group. It isn't my place to judge the wisdom of the decisions made under exceptionally difficult circumstances, but on the basis of precise information we received, I can testify to the fact that Dalal al-Maghrabi and her companions wanted to avoid bloodshed. They knew perfectly well that civilian deaths would be exploited as usual by Israeli propaganda in order to present the Resistance as a band of murderers. Naively believing that the Zionists wouldn't dare open fire on their own compatriots, they seized a bus and its passengers to assure themselves safe-conduct to Tel Aviv.

The international press gave a great deal of coverage to what followed. Israeli security forces erected roadblocks between Haifa and Tel Aviv before coldly opening fire on the bus, killing some passengers as well as motorists traveling in the opposite direction. They thus provoked the battle and consequently the slaughter: Dalal al-Maghrabi and eight of her comrades were killed at the price of the massacre of about thirty Israelis.

The tragic epilogue was hardly surprising. In every analogous instance in the past—for example the Munich Olympics operation of 1972—the Zionist state always preferred to sacrifice its own citizens rather than allow us to score a political success. When Golda Meir headed the government, she explained the motives behind this callous behavior by declaring that if she yielded even once to Palestinian blackmail, nothing would prevent the fedayeen from demanding that the Israeli prime minister be exchanged for a group of hostages.

In the last analysis one can understand if not approve this unscrupulous calculation. But the cynicism of the Israeli leaders exceeds all
bounds when they try to saddle us with the sole responsibility for the
death of innocent civilians; or when they demand, as they did after the
Tel Aviv bus incident, that all Western governments that recognize the
PLO break off relations with us; or when the Knesset adopted (unanimously except for the communist votes) a resolution in March 1978 authorizing the Israeli secret service to kill Palestinians throughout the
world as part of their "struggle against terrorism." To legalize and insti-
tutionalize the murder of political enemies, to say nothing of members
of a hostile national community, is without precedent, even—if I'm not
mistaken—under the fascist regimes.

The March 11 operation was also used as a pretext for the full-scale offensive against South Lebanon three days later. I say pretext, because
two months earlier we had received a report from friends in the United
States mentioning an Israeli plan to destroy our military and political in-
frastructures in a blitzkrieg to last twenty-four to forty-eight hours. The
disaster inflicted on the Palestinians was supposed to be as devastating
as the one dealt to the Arab countries in June 1967. We also knew as of
early November 1977 that the Zionist authorities were warning the
Beirut government not to allow Lebanese army units to penetrate the
border areas under the control of their puppet, Major Saad Haddad, and
the Christian militias of the extreme right.

Israel attained only a minuscule part of its objectives through its invasion and occupation of South Lebanon. Without question it succeeded
in maintaining the so-called "security belt" about ten kilometers wide all
along the border. It also got UN forces stationed in South Lebanon.

But Mr. Begin failed in the essential. The blitzkrieg he dreamed of
didn't come off. By the admission of no less a figure than General Gur,
at the time Israeli chief of staff, the performance of our guerrillas was remarkable and generally effective. Despite the enormous resources committed to the battle—despite the air force, heavy artillery, cluster
bombs, and 30,000 infantrymen—the Israeli army needed eight days to
overcome the heroic resistance of the fedayeen. The guerrillas, moreover, withdrew in an orderly fashion and only suffered light losses in
men and matériel.

The main thing is that the Palestinians did not suffer the "June 1967"
promised. Their forces and striking capacity remained intact, as witnessed by the almost daily attacks launched on the occupiers since then.

Neither the presence of the UN "Blue Berets" in South Lebanon nor the right-wing militias in the Christian enclaves along the "good fence" with Israel have been able to curtail fedayeen activities in the area.

Basically, what Israel really wants is to keep up the instability and armed clashes in Lebanon. In the eyes of the Zionist leadership, such a situation would exhaust its adversaries—the Syrians, Palestinians, and Lebanese left—in marginal battles while at the same time giving Israel a ready excuse to intervene in the name of "defending the Christians" any time Mr. Begin faces a thorny political or diplomatic problem such as that posed by Sadat's "peace initiative."

By the time Sadat went to Camp David, he had lost much of the sympathy he had attracted through the illusion that he was going to put an end to the Israeli-Arab conflict. Israel's invasion of South Lebanon made him appear ridiculous. When he arrived in Jerusalem in November 1977, hadn't he declared that there would never again be a war between the Zionist state and its neighbors? He was in trouble at home, too. The Egyptian people had noted that he hadn't kept any of his promises, that no peace was in sight, and that their economic and social conditions had continued to deteriorate.

So the United States and various Arab countries tried to save him. Saudi Arabia proposed organizing a summit to bring Egypt back into the Arab fold and pressed for its reconciliation with Syria and the PLO. The Egyptian president refused to make suitable amends, however, and confined himself to expelling the permanent Israeli military mission that had been set up in Cairo. Even then, Sadat made two attempts to avoid a definitive break with Begin, the first in July at the Leeds Conference, where he was represented by his foreign minister, and the second by agreeing to participate in the Camp David meeting. Sadat wasn't the only one who nurtured illusions about the Israeli prime minister's mentality. He and Carter both clung to the belief that the Likud leader, an intractable terrorist who believes only in violence, was capable of rising above his own mystical fanaticism. The Camp David agreements are a catastrophe for the Arab cause, but at least they unmasked the Americans and their Israeli allies once and for all.

It is conceivable that Sadat will be able to hang on to his power for some time. His Arab and American friends, the CIA in particular, guard over the security of his regime even while remaining on the lookout for a valid substitute. In the meantime, he will have done inestimable damage to the Arab cause, among other things by eliminating the alternative of war. General Shazli, chief of staff during the October 1973 conflict, told me in July of 1978 after he left his post as ambassador to Lisbon that the dispute with the USSR had compromised the operational capacities of the Egyptian army for at least a generation.

Epilogue: Taking Stock

MORE THAN THIRTY YEARS HAVE PASSED since the exodus of the Palestinian people, and more than twenty since the creation of Fatah. The hour of reckoning has come. It is with profound bitterness that I must admit that our situation today is much worse than it was in 1958 when we were led to found our movement. I greatly fear that all must be started from scratch.

Of course, I don't deny the successes scored. I am proud of my people and of the sacrifices they made to win victories on the battlefield in the face of terrible odds, against an enemy whose overwhelming power needs no demonstration. I take pride, too, in the PLO's position on the international scene. Recognized as the sole legitimate representative of the Palestinian people by most states, its success in wresting an observer seat at the United Nations was no small achievement.

This having been said, after twenty years of bitter struggles, the plight of my people remains heartrending. We still are without a country, without an identity. In actual fact, our position has deteriorated. Israel today occupies not half but the totality of Palestinian territory. The United States, guarantor of the Zionist venture, has spread and consolidated its grip on the Arab world. Egypt, the largest and most influential of the Arab countries, went under at Camp David. The "southern front" is thus frozen.

The "northern front," meanwhile, is paralyzed by the chronic conflict

219

between the Syrian and Iraqi regimes. If the quarrel between the rival
Baathist factions of Baghdad and Damascus persists, King Hussein will
be able to pursue his intrigues against the PLO. Arab oil, which could
have been used as a formidable political weapon, is no longer anything
but a simple trade commodity. The Arab world, which has offered concession after concession to Israel these last years without getting anything in return, seems on the brink of shameful surrender. For the time
being, it is neither in a position to conclude a just and lasting peace nor
capable of resorting to force, without which peace is not possible.

The Palestinian movement today does not have the means it enjoyed
in June 1967. At that time, the Arab disaster did not prevent us from
pursuing and intensifying our guerrilla activities, thus showing the Zionists that the war wasn't over despite their brilliant victory. At the same
time, we raised the morale of the Arab masses, projecting a ray of hope
in the darkness of defeat and occupation. We had strongholds from
which we could launch our raids against Israel. The prestige we enjoyed
enabled us to exert an influence, sometimes decisive, on the policy of
various capitals. The Arab regimes didn't like us any better then than
they do now, but at least they feared us and took our opinions into account. Without exaggerating, I can say that we contributed to the psychological preparation and triggering of the October 1973 war, just as
we hadn't been foreign to the June 1967 conflict.

Despite its ups and downs and the obstacles set in its path, Fatah has
been able to guard its autonomy, thus avoiding the capital error committed by our predecessors at the head of the Palestinian national movement. Considering our financial and logistical dependence on the Arab
countries, this in itself constitutes a veritable tour de force. By diversify-
ing our resources and relations and by making use of the political contra-
dictions inherent in the region, we managed to exercise our will freely.
In so doing, we came into conflict successively with Gamal Abdal Nasser
(when he accepted the Rogers plan in 1970), with King Hussein (when
he tried to neutralize us), Colonel Qaddafi (who attempted to make light
of our autonomy), President Sadat (after his Jerusalem trip), and with
still others. On that score, we have no reason to reproach ourselves.

If it's true that we avoided many errors committed by our predecessors, our own errors caused us grave, sometimes irreparable, damage.
We concluded what we thought were strategic alliances with Arab
regimes only to discover later, at our own expense, that they were extremely provisional. Such mistakes brought us profound disappointment
and unexpected reversals. We thought, for example, that Egypt would

be with us forever; that Syria would never, not even briefly, side with the Christian right against us in Lebanon. We never imagined that Iraq, whatever our political differences, would stoop to having our most eminent militants abroad assassinated!

In addition to misjudging the realities of the Arab world, we were guilty of a miscalculation. Faced with a situation of conflict within a given country, more often than not we opted to safeguard our relations with the regime in power at the expense of our relations with the masses who contested it. We thus neglected what should have been a guiding principle: Our real force would have derived far more from the sympathy we could have generated among the masses than from the support we received—and grudgingly at that—from the governments. It's true that we sometimes maintained clandestine relations with the opposition groups at the same time. But public opinion, which knew nothing of our behavior, got the impression that we were following an opportunist policy.

Fatah's entry into the PLO in 1968 compromised its revolutionary character. What we feared most of all, and what caused us to have reservations at the time, has happened: Our movement has become bureaucratized. What it gained in "respectability" it lost in militancy: We have acquired a taste for dealing with governments and men of power. We take their opinions and wishes into account. We have let ourselves be dragged into the Byzantine intrigues of inter-Arab relations, and whether we like it or not we "went into politics" in the least flattering sense of the term. Recoiling from accusations of terrorism, extremism, or adventurism by more or less well-intentioned professional diplomats, we knocked ourselves out to demonstrate at all costs our moderation, flexibility, and conciliatory spirit, forgetting that such was not our primary vocation.

So we came to be seen less as revolutionaries than as politicians. It goes without saying that this change in our image was very damaging for us among the Arab masses, who had expected more from us. Yet this loss was by no means compensated for by a corresponding rise in sympathy on the part of Americans and Europeans. It's true that unlike our Zionist enemies we had neither the means nor the experience necessary in the field of public relations. But the main reason for our failure lay in our ignorance of Western society and the complexity of the democratic mechanisms that govern it. Most often—and particularly in the case of the United States—we had difficulty distinguishing between the imperialist policy practiced by the government and the psychological motivations, in themselves perfectly valid, which formed the population's attitudes toward us. It was such confusions which led us either to take initiatives doomed to alienate Western opinion even further or to seek refuge in the passivity of despair.

Furthermore, we were unable to unify the Palestinian movement, or at least keep its fragmentation to a minimum. There were, of course, objective reasons that prevented us from achieving this aim. When we created Fatah, we envisaged it as a wide front grouping all Palestinians without regard to ideological distinctions or political inclinations. Without resorting to force—which was out of the question—we could not induce authentic leaders such as George Habash or Nayif Hawatmah to join our ranks or prevent them from forming their own organizations. On the other hand, it would have been perfectly feasible for us to firmly oppose the creation of the groups set up by various Arab regimes with the sole purpose of serving as their political or military tools. Given the present force equilibrium, it is no longer possible to demand their dissolution or expulsion from the PLO. But if we had shown firmness when they were first created in the wake of the June 1967 catastrophe, the Arab regimes—vanquished and weakened—would have been hard pressed to resist our will.

These puppet Palestinian formations not only undermine the Resistance by reducing its cohesiveness and effectiveness of action, they also sometimes play a role both negative and decisive. Through their outbidding and provocations, and also through the foreign support they enjoy, they have sometimes succeeded in dragging us into adventures we could otherwise have avoided. In the realm of international relations—to use a well-known example—it isn't unusual for a small country without importance in itself to impose a detrimental policy on an allied great power.

It's true that on several occasions we were able to resist the pressures to which we were subjected. After the Arab Deterent Force (ADF) entered Lebanon in the fall of 1976, for instance, the Syrian-dominated Saiqah tried to persuade us to liquidate the Rejection Front organizations, certain of which are linked to the Iraqi regime. They suggested that the operation be led by Fatah, Saiqah, or the two organizations jointly. We rejected all three formulas, not only because we believe in the principle of democratic dialogue among Palestinian organizations, but also because we had no desire to be implicated in the infighting and score-settling between rival Arab regimes.

We Arabs are generally quick to raise the cry "imperialist plot" every time a marginal conflict deflects us from our principal objective, the struggle against Zionism or more generally against colonialism. This doesn't prevent us, unfortunately, from plunging headfirst into the fray whose damaging nature we're in the very process of denouncing. A case in point was the armed clash between Palestinians and Syrians which went on for months on end in Lebanon, to the great satisfaction of the Americans and Israelis.

Our errors of judgment, shortcomings, and mistakes are not sufficient to explain the delicate situation in which the Resistance now finds itself. It must be said in our defense that we have assumed a task whose difficulties make it without precedent in history. We are leading a movement which by its very nature cannot benefit from a coherent base. The people we are trying to mobilize are dispersed geographically, given to disagreement psychologically, and run the whole gamut politically. Palestinians live under different and sometimes contradictory socioeconomic regimes, which inevitably influence their ways of thinking. They are subjected to authoritarian systems which don't tolerate dissent, especially when divergences or conflicts arise between the state and the Resistance. In such cases, to avoid probable reprisals, my compatriots have no other choice but to rally to the official line or hide behind an apparent neutralism.

To spare them such risks, we are obliged to deal tactfully with the governments, to close our eyes to unfriendly behavior we otherwise wouldn't have tolerated. In a way this limits our freedom of action, and explains the range of apparently contradictory attitudes we adopt according to the Arab regime we're dealing with. We are like the traveler moving between the Northern and Southern hemispheres, who is obliged to carry winter and summer clothes to protect himself against strongly contrasting climates. It is not a question of opportunism, as some claim. It is a question of survival.

Bitter experience has mandated prudence. To illustrate this, I would like to cite an example that haunts our memories. After a conflict between Nasser and King Saud in 1957, Nasser demanded that the Palestinian Legislative Council in Gaza, a mere tool of the Egyptian government, adopt a motion criticizing the Saudi monarch. Whereupon Saud in reprisal promptly expelled all the Palestinian teachers employed in his kingdom. Seventy thousand persons, including the teachers' wives and children, thus lost once again their homes and their livelihood. And yet Saud knew full well that the Gaza Legislative Council had no choice but to apply the directive from Cairo. His vengeance would have been a thousand times crueler had he been criticized by an autonomous organization like Fatah. This gives some idea of why we must go to such lengths to avoid a confrontation with this or that Arab regime, at least when a crucial or fundamental issue is not at stake.

To understand our attitude, one must understand that every Palestinian aspires above all to a haven, however minuscule, to a consulate he can appeal to when he considers himself injured or threatened. Not to understand this point is to understand nothing of the Palestinian movement. Are we less deserving than the citizens of some Gulf emirate? Most Arab states refuse to grant citizenship to Palestinians. So be it! We don't complain of that, since in a way they are doing us a service, perhaps unintentionally. In so doing, they are helping us preserve our authenticity and reinforcing our determination to have a country of our own. The day we succeed in establishing a state in the liberated territories of the West Bank and Gaza, the first thing we'll do is deliver identity papers.

It is possible that for practical reasons many Palestinians will decide not to live in the new state. But what does it matter? They could live in the Arab state of their choice, without complexes and without anxiety! They would finally be treated on an equal footing with all those who have a passport to show. And if they feel threatened for one reason or another, they would always have the option of packing their bags and going back to Palestine, where they wouldn't be treated as pariahs. More than half of the Lebanese people live outside Lebanon; yet no one has ever contested their right to a state.

The arguments developed by those who deny us our right to a country are specious. They say that a Palestinian state on the West Bank and Gaza would not be economically viable. They pretend to ignore the fact that many young nations that became independent since the last world war had much less going for them than we do. The Palestinians have an abundant labor force, numerous technicians and executives with higher university degrees, a bourgeoisie rich in capital. We can also count on considerable financial aid from the Arab oil-producing states. In any case, we are certainly as "viable" as the state of Israel.

Our enemies also pretend that an eventual Palestinian state would become a sort of communist base implanted in the heart of the region, a springboard from which terrorists would harass Israel. These allegations are ridiculous. We are not, as everyone knows, Communists. The Marxists among us are a tiny minority. And whatever our political preferences, all of us are fervent nationalists who would defend the newly acquired independence and sovereignty against all comers.

The most ridiculous argument of all is that we would constitute a threat to Israel. First of all, is it not paradoxical, to say the least, that the greatest military power of the region, which singlehandedly holds twenty Arab states at bay, could pretend that its minuscule neighbor would be a threat to its security and existence? Personally, I am convinced that once we have a state to run, and above all to preserve, Palestinian subversive activities will vanish. Extremism will disappear from our ranks, even within the Rejection Front. George Habash, for instance, may not renounce his ideas, but his opposition would be respectful of the institutions and laws the Palestinians gave themselves. He would no longer resort to violence to make his opinions prevail. He would act no differently from the Israeli parties or oppositional leaders who contest Zionism, such as the Rakah Communist party or even those who question the very legitimacy of the Jewish state, such as the religious group Neturei Karta. This is not wishful thinking on my part. I know what I'm talking about. I know the profound patriotism and sense of responsibility not only of my comrades, but also of our political adversaries within the Palestinian movement.

If ever reason prevails over the territorial ambitions of the Israeli extremists, if ever peace—a just peace, not that of Camp David—comes to the region, it would be very natural to have open borders between Israel and its Arab neighbors. It would be logical and normal for a flow of exchanges to open and develop between entities which would be complementary in more ways than one. How could it be otherwise when more than 500,000 Palestinians live within Israel's 1948 borders and would want a bridge linking them with their brothers living in the West Bank, Gaza, the Hashemite kingdom, and beyond in various other Arab states?

As the leaders of the Palestinian movement, we are not hostile to open borders in theory. On the contrary, we remain faithful to our ideal—to our "dream," as Yasir Arafat calls it—which provides for the reunification of Palestine in a secular and democratic state shared by Jews, Christians, and Muslims rooted in this common land. Open borders would of necessity lead to dialogue, and ultimately to an understanding with a view toward such a reunification. Instead of a nationalist confrontation, there would be a class struggle pitting the Arab and Jewish masses against their exploiters and the imperialists, those very groups which stirred up hatred between our two peoples in the first place.

The obstacle to such an evolution does not lie in our camp. It is the

Israeli government which doesn't want a comprehensive and final peace. It is the extremist Israeli leaders who fear open borders, perceiving them as a threat to the cohesion of the Zionist state and its expansionist policy. On the contrary, they seek to keep alive the tensions and drive the wedge between our peoples even deeper. By nurturing the Israeli people's fears, the Zionist leadership assures their docility while at the same time pursuing the colonization of what Mr. Begin calls Judea and Samaria.

All this does not leave much room for optimism. I know that as a revolutionary leader my role is to inspire hope, to strengthen our people's resolve to pursue the struggle. But it is also my duty not to mislead them, not to nourish illusions which are more dangerous than painful disappointments. To be perfectly frank, I don't believe my generation will have the joy of seeing the birth of an independent state on even an infinitesimal fraction of Palestine. I must specify that for me, as for the vast majority of my people, a truly sovereign state is inconceivable unless it is founded and governed by those who have led the national movement for the past twenty years. Nor can a lasting peace be initiated without the authentic representatives of the Palestinian people.

Of course, nothing can be determined in advance. There are too many intangibles in the regional and international equation to be able to predict the future. Nothing would make me happier than if my pessimism were to be disproved by events in the short or medium term. But if a victory in the foreseeable future remains a possibility, so does a catastrophe—the paralysis or even destruction of our movement. It would be neither the first nor the last time that reactionary forces would succeed in aborting a revolution.

Nonetheless, our people will bring forth a new revolution. They will engender a movement much more powerful than ours, better armed and thus more dangerous for the Zionists. There is no doubting the irrepressible will of the Palestinian people to pursue their struggle, come what may. It is in the nature of things. We are determined to survive as a nation. And one day, we will have a country.

Index

A

Abdallah (king of Transjordan), 32, 105, 137
Abdallah, Sheikh Saad, 86
Abdel Aziz (king of Saudi Arabia), 53
Abu Ali Ayad, 45, 50, 73
Abu Amer, 198
Abu Arz, 170
Abu Daud, 99-103, 126
Abu Garbiyya, Bahjat, 75
Abu Gharbra, Bahjat, 82-84, 86, 89
Abu Iyad (Salah Khalaf)
Kamal Adwan and, 114-18; job at the Al Kamal coffeehouse; 15-17; tour of Arab countries (December 1975), 172-74; student strike against the Arab League, 21; speech at Arab University (February 1974), 134-36; first meeting with Yasir Arafat, 19-21; meetings with President Asad, 183-85, 198-201; assassination attempts on, 119-20; BEA plane hijacked to Tunis and, 149-54; beaten and arrested in childhood, 7-9; birthday celebration for, 157; meeting with Camille Chamoun, 165; childhood of, 3-12; on coexistence with Israelis, 139; visit to Cuba (1970), 70-72; at Dar al-Ulum (college), 18-19; on evolution of the liberation movement, 136-38; meeting with Suleiman Franjieh, 165-70; schooling in Gaza, 13-15; teaching career in Gaza, 25-28; teaching career in Gaza, 25-28; underground activities in Gaza, 27-28; youth in Gaza, 13-17; review of Fatah history, 219-26; first meeting with King Hussein, 75; on Israeli terrorist operations, 103-106; family's relations with Jews, 5; first job, 14; jumps off roof, 16; battle of Karameh and, 57-60; exile in Kuwait, 38; trip to Kuwait (1975), 172-74; Lebanese civil war and, 159-201; marriage of, 28; ministate proposal and, 134, 138, 142-43; on Munich Olympics operation, 106-12; Yusuf al-Najjar and, 114-18; Kamal Nasir and, 114-18; death of Nasser and, 90-91; meets Nasser, 22-23; in North Vietnam, 67-70; the October War and, 121-33; post-October War peace attempts and, 134-58; Palestinian exile of 1948